---------- **THE** ----------

COLLECTION
ALL AROUND

ALA Editions purchases fund advocacy, awareness, and accreditation programs for library professionals worldwide.

THE

COLLECTION

ALL AROUND

*Sharing Our Cities, Towns,
and Natural Places*

JEFFREY T. DAVIS

An imprint of the American Library Association
Chicago / 2017

Jeffrey T. Davis *is a branch manager with the San Diego Public Library. He has worked in branch and central libraries from the South Bronx (New York City) to downtown San Diego. His previous experience includes collection development and electronic resources management. He is interested in all things library, with a current focus on early learning spaces and the collection all around.*

© 2017 by the American Library Association

Extensive effort has gone into ensuring the reliability of the information in this book; however, the publisher makes no warranty, express or implied, with respect to the material contained herein.

ISBNs
978-0-8389-1505-9 (paper)
978-0-8389-1581-3 (PDF)
978-0-8389-1582-0 (ePub)
978-0-8389-1583-7 (Kindle)

Library of Congress Cataloging-in-Publication Data

Names: Davis, Jeffrey T. (Jeffrey Trapp), author.
Title: The collection all around : sharing our cities, towns, and natural
   places / Jeffrey T. Davis.
Description: Chicago : ALA Editions, an imprint of the American Library
   Association, 2017. | Includes bibliographical references and index.
Identifiers: LCCN 2017004874 | ISBN 9780838915059 (pbk. : alk. paper)
Subjects: LCSH: Libraries and community—Case studies. | Libraries and
   community—United States—Case studies. | Community information
   services—United States.
Classification: LCC Z716.4 .D385 2017 | DDC 021.2—dc23 LC record available
   at https://lccn.loc.gov/2017004874

Cover design by Alejandra Diaz. Imagery © Shutterstock, Inc.
Book design by Kim Thornton in the Expo Serif Pro and Adelle typefaces.

♾ This paper meets the requirements of ANSI/NISO Z39.48-1992 (Permanence
of Paper).

Printed in the United States of America

21 20 19 18 17   5 4 3 2 1

For Naomi and Theo

CONTENTS

ACKNOWLEDGMENTS

THANKS TO EVERYONE WHO SPOKE WITH ME ABOUT THE work they are doing. Robert Anderson, Richard Beeland, Brett Bonfield, Shaun Briley, Chris Brown, Amy Calhoun, Mary Pom Claiborne, Sue Considine, Gretchen Crowe, Stacie Deng, Amanda DeWilde, Katrina Farrow, Kathleen Ferrier, Bill Folden, Jennifer Hoffman, Sarah Houghton, Nancy Howe, Rachel Hudson, Jennifer Inglis, Sandy Kallunki, Kara Logsden, Stephanie Loney, Katherine Malmquist, Lexy Mayers, Suzanne McGowan, Tim Moreland, Chris Olson, Anne O'Shea, Diana Plunkett, Carla Powers, Rebecca Ryan, Almis Udrys, Christina Wainwright, and Lisa Zicherman.

Thanks to the New York Public Library and the San Diego Public Library for the opportunity to learn and practice public librarianship.

Thanks to Chou, Gabi, Harriet, Leng, Luan, Michael, Ming-Lan, Nathan, Thao, Thuy, and Tomoe for your dedication and spirit.

Libraries Take on the World

"...and the walls became the world all around"
— Maurice Sendak, *Where the Wild Things Are*

L IBRARIES DO A LOT. WE SHARE BOOKS, E-BOOKS, CDS, DVDS, databases, and expertise. Sometimes we share tools or seeds or toys. We provide shared computers and Internet access. We share 3-D printers. We offer classes. We share programs ranging from storytimes to yoga to book clubs to concerts to lectures. We share spaces to read, to work, to focus, to play, to explore, and to be at ease. The great range of library offerings attracts people of all kinds, matching a need or curiosity to the library's many offerings. It's no surprise that in every city and town the library is a magnet and an anchor.

But there's much more, of course, that people ask of the places they live that isn't a part of libraries and needn't be. Cities and towns have parks, recreation centers, and nature. They have museums and dance studios, streets and transit, meetings and activities, history and all the stuff of local community, culture, identity, and civic collaboration. The places around us are made up of wonderful, incredible resources that aren't the library and that the library doesn't have to duplicate. Good news! They weren't all going to fit in the library anyway.

But access to those riches isn't as broad as it could be. Barriers of cost or of social, economic, or cultural inequality exist. Not every local resource is as welcoming or as community-focused as the library is. Many of the great assets of cities and towns are poorly shared. That's where libraries come in. Shared access—help with access—is what libraries do.

Think, then, of the city, the town, the community, and all that it has to offer as a potential collection. The collection all around.

How do libraries help their communities use that collection? How can library members be helped to access the resources around them as easily as a storytime or a best seller? How can librarians help move city and town resources toward the public-goods end of the scale? Can librarians help local organizations meet the public halfway? That's what this book explores.

It's interesting. Content the world over has gotten immeasurably more available. While barriers remain, the stuff of books and movies and music and research and knowledge is now unquestionably more abundant and accessible, thanks to the Internet, e-commerce, electronic bazaars and swap meets, digital communication technologies, user-generated content, and other online resources. Whether paid or free, digital or physical, the barriers to getting access to content are not what they used to be. Access can be confusing and often costly and there's much farther to go, but the change is undeniable. The skills and tools that libraries developed when content was scarce are now in less demand. Libraries are still navigating this sea change. Meanwhile, access to the local museum, theater, enrichment class, and neighborhood improvement process remains about where it's been for decades. It's difficult for most people. There are barriers of cost and complexity, language and know-how, connection and convenience. Fortunately, the same skills and tools that libraries developed to facilitate access to content are valuable here. Librarians can help.

And they do! Countless programs of local access have sprouted up in libraries in recent decades. Libraries everywhere are engaged in efforts to improve access to the resources of our cities, towns, and natural places. An impressive variety of library work contributes to this goal. I set out to find diverse examples of this work and to introduce them to a wider audience. Exploring these programs should be valuable to librarians, library strategists, and community members looking for help in accessing their world. Importantly, these efforts cohere as a largely unarticulated service model: libraries and librarians as agents on behalf of the public to our great local resources all around.

Direction and Innovation

There is no shortage of innovation in libraries right now, but this book is not a guide to cool or worthwhile things that libraries are doing. There are lots of great new ideas. Too often, though, those new ideas are either novelties or bear little relation to library strengths. They don't generate momentum, accrete to anything new, or taken together help clarify what libraries are and what they do.

Work that is aligned—that variously contributes to a platform for going farther, that builds institutional strength—will be more lasting and consequential. This book explores and reappraises many projects old, new, and prospective that share a strategic direction: providing or expanding access to local resources. Most of these projects have received relatively little attention; in some cases, despite drawing on new technologies. A more purposeful mode of innovation can better harness the great energy and dedication in libraries.

This book is about libraries improving access to the resources around us that aren't part of the library. By way of contrast, this is not

- embedding librarians and library resources in the community: decentralizing library services and resources, the library without walls
- bringing new resources into the library like makerspaces, media labs, online forums, tutoring, publishing, and other library services, performances, and events

While these all have great value, they represent a different direction and a somewhat different set of skills than what's explored here.

With little fanfare, librarians have been developing new or updated programs and services of great depth and breadth, bringing together their members and the wealth of their (nonlibrary) local resources. I hope to credit that work and show how these programs situate the library in ways that draw on library traditions, skills, and strengths. Where these projects have gotten attention, they haven't been contextualized as part of a broader strategy. Why not? Probably, first of all, because libraries haven't organized their work around it: The position of "local access librarian" hasn't been represented in any job or division titles that I've been able to find. Which library will be the first to create that job in its organization?

Our conceptual categories also explain some of why this is. We know that libraries have collections. We know that libraries have programs attended by members. Libraries do outreach. Libraries have facilities. Libraries have technology. And then there's all the other offerings and work libraries do that has a foot in one of these and the other foot vaguely in "services." Like any framework, these categories create some blind spots that affect our thinking and decision-making. They shape how we understand what libraries do and what they do next. Considering a new paradigm—local access—illuminates many things that we may not have realized our libraries are already doing.

Playing to Strength

Libraries continually evaluate potential projects and directions against a background of clamoring possibilities. There's a world of cool things that libraries can do that are consistent with our mission and have a positive impact in our communities. And we should have high expectations about extending librarians' skills in new directions. But strategic thinking has to go beyond "Could we do this?" to "Is this something we can do better than someone else?" If another organization—schools, a social service agency, the health department—decided to offer an equivalent program, would the library's effort be superseded?

Libraries neither need to become all things to all people nor retreat into the familiar. There are real competitive advantages that libraries have as agents of access to the collection all around and that they are practicing already. This direction aligns with librarians' core skills and the library's context in the community. It plays to libraries' strengths.

- The collection all around builds on the existing skills of librarians. The work of improving local access combines outreach, customer service, event management, collection development, and acquisitions. It benefits from good design thinking and thoughtful metadata. It depends on comfort with new technology and creative thinking about how to apply it. It's in librarians' wheelhouse.

- The collection all around scales well. With a local access service established, greater and greater numbers of community members can be served without comparable increases in cost. For much of library programming and other services—as valuable as they are—providing twice as much service requires nearly twice the work or resources. Programs of access to local resources generally have staff-to-user ratios and users-per-hour capacities that allow and encourage their growth.
- It lasts. Many of the projects described here, having been established, require much less work to maintain. Having brokered local access, the relationship is easy to renew every year or so. The initial work pays ongoing dividends. That longevity is internalized by the public. They use a service and then use it again on their schedule, year in and out. The library as an avenue of access becomes an ordinary expectation, like circulating books.
- It builds on the position of libraries in their communities. Libraries know their communities as well as or better than anyone. There is goodwill and trust that libraries have built and continually restore. Local access work forms a virtuous circle with libraries' place in their communities. As these projects become visible and are enjoyed, they strengthen the support of libraries, which improves access to community resources, which raises visibility and strengthens support, which . . .
- That same community position makes libraries among the most effective interfaces for the public to access local resources. Libraries are approachable and familiar in ways that the symphony or community board are not for many. Unfamiliar government agencies and private institutions can all be intimidating at times. This can be especially true for underserved communities. The library is a trusted gateway and a source for personal attention.
- Brokering public access to local resources is a "blue ocean." Borrowing the metaphor from Blue Ocean Strategy, local access is an area of little competition.[1] Where do people turn for help with better access to their local resources? It's an open space. Crowded, contested spaces like education or events are important places for libraries' communities, of course, but libraries inevitably compete there with businesses, schools, and the wide

Internet. Shared access to local resources is a space in which libraries have a unique position and a competitive advantage.

The Collection All Around

The projects described in this book are grouped into five thematic chapters.

1. *Membership.* The programs described in this chapter don't all fit entirely in the framework of improving access to nonlibrary resources (though some do). Membership, though, acts as a linchpin for the projects that follow. Providing access to nonlibrary resources doesn't make the library invisible. It makes the library, and library membership in particular, a gateway to those, to the collection all around. Reaffirming the place of library membership in library work is an illuminating place to start.

2. *City Passes.* These are the quintessential local access programs: librarians broker direct access to museums, pools, classes, performances, and venues of all kinds on behalf of the public, with new opportunities and benefits to those institutions as well.

3. *Guides.* Much of the world around us can be made more accessible simply by making it more comprehensible and welcoming, sometimes through providing modest assistance. This isn't always work that other agencies have a stake in. It is something that librarians understand and excel at providing.

4. *Placemakers.* Access to the world around us includes access to the ordinary stuff of our neighborhoods. Can we get around? Are there places for us? Are the streets and squares and built environment that we pass through ours to shape or someone else's business? Libraries are working to make neighborhood places more responsive to their members.

5. *Rangers.* The barriers limiting access to nature are subtle. Most natural settings are apparently accessible. But there are important roles that librarians can play to provide assurance, expertise, and assistance that are otherwise scarce and that help make connections to nature more available to all.

A conclusion, *All Together Now*, reflects on the ways a local access agenda can be helped forward. I'll be discussing the value of these projects primarily in terms of access, or ultimately in terms of access. That's not the only value they each have, of course, and it's not the frame in which those projects' leaders necessarily think of them. For example, these projects are each variously educational, service-oriented, or community-building. That's all true. What these projects do in common, though, is share local access. They can contribute to a common direction and vision.

Because the process of planning and implementing these programs is an extension of other work familiar to librarians, I haven't spent much time on the basics here. There's good coverage and coursework on outreach and community partnership methodology elsewhere. From the American Library Association (ALA), consider *Librarians as Community Partners: An Outreach Handbook* and *Successful Community Outreach: A How-to-Do-It Manual for Librarians.*[2] Throughout this book I refer to the people doing this work as librarians, irrespective of classification, for the sake of simplicity, and I refer to library patrons and customers as members.

Not every relevant program is included in this book. I selected a representative program where there were many. I didn't find or know how to find countless more. And more programs are still being created. This is all being done without library staff in defined local access roles or departments. Imagine how many more ways will be found to bridge the library public to the riches all around when that's made an assigned responsibility, a strategic focus, and a topic of shared expertise.

The programs described in this book range from the attention-getting to the taken-for-granted. Many are consequential updates of traditional programs, often using tools that weren't available until recently. That many superficially look like traditional offerings perhaps explains their being relatively less visible. Hopefully, exploring these projects side by side shows that what's important about each of them is not their buzz or isolated impact. It's how they have the potential to reinforce one another and achieve something bigger . . . For example, it isn't being able to borrow best sellers or Spanish-language board books or jazz CDs or Korean movies or market research each in isolation that makes those things cool. (Though they each are.) It's that borrowing what you want is a thing you can do at the library, with offerings matched to each community.

The same is what's relevant with the city, town, and nature access programs described in this book. As they become a collection, reaching the treasures and ordinary resources all around becomes a thing you can do via the library. That is what can be achieved. Equitable, widely shared access to our cities, towns, and natural places is ambitious and lofty and utopian. But not too much so. It's grounded in the library as an institution and in the work of librarians.

On the other hand, making the world a better place and empowering people are, of course, tremendous callings. But people looking for providers of these things shouldn't be expected to think of the library first. Which is the institution that makes the world a better place? Public health agencies, for many. Or a socially engaged church. Which is the one that empowers people? Community organizers and civic groups, for some. Which educates? Schools, of course. Libraries aren't the answer to every question.

So, to which question are libraries the answer?

How about: "Which institution helps me access the world around me?"

Yes. That's the library and the collection all around.

NOTES

1. W. Chan Kim, and Renée Mauborgne, *Blue Ocean Strategy: How to Create Uncontested Market Space and Make the Competition Irrelevant* (Boston: Harvard Business Review Press, 2015).

2. Carol Smallwood, *Librarians as Community Partners: An Outreach Handbook* (Chicago: American Library Association, 2010); Barbara Radke Blake, Robert Sidney Martin, and Yunfei Du, *Successful Community Outreach: A How-to-Do-It Manual for Librarians* (New York: Neal-Schuman, 2011).

CHAPTER ONE

It Starts with Membership

THE ROMANTIC APPEAL OF LIBRARY CARDS IS HARD TO deny and probably speaks to anyone reading this book. It's evergreen too. A look anytime at the hashtag #firstlibrarycard on social media will reliably turn up the latest sharing of stories, photos, and enthusiasm about the milestone of receiving one's first library card. (It's a nice pick-me-up on Instagram, especially, go see.) A number of libraries recognize this with "My First Library Card" marketing promotions for young children.

But in the end, a library card doesn't mean that the holder has checked out an item. It doesn't mean that the holder has been to a library program, searched a library database, or used a library computer. Someone with a library card might never even set foot in a library. Having a library card does correlate with more library engagement, of course, but ultimately the card is just an account. It's a by-product, an administrative hook for library services and the real work that we do.

But no. That's not right either.

Whether they're used or not, library cards are tokens of belonging and potential. Very often, for kids, a library card is their first tangible membership in grown-up society as an individual who is independent of his or her family.

Library cards come with privileges and responsibilities and a whole new relationship to the world. They're a big deal. It's a wonder we don't make elaborate ceremonies out of awarding these talismans.

Library cards represent belonging for adults as well. For new immigrants, for example, a library card may be the first tangible sign of membership in their wider new community, an unhyphenated membership in common with one's neighbors. Whether one is a first- or fifth-generation American, the community library is the same, membership is the same, and the card is the same.

The 2014 Pew Research Center survey and report *From Distant Admirers to Library Lovers—and Beyond* derived types of public library engagement in the United States.[1] In the two groups least engaged with libraries—"Distant Admirers" and "Off the Grid"—28 percent nevertheless reported that they have a library card. That's kind of remarkable.

The Thing Itself

It makes sense, then, to start with a noninstrumental view of library cards. They have meaning to people whether or not they are used. The cards confer civic membership. They embody access to and a place in the city. From that starting point, we can extend library cards' meaning and use in practical ways.

Used frequently or infrequently, the cards themselves are carried around, seen, and handled by library members. Their designs affirm the library's brand and can communicate in other ways. The San Diego Public Library created limited edition cards for Comic-Con (the vast comic book convention held there every summer) and issued them with library registration held at the event (see figure 1.1); special library cards were created for the opening of their new Central Library; and standard-issue cards are available in five colors. When new members register, they're surprised and delighted to be asked to choose the color of their library card. The cards create a connection with members. Using one of them may remind users of the time they got their card—their membership—at a special event or a local occasion, or when they just selected their own color. They're part of the library community with a history that is both personal and shared.

FIGURE 1.1
San Diego Public Library/Comic-Con
Toshwerks & San Diego Public Library
Comic-Con 2016 Library Card

Similarly, the Seattle Public Library created cards in partnership with the NFL and Seattle Seahawks. The Brooklyn Public Library featured a Sesame Street card to accompany a major exhibition. The Cleveland Public Library created a card honoring local author Harvey Pekar. In 2015, a number of libraries piggybacked on the ALA's licensing of Peanuts for Library Card Signup Month that year.

Libraries have led library card campaigns for years, and in 1987 the ALA launched the September observance of Library Card Signup Month. That effort originated with then Secretary of Education William J. Bennett who said, "Let's have a national campaign . . . every child should obtain a library card—and use it." Every September, thousands of public and school libraries join in this national effort.

Students Belong Here

The recognition of library membership as a valuable focus in itself continues to grow. In 2015 the Obama administration's ConnectED initiative set a Library Challenge goal of registering every enrolled student in thirty partner cities for a library card. The Challenge is supported by the Institute of Museum and Library Services, the Urban Libraries Council, and the ALA.

In some cases, the Library Challenge goal is being pursued through traditional means: essentially, library card campaigns partnered with schools. In others cases, library membership is being directly integrated with school enrollment. Library registration and activation are automatic via school enrollment in each of these districts:

- 154,000 Charlotte-Mecklenburg (NC) public school students' IDs function as library cards.

- 60,000 Nashville (TN) public school students' IDs function as library cards.
- 15,000 Kansas City (MO) public school students' IDs function as library cards (the ID numbers require a library prefix for operation).
- 70,000 Washington, DC, public secondary school students receive the city's DC One Card, a school and municipal ID that is also available to adults. The ID card provides access to Park and Recreation centers and programs, serves as a transit pass, and is an activated library card.
- 20,000 Boston (MA) public high-school students receive the city's Boston One Card. The student ID card also serves as a library card, community centers pass, and transit pass.

Some systems provide mechanisms to opt out of either borrowing privileges (leaving digital services in place) or out of library membership entirely. As another way to address concerns about automated account creation, some systems do not generate fines for late materials on these cards. Coordination between library vendors and school ID providers must be undertaken to ensure the compatibility of numbering schemes and to avoid duplication.

Like the DC and Boston cards, one way to build on library membership is to make the library card the hub of access to other community resources. The MyDenver card is an ID/pass for Denver youth from ages five to eighteen. The program first developed as a teen pass to city parks and recreation facilities and programs that was issued by public schools on an opt-in basis. The pass provides access to twenty-seven recreation centers where youth can take advantage of amenities and participate in structured drop-in activities revolving around sports and wellness, arts and culture, science, technology and education, community engagement, and social recreation.

A bond measure in 2012 included expansion of the program to all Denver residents ages five to eighteen. Card registration then moved from schools to online sign-up and was administered by the Denver Parks and Recreation Department. The city's Office of Children's Affairs now oversees the program and coordinates with the Denver Public Library (DPL).

Use of the MyDenver card for library services began in January 2013. Youth using the library then activated their MyDenver card for library use, but no forms were required. The library had access to the MyDenver database and imported records into its integrated library system (ILS) as needed. Beginning in 2016, all Denver public school students are now issued a MyDenver card via school registration with a simple opt-in. The schools provide the DPL with a data file that is loaded into the ILS. These accounts require no other activation for database and e-book access. For circulating materials, youth using the library obtain a library bar code to add to the record, but no other forms or permissions are required.

Jennifer Hoffman, manager of books and borrowing at the Denver Public Library, explains that "the big thing is making it really clear and easy for parents. One of the things that we realized early on is that the kind of parent who's going to see the library as a benefit for their child probably has already signed their child up for a library card. So we have to be prepared for duplication and how to deal with that. The other thing is that we have different ways that we work with the schools in terms of registering whole classrooms for cards." The DPL is working "to make signing up for the MyDenver card the preferred method of getting a library card for any child who's in the Denver public schools system." While the MyDenver card started independently of the library, the library was envisioned early on as a partner. Today there are 70,000 MyDenver cards activated for online services with the DPL. No visit to the library is needed for that level of membership. To activate a MyDenver card for full borrowing privileges, students only need to visit the library and present their card.

Just as importantly, Denver's Office of Children's Affairs has worked with partners at the Denver Art Museum and the American Museum of Western Art to add museum admission benefits and discounts to the MyDenver card. The expanded school, library, and recreation center core now includes benefits with the Denver Botanic Gardens, Denver Center for the Performing Arts, the Denver Zoo, the Denver Museum of Nature & Science, and many more. Work is under way to include mass transit access.

All of this places the Denver Public Library, through its joint-use card, at the hub of Denver youths' access to local arts, culture, recreation, and education. That's real community membership.

One for the Power Users

The Brooklyn Public Library (BPL) is experimenting with a "Power Users" program to build a closer relationship with its most active members. The program, which was launched in October 2015, used circulation totals to identify 150 patrons who had checked out over 5,000 items (over the available lifetime of ILS data, in their case, since the mid-1990s). A letter was then mailed to each of these patrons to invite their participation in the Power Users program. Less than a month into the program, over 10 percent of the patrons notified had brought their letter in to staff at a Brooklyn Public Library location. The first patron to do so was met with a round of applause.

Power Users get a branded library card, a tote bag, and a water bottle. Other perks are being explored, but for now patrons are responding mainly to the recognition. The Brooklyn Public Library asks Power Users if they're willing to advocate on behalf of the library. The BPL hopes to cultivate these super-fans as advocates for library members, with their advocacy addressed to the library system. Brooklyn Public Library's strategic initiatives manager, Diana Plunkett, explains that the program "creates an opportunity for us to have conversations with our heaviest users and have them help guide us. It's a great way to have a dialogue with people who are really invested in the library, and it can help us learn how we can make the experience for themselves—or for others who might not be at their level—even better and more powerful."

Early participants are also being asked to help shape the program, which is expected to evolve, and to act as ambassadors to the next 150 invitees. So far the Power Users tend to be older, but the first group of invitees did include families and teens, plus a local government official. As the library makes contact with the invitees, it's learning more about who the library's most active users are—their demographics, geography, local branch, and interests—and also at how that picture changes as circulation thresholds are reduced to expand the membership in the program.

The "superfan" identity quickly raises a question about using circulation counts as an indicator. Circulation is only one measure of library use, of course, and the library is experimenting with other metrics for the Power User recognition. The BPL would like to include program attendance, for example, and it has experimented with card swiping. Plunkett reports that program attendees were comfortable with that, but didn't always have cards with them and that it was a poor fit for caregivers and class visits. It's a question the library is still looking to resolve. PC and Wi-Fi usage are other measures it's looking at.

Going Cardless

We've been talking about library cards as physical things, but one could just as well be wondering about digital "cards" and other forms of secure identity. An account needs only an ID and PIN combination. A digital token can be passed from a smartphone, watch, NFC (near field communication) bracelet, and so on to accomplish anything a library bar code does ubiquitously now.

What about that? Is a virtual card different? Does it matter that it's less substantive? If we can't hold that totem and scrawl our name on it, can we still attach the same mystery and power to it?

Los Angeles Public Library Card
Card designed by Shepard Fairey. Illustration courtesy of Shepard Fairey/ Obeygiant.com

We'll see.

But whether physical or virtual, at hand or regularly lost, the role of the card doesn't change. The important thing is that meaning and utility both are bound up in library membership. Online and in plastic, there's a place for libraries to leverage art and branding. And of course, both physical cards and virtual cards can and do coexist and will both be used.

Circulation, too, is not simple. The library's measure doesn't include e-book circulation, for example, because data on individual patron usage resides with e-book platform providers, not with the library. The BPL is working to get those numbers, but they're not ordinarily available to client libraries. The noncirculation use metrics are increasingly important to libraries. An emphasis on membership and the collection all around may push this farther, and using a metric like card swiping might become more common and taken for granted. Library privacy policies and data aggregation and anonymization should follow into these areas.

The web page explaining the Power Users program (www.bklynlibrary.org/poweruser) lets all BPL card holders look up their lifetime tally and compare that to average and maximum totals for the system or for a zip code. Very cool. (Individual lifetime circulation totals are a standard part of Brooklyn's Innovative Sierra ILS, but not all ILSs tally this.) Plunkett notes that "it's a bit of a challenge to think about what the library can do in a benefits program when everything is free." The BPL has shown, though, that for some libraries this is a terrific way to highlight and build on library membership as a value in itself.

What Else Is This Card Good For?

While multiuse community membership cards are fairly new to public libraries, they're well established in academic settings. Although they don't share public library cards' mystique, student ID/campus cards are multifunctional and are unmistakably tokens of membership on college and university campuses. The campus card combines identification and a library account and usually also includes debit, meal plan, and digital and print services. Often it integrates facility access/electronic door management, transit, event ticketing, and more. Off-campus merchant support is increasingly common.

At many colleges and universities, this very multipurpose campus ID card is a library offering. Bill Folden, library circulation supervisor at Humboldt State University in northern California, shared a window into their particular experience. At that school, campus ID cards are made in the library but are administered separately.

> Traditionally, [campus cards] were looked at as separate from library work. But we had the space in the library to make them. It was convenient and we were open more than any other building on campus. There was a natural tie-in with issuing ID cards and checking out library books.
>
> Now we're trying to do away with the [separate] office, to make it more a part of regular library services. Our next step is to bring the ID functions out of this office, bring it out to the checkout desk, and transform that checkout desk to a library services desk, to expand the services we provide. People

walk up to the checkout counter, they need an ID: "Great, stand over here, take your picture, here's your card."

Humboldt State University ties a number of complementary functions to its campus card, including arrangements with three transit systems for unlimited free bus service. The transit pass is tied to a student ID number encoded in the ID card's magnetic stripe. The same number is used as a "convenience card" account to access stored funds and to receive discounts. Businesses on and off campus accept the debit cards, which also work with print/copy networks, vending machines, laundry, and more.

The functions are handled by different software systems. In Humboldt's case, PeopleSoft is the campus administrative system software which manages student IDs, course records, and finances. Another product, ID Flow, is used to generate cards and integrate them with ID records, secure entry (facility door) systems, debit systems, and with the library ILS. While other campus agencies manage each of these back-end systems, the primary student-facing touchpoint for the campus card is the library. In other words, the place to get your debit card for campus laundry, which is also your dorm room key, your bus pass, and your campus membership, is at the library circulation desk from library staff. That's fantastic and has been easy to take for granted. It's also a reminder to public libraries that the possibilities for attaching managed membership services to the library card are there and that a technological foundation for doing this has already been developed by universities.

Public libraries are borrowing from the campus model and finding applications of their own. Public library cards often integrate with managed printing, photocopying, and computer reservation systems. This integration is valuable and is a feature that public libraries can look to extend. Just as the campus card provides access to computer and print services campus-wide, PC management products might give public library members access to computer and print services around town. A meaningful share of library computer lab and copier use is for simple tasks like printing passes, coupons, applications, resumes, and so on. Could this be a portable feature of a library membership that is available at community centers, shopping plazas, or cafes?

The Iowa City Public Library maintained an off-site computer lab at a police substation. Kara Logsden, community and access services coordinator for the

Iowa City Public Library, explained that the program came out of their strategic planning. They had data on "who was using their library card to sign in to our Internet computers. We saw that on the southeast side of Iowa City, that that part of town was using the Internet computers [at the downtown library] more, and that they would benefit from more computer access in their neighborhood. We put a computer lab out. Our city had a police substation in that neighborhood and so the facility was there, they had a really nice conference room, the city's Internet was already there . . . The reality was, nobody came. They didn't want to come do Internet in a police station." There were also difficulties with the limited schedule the computer lab was on.

Although the program was discontinued after a year, the identification of the need and the lightweight response deserve credit and are an interesting example of making a library membership benefit portable.

Who Needs a Ride?

Another innovative partnership developed out of the Iowa City Public Library's strategic planning process. The library does a community survey every five years. The library had frequently seen that its members wanted easier access to their downtown library, in part driven by perceptions of limited parking downtown. The library also had data showing that its patrons came from all over the city, but that some underserved neighborhoods had transportation barriers impeding access. Making it easier to access the library became a strategic plan initiative.

They first experimented with a "Ride and Read" program which allowed any patron at the library with a valid library card to receive a pass for a bus ride home that same day. The program was good for Tuesdays through Thursdays and was available from all library public service desks. The limited schedule proved confusing, though, so it was later expanded to all six days with bus service. A simple tracking program limits patrons to two uses per week. Kara Logsden explained that the library next heard from teachers "who were very concerned about children having access to the library in the summertime." The library decided to complement the Ride and Read return-trip program with a "Summer Library Bus" to the library, free to students up to age eighteen

FIGURE 1.2
Promotion for the Iowa City Public Library Summer Reading Bus
Graphic courtesy Iowa City Public Library

and the adults riding with them. Their library card was the bus pass.

At first, the Summer Library Bus program used a dedicated, decorated shuttle bus operated by Iowa City Transit on a limited schedule. This was successful, but it proved to be too constrained by the route and schedule. The program grew to allow children or teens and accompanying guardians to present a library card for a free ride downtown on any Iowa City Transit route, weekdays off-peak (9 a.m. to 3 p.m.) all summer, from the day school lets out for summer to the day before school starts in the fall. (See figure 1.2.)

The already established Ride and Read program provides the bus rides home, and "if there's a student who wants to use it more than twice a week, we're flexible and we'll give them more passes." The bus rides are all charged to the library at a discounted rate by Iowa City Transit. Buses record the number of rides given and the transit system bills the library monthly. The library budgets for the cost, which was a little over $2,000 in 2014. Because the library and the transit system are both operated by the city, the city does the charge through internal accounting. "We think it's money that's very well spent."

Statistics on the program show strong and growing use. In summer 2015 there were over 3,200 Summer Library Bus rides downtown. The Ride and Read return trips for all of 2015 exceeded 1,500. While the usage is measurable and has tangible benefits, investing the library card with "real-world" applications like this has intangible value as well. The membership role of the library card grows. Members have access to the library and to their city: books, public places, programs, and . . . mobility. Logsden continued:

Our transit system is wonderful and great to work with. We've been doing some cross-promotion where we go out to the schools in the spring to get kids signed up for library cards and transit comes out with their bus. We have the stand, "Sign Up for a Library Card," and we have the bus right there. We have bookmarks about the Summer Library Bus.

We've been doing a lot of cross-promotion, specifically targeting Title I schools or a school in need of assistance. It's worked really well and the use is pretty amazing. It's wonderful to go to a school and say, "Hey, if you have trouble getting to the library, all you have to do is show your library card and you can hop on a bus!" It's brought a lot of kids into the library.

Librarians brokering improved access to cities and towns—in this case through a thoughtful and valuable transit benefit, negotiated with a civic partner—has expanded library membership. Access to the resources around us can be a matter as literal as getting there. Mobility is a promising piece of the collection all around.

Financial Connections

Access to the world around us is also built on basic economic participation, on having a means of receiving, storing, and spending pay and benefits. The "I Love My Library" card, an experimental pairing of library card and prepaid debit card, was developed by the library automation vendor SirsiDynix and was piloted at three libraries starting in 2014. Maryland's Frederick County Public Libraries, Illinois's Lansing Public Library, and Mississippi's Lamar County Library System participated.

Prepaid debit cards offer unbanked patrons a convenient way to store and save money, similar to a checking account but without requiring a bank account or credit check and without the extraordinary fees of check-cashing services. Despite limited consumer protections, prepaid debit cards are widely used. A total of $167 billion was projected to be loaded into prepaid card accounts in 2014, an increase of 42 percent from the amount loaded in 2010. Most cards accept direct deposits and carry loss and fraud protections. Social Security and Supplemental Security Income recipients are required to receive their payments electronically, for example, and the cards are one way that many people do receive these payments.

Many prepaid cards carry high fees, however, and have opaque fee structures. The product partnered on by SirsiDynix carried fees that were average for the category. An expectation held by SirsiDynix and the libraries is that by pairing debit storage with a library card, users will be more likely to retain the dual-use card longer than is typical for prepaid cards. This avoids activation and other fees when obtaining a new one. According to a 2012 study by the Federal Reserve Bank of Philadelphia, prepaid cards have an average life span of only six months. The SirsiDynix card also featured affinity card functionality, allowing local businesses to offer discounts that would be automatically applied when the card was used. Controversially, a portion of the card's fees was returned to the library as revenue. Although activation and funding rates were higher than forecast early on, ultimately, the product didn't align well enough with library principles and didn't offer exceptional value for members. It was discontinued in August 2015.

Banking remains an important component of community membership and access in the meantime, though. Libraries educate and assist on financial literacy, but going farther, the place of libraries in their communities makes them good prospects for connecting the public with banking and credit services. Cooperative banks and community-development banks may be partners to consider for their membership and community benefit missions. Librarians that are able to broker financial services between the public and financial partners, particularly in communities that are unbanked at higher rates, could provide a valuable service. The practical utility of this is clear and foundational, and the contribution to community membership and belonging is also important. Facilitating library-assisted and member-serving economic participation is consistent with the library as a gateway to local access and is a challenge for librarians to consider.

Local Citizens

Discrete programs like these are excellent ways that librarians have extended library membership. Local governments have also led noteworthy programs of civic membership, usually with ties to libraries. Municipal IDs are photo IDs provided by an increasing number of cities and counties. The cards help community members who have difficulty obtaining state-issued IDs—for example, undocumented immigrants, the homeless, foster youth, the elderly, and formerly incarcerated individuals—to gain better access to civic and economic life. As described in the Center for Popular Democracy report *Building Identity: A Toolkit for Designing and Implementing a Successful Municipal ID Program*, "typically all government agencies and officials (including the police) will accept the card as proof of identity in any interaction with a community member."[2]

Without the right form of ID, a person may not be able to open a bank account or cash a check, see a doctor at a hospital, register their child for school, apply for public benefits, file a complaint with the police department, borrow a book from a library, vote in an election, or even collect a package from the post office. A municipal ID removes all of these barriers with a single stroke. A municipal ID can be a powerful symbol of inclusion and welcome extended to marginalized community members. Young people, especially those with unstable home environments, often have trouble obtaining official IDs either because of the cost or because they do not have access to the necessary documents. Having a valid ID can help them avoid being detained by the police or being issued a summons.

The largest municipal ID program is New York City's IDNYC, with 863,464 cardholders as of June 30, 2016. Library registration is not automatic, but the IDNYC card can be tied to existing library accounts or used to open new ones at all three library systems covering New York City's five boroughs. About ten other cities offer municipal IDs and an equal number are seeking them. In most cases, government agencies run the service but there are also private and nonprofit-administered programs.

A survey of 70,000 IDNYC cardholders found that among immigrant cardholders, 36 percent rely on the municipal ID as their only form of photo identification and 77 percent reported that their IDNYC card has increased their sense of belonging to the city.[3] IDNYC and other municipal ID programs have developed additional benefits paired to the IDs, including discounts at cultural institutions and local businesses, access to park and recreation centers, and the inclusion of emergency and medical information. Over half of IDNYC survey respondents have used the card to obtain free memberships to forty cultural institutions—such as museums and performing arts centers—and to receive discounts on groceries, pharmacies, and fitness centers.

A similar card is offered nationally in Scotland: the National Entitlement Card provides library membership and works as a smart card for transit, debit and prepayment, printing and photocopying, door access control systems, and discounts at cultural institutions. Another membership model is Canada's Cultural Access Pass, which is available only to new citizens. The pass is free and valid for one's first year of citizenship. The pass includes free admission to hundreds of Canadian museums, national and provincial parks, events and performances, and discounts on travel and hotels. A number of libraries act as pass distribution sites.

While these programs have not originated with libraries, libraries have been active partners in them. Where localities do not have the interest or capacity to lead on municipal IDs, libraries might pursue a leading role. They have relevant experience in all aspects of these projects. Where the IDs are led by other city departments, libraries should be primary enrollment centers. (In New York City, a select number are.) The fit with libraries' mission and expertise is clear and is consistent with the fundamental role of membership and community identity in library practice.

A Home for Community Membership

Library membership has an important place in facilitating access to the world around us. It ties the wide variety of those programs and services together. It's where the collection all around starts. Library membership is also a reminder that the work of making the valuable resources around us more available to all has a long-standing institutional home and practice: the library and librarianship.

There are many directions for benefits attaching to library membership yet to come. The thoughtful, deliberate work of "local access librarians" will yield some efforts that we can all learn from. We know that librarians have the expertise, experience, connections, and place in the community for the job. Let's see what they come up with.

NOTES

1. *From Distant Admirers to Library Lovers—and Beyond: A Typology of Public Library Engagement in America*, Pew Research Center, 2014, http://admin.issuelab.org/permalink/resource/17490.

2. *Building Identity: A Toolkit for Designing and Implementing a Successful Municipal ID Program*, Center for Popular Democracy, 2015, populardemocracy.org/sites/default/files/Municipal-ID-Report_WEB_Nov2015_0.pdf.

3. *IDNYC: A Tool of Empowerment—A Mixed-Methods Evaluation of the New York Municipal ID Program*, Westat, Inc., 2016, www1.nyc.gov/assets/idnyc/downloads/pdf/idnyc_report_full.pdf.

CHAPTER TWO

City Pass
Agents Share
the Wealth

MUSEUM PASS—OR "CITY PASS"—PROGRAMS ARE THE quintessential example of librarians improving the public's access to local resources. Through the library—with the library in the role of agent or broker—members borrow short-term passes to remarkable area venues, large and small, each showcasing unique treasures, talent, and expertise. Like most projects discussed here, these programs are not entirely new and they're not uncommon. Most larger libraries and many smaller ones have had a museum pass program for many years. I couldn't identify the "first museum pass program," but the Boston Public Library is a contender. Theirs began in 1995.

Typically, museum pass programs consist of printed passes for a local museum and they circulate like a book or other material with a comparable loan period. A library might have several passes for one institution, another batch for a second venue, and another batch for a third. In a multibranch library system, some allow the passes to travel from branch to branch, while others don't. Some allow hold requests to be placed on the passes, and some don't.

These basic city pass programs are great successes and are very popular. The Chicago Public Library offers passes to each of fifteen different institutions on this model, with no holds permitted. At the San Diego Public Library, where passes are available for three local institutions, queues often run to over 1,000 requests for a single venue (each with about 40 circulating passes). The passes have given libraries' communities access to art museums, children's museums, zoos, gardens, pools, and a host of opportunities that are otherwise a challenging cost for many. Most passes offer free admission. In some cases, they provide free admission to kids with discounts for adults. For venues that are free to begin with, some passes offer free parking or store discounts.

The Vancouver (BC) Public Library's Inspiration Pass combines free access to twenty-seven area sites in a single circulating pass that is good for a group of four. (See figure 2.1.) Anne O'Shea, manager for programming and learning at the Vancouver Public Library, explained that the two-week pass "gives you access to a huge number of organizations: the aquarium, the symphony, the museum. All sorts of things. You can bring your family or a few friends with you." Circulation restrictions limit members to borrowing the pass once per year and to visiting a venue only once over the two-week loan period. A "passport" page is stamped as a simple way to record visits. Restrictions like these help meet the concerns of partner venues that the passes won't compete with

FIGURE 2.1
Vancouver Inspiration Pass
Images courtesy of Vancouver Public Library (Vancouver, B.C., Canada)

their own membership sales. Despite the modest restrictions, the program sees long request lists and wait times, a testament to (and a limit on) the program's success.

The types of venues made available through pass programs reflect the diverse communities in which they're found. Passes from the Kimball Library (Atkinson, NH) are available to sites around the region, including the Strawbery Banke historical waterfront museum in Portsmouth and the Imagine That kids' museum and indoor play space in Lawrence, Massachusetts. The North Babylon (NY) Public Library provides passes to Old Westbury Gardens and the Fire Island Lighthouse. The Glen Ridge (NJ) Public Library takes you to the Aviation Hall of Fame. The Seattle Public Library gets you in to the Log House Museum, Seattle Architecture Foundation Tours, and the Center for Wooden Boats.

At the Sacramento Public Library there are four varieties of circulating Crocker Art Pack kids' backpacks. The backpack itself acts as a free pass to the Crocker Art Museum for an accompanying adult or an older child (kids six and under are free). The "Color Garden" edition of the kids' backpacks contains five themed books, a CD, a color discovery box with soft toys, a game, three colored scarves, a color wheel and maze, an animal voice box, and other activities for exploring the theme.

Libraries know their communities as well as or better than anyone. They have existing relationships with local venues that represent first steps already taken toward starting pass programs. Collaboration on city pass programs, in turn, affirms and strengthens those institutional relationships. For participating venues, the passes bring in new attendees and new customers and help reach underserved communities.

The Value Is Clear

For libraries and their communities, the demand, use, and value of pass programs are practical and measurable. Pass lending is recorded. There's a corresponding dollar value to the use of a pass. Chris Brown, deputy county librarian for community library development at the Santa Clara County (CA) Library District, explained that "a lot of library programming is difficult to report out the value of. When you're reporting out to your commission or your city manager or in your annual report, with [the pass program] it's very easy to say, 'Here's the dollar value our users got back from this service.'"

Beyond simple accounting, there's a growing appreciation in libraries and education that "enrichments," including the experiences that these venues specialize in, are serious business. Kids' early learning depends on play and exploration. Children's museums, play centers, children's gardens, science centers, and many other venues heighten and expand kids' everyday learning experiences. Serving early learning is a part of libraries' charge, and city passes are a way to bring those experiences to all the children in a city, town, or county. For adults, access to our cultural treasures, history, and recreation—besides being its own reward—enhances our local connection and understanding.

Pass programs which circulate a printed pass contend with a number of limits and inefficiencies. If placing holds isn't permitted, passes can sit unused. When there are holds, passes still sit unused going through delivery and waiting for pickup. For the public, physical passes mean long waits for passes, trips to the library for pickup and return, plus potential late fees. For the participating venues, physical passes are typically good anytime and so compete with memberships and paid admission. There are few ways to shape who borrows the passes so as to meet the institution's goals. And there are few ways to limit repeat use by library patrons in order to increase exposure and nudge users toward membership. And finally, there's no way to shape the number of passes available from season to season or day to day with any agility.

As much as traditional pass programs have been valued and applauded, for these reasons it's been difficult to expand the number of partners participating under the circulating physical pass model. But things are changing. Online technology has made it possible to manage very complex availability schemes efficiently and with much greater convenience for library members and partner institutions. The key to taking advantage of this is turning circulating passes into admission *tickets* that can be booked and retrieved online on one's own or through library staff. On its face, tickets are an incremental change to a long-standing program. In practice, they're a qualitative leap to something very new.

From a Feature to a Collection

The Discover & Go ticketed pass program was started by the Contra Costa County Library (CCCL) in the California Bay Area in 2011. In 2012 CCCL was awarded the National Medal for Museum and Library Service for the program. It is truly remarkable. Today, Discover & Go offers library users from 44 participating library systems ticketed day-passes to a total of 92 California museums, parks, pools, zoos, galleries, theaters, gardens, and other attractions. Currently, all but a few of these attractions are in northern California, but a southern California program has recently started. The program has supported over 500,000 visits since it started. Here are just a dozen of the 92 participating attractions, large and small.

> California Shakespeare Theater
> Charles M. Schulz Museum
> Chinese Historical Society of America Museum
> Coit Tower
> GLBT History Museum
> Hamilton Swimming Pool
> Lindsay Wildlife Experience
> Museum of the African Diaspora
> Oakland Zoo
> Sacramento Children's Museum
> San Jose Museum of Art
> Santa Rosa Symphony

What is this but a collection? It is a big regional shelf of titles—some brightly colored, some classic—to pull down, peruse, and dive into. The library card, as ever, is one's key to using this remarkable collection all around us. Here it is "on the shelf," through the work of librarians brokering and facilitating access, and doing old work in a new way.

Despite the program's success and award recognition, Discover & Go and other ticketed pass programs strike me as underappreciated in the library community. There have been few articles on them, no books, no conference tracts. Why not? Maybe because they resemble the circulating pass programs that preceded them and, so, don't look "new." (Though those warrant more attention as well.) In any case, ticketing creates such an increase in scope from earlier programs that it becomes a difference in kind. The online ticket management systems that make these programs possible are enabled by technology that wasn't practical and affordable until very recently. They are new and rich and warrant inquiry and exploration.

I spoke to the information systems programmer at the Contra Costa County Library, Stacie Deng, who was part of the launch team and administers the program today. Starting out, Deng knew that they wanted an online ticketing system that could pool tickets for all of their twenty-six library locations, support a consortium of systems with different needs, and allow customization as the program grew. They found one software application that they thought might work, but they couldn't work out affordable licensing. With a clear, ambitious vision for what they wanted, they decided to have a new application developed just for their needs and to find grant money to make it possible.

Cathy Sanford, then deputy county librarian for support services at Contra Costa, initiated the project and secured a grant of $45,000 from the Bay Area Library and Information System (BALIS), their regional cooperative. The grant included funding to work with the library software developer Quipu Group, with whom CCCL had worked previously on other library utilities. Quipu hosts the Discover & Go software and the relationship has continued through numerous modifications and revisions. An important requirement of the grant was that the program support a consortium of library systems. This requirement was formative for the program's eventual flexibility and broad appeal.

Patrons log in with their library card and the system applies a number of filters—library membership, city, zip code, age—to determine what tickets are available to them and what they see. Tickets are also limited in a number of ways. For a particular venue, individual users may be allowed only one ticket per year or per month. Library systems each receive a limited number of tickets. Some programs have age requirements.

I spoke with Robert Anderson of the Quipu Group which developed the ePASS software that Discover & Go runs on. Anderson was struck by the clear value that CCCL's program was providing the public:

They shared with us comments coming in from the patrons. "I'm a single parent of three and I can finally take them to the Tech Museum!" Contra Costa saw that once they released Discover & Go, neighbor said to neighbor, "We're going to the museum because we got these free passes from the library." They saw more people signing up for library cards because of this type of community outreach. It's been one of my favorite things that I've ever done. We got a great response from patrons, a great response from the libraries, and from the attractions. It was very win-win-win.

The other wonderful thing about ePASS, and that was one of the major goals, was access for all. One of the issues when they were circulating physical passes was that there were lines at the door for people trying to get museum passes. This system was set up so that no one patron could dominate the system.

Chris Brown was Discover & Go's project manager and was responsible for the opening-day collection. He emphasized the ticketing technology's outward simplicity as being of critical importance to the program's success with the public. "For the user," Brown explained, "Discover & Go was an example of building a service modeled on the convenience of other services in the for-profit world. You go and you order tickets to a concert you want to go see. Or you book reservations for a restaurant you want to go to. It was built in a similar model of access as other products that people would purchase with their credit card . . . It was modeled on the convenience that was becoming a baseline for any other service industry." (See figure 2.2.)

FIGURE 2.2
Discover & Go Logo

Tickets and Reporting Make All the Difference

Contra Costa hadn't had a circulating physical pass program in place, so they were starting from scratch. They began approaching museums in their county, starting with ones they'd partnered with on other programs. The first partner was the Lindsey Wildlife Experience in Walnut Creek, which had led many children's programs for the library. The second was the Oakland Museum of California, with whom they also had a relationship.

The Discover & Go team hoped for a launch collection of five museums. Ultimately, they had an opening-day collection of over *forty*. "It was just amazing!" Deng said. "The responses we got from the museums were very, very positive. We weren't expecting that this many people would say, 'Okay, here you go!'"

Brown related the progression that venues went through when he approached them asking for donations and the leap that the ticketing software represented:

> I was asking all those museums for donations. You'd find some who immediately would say, "No, I don't want to do this." And you'd say, "Well, what if we could guarantee that it wouldn't get abused? That a cardholder could only use one pass a year?" And suddenly they'd say, "Oh, well that's kind of interesting."
>
> And then we'd talk some more and we'd be able to say, "Well, what if you could give a set of universal passes and maybe another batch of passes that would only be accessible to a zip code that you wanted to reach?" Suddenly they'd say, "Oh! Well, this is making it worthwhile for us."
>
> It felt like a real partnership in that sense, that you could do something through the technology that you wouldn't be able to do if you just had a physical pass from the library. You can literally say, we want X number of passes to go to underserved communities. I think that helped the museums feel like they were getting something out of this as opposed to only donating resources.

Deng elaborated on the ability to amplify access in underserved communities and the relevance of that function to the partner institutions. As she explains, it was an important piece of their decision-making and a reason why so many got on board with Discover & Go, even before it had launched and had a track record. "I found out later that the museums usually have allocated money to serve underserved communities," Deng said. "Our software is able to address that. When we approach them, they say, 'Can you do this? Can you do that?' and the answer is 'Yes, we can.' The California Academy of Sciences would give us, let's say, 4,000 tickets a year and then say, 'Okay, I'm going to give you 800 more and those 800 need to go to certain income-level patrons.' So we look at the census data and say, 'In the city of Richmond, the median income is within your guideline.' We can limit the distribution of the 800 to just those patrons. We have several museums that will only take patrons from certain zip codes. That is a big sell."

Usage reports are the component that brought home the benefits of shared ticketing for the venues and underlined the control that it offered them. They could plan to reach target populations by allocating tickets in a particular way. It was the reporting that let them see that the system was working. The reports satisfied their funding and budgeting requirements and informed their planning.

> We are able to provide them a report every six months about how many tickets are distributed to each zip code. They love those reports! They use the reports in their board meetings, in their grant applications. I heard multiple times that in the past they would just give tickets to libraries but that they had no statistics on how the tickets were distributed or used. We were the first ones that were able to provide that to them. That was a big selling point.

For example, one report showed that the California Academy of Sciences had 21,214 Discover & Go visitors in 2015. A total of 1,384 of these visitors belonged to the San Francisco Public Library, 1,147 were from the Contra Costa County Library, and on through the Oakland Public Library, the Berkeley Public Library, Alameda County . . . Geographically, visitors came in descending order from San Francisco, Oakland, Berkeley, Freemont, Concord, and so on. The Discover & Go software tracks which tickets go from being reserved to being printed. Tickets that aren't printed by the day before they're valid are returned to the pool for access by another patron. Though not all venues do this, the printed tickets have bar codes that many venues scan to collect additional data showing which tickets are in fact used and when.

Follow-up surveys are e-mailed to patrons after their ticket dates asking "Would you return? Would you visit this venue again even if you have to pay? Are you going to consider membership?" Comments received in the California Academy of Sciences surveys included "Thank you for providing this service. It allowed me to check out the venue and buy membership." And "Thank you for the very enriching experience! We learned a lot and had so much fun!"

When the Yolo County Library was joining Discover & Go, the regional manager, Rachel Hudson, and her team brainstormed how they could use the program to show off what their largely rural county had to offer. "Where do we take our friends when they come from out of town? What do we really like about our county?" Librarians at Yolo County began with the county historical museum, the Gibson House, a historic estate and grounds, and are working to create partnerships with local performing arts centers. The reports are an important part of their outreach. "Gibson House was really excited about all the new people that were coming to town. When you look at the report, it's not Yolo County residents that are going to the exhibit, it's people from outside Yolo County. That was really interesting." Hudson has used the interest of those visiting from outside their area as a selling point for another venue they're working with. "Because this other venue has a static exhibit, their concern has always been, once people have been there, they've seen it. They were looking for ways to reach out beyond Yolo County and bring people in. Seeing the reports, they said, 'Oh, this would be just what we need!'"

Hunting for Free Treasure

Another important feature for Discover & Go's participating libraries' partners has been the ability to select days on which to make day-passes available. The system maintains a calendar for each venue to know which days they're open, but, Deng explained, "some museums will say, 'Okay, my weekdays are slower and my weekends are busy, so I don't want to offer weekends to you.'" Some venues like to limit day-passes to days with docent tours available. The ticketing program is able to apply all of this.

I find this aspect the most intriguing one. In effect, the librarians and venues are identifying *surplus availability*—access with little to no marginal cost to the venue—and making it free to the public. The venues can do this in a managed way. (It's not just a free day that is open to everyone. The number of admissions is limited.)

Stacie Deng described the evolution of this aspect of the program. "When we first started, the software didn't have that many features. Then, pretty much every time when we added a new museum they had new specs that we needed to meet. They would say, 'I'm going to give your county Monday and Tuesday, but I want to give another county library system Wednesday and Thursday.' Smaller venues are not able to accommodate too many people on the same day, so we spread them out."

For passing along their surplus availability the venues get something in return: exposure to new audiences while preserving the value and incentives of membership. The venues are not overcrowded—that is managed—and membership offers access at choice times plus other benefits.

Identifying and harvesting our communities' surplus wealth—surpluses that have been there all along—and then sharing that harvest in a managed way through library membership is new and exciting. A "surplus wealth" framework might lead libraries to explore new frontiers in the types of resources that they can share: open seats at university classes or low-speed cellular data connections. This idea isn't new, but the technological platforms allowing libraries to efficiently support it is. I think libraries have only just started experimenting with this.

Negotiating Partnerships

The process of bringing partner venues on board is aided by a library's existing relationships and place in the community. As Brown explains, "The other thing that's incredibly important is the goodwill that libraries have. There's not a lot of other institutions that could provide this service. We're mission-based. We're not making a profit. We're doing this solely to expand the informal learning opportunities of our public. The museums understood that libraries are coming to the partnership with a similar mission as themselves."

The position of libraries in the community gave the Discover & Go team a position of some strength and they have been incredibly effective at negotiating on behalf of the public. Deng explained that in some cases, the partner venues don't want to offer a full family day-pass and have proposed discounts. "I'm not really interested in the discount stuff," Deng said. "I want to have at least one child free. I don't want them to use us as an advertising source." Libraries should be attentive to this: there's potential for venues to misuse the program for marketing alone. Other venues are interested in serving only their local area, so, for example, the San Francisco Zoo is only available to cardholders with a San Francisco city zip code. Discover & Go is generally able to accept this latter sort of restriction.

I asked Deng about other incentives for the partners. Is access ever purchased? "There are museums that charge us an administrative fee. For example, the San Jose Art Museum charges each of the libraries that wants to join them $75 a year. The other opt-in is the Asian Art Museum in San Francisco, and they charge $300 per year for 45 family day-passes per month, for each system opting in."

It's striking to me how affordable their opt-in partners are: $75/year or $300/year. That's an easy purchase in the context of collection development. The Contra Costa County Library has approached some venues about paying for a greater number of tickets and has been refused. In those cases, the venues feel that they're providing shared access at a level that meets their goals. Sometimes that's lower than what the library would like.

When a new library system is brought on board, that system enjoys access to the large Discover & Go "opening day collection," which for many is enough. They're encouraged, though, to bring in new partners that are local to them. The Discover & Go team coaches new systems on how to approach partners, and provides sample letters and talking points. (See "The Playbook" sidebar later in this chapter.) When participating libraries approach new partners, they're aided by the presence of major institutions already in the roster, which generates ready interest and confidence in the program.

Bringing new library systems into the program carries with it technical and policy hurdles, namely the diversity of library automation systems and associated library policies that have to interoperate. Patron status and eligibility are basic components. The ePASS software that automates Discover & Go needs to authenticate users and retrieve information about them in order to present appropriate offers. Meanwhile, the ILSs used by the many libraries in the consortium have different behaviors. As Robert Anderson of the Quipu Group explained:

> Most libraries have SIP2 [the Standard Interchange Protocol for communication between library automation applications] and usually it can bring back the particular information we need. For some ILS vendors, we have to use APIs for patron authentication because their SIP2 implementation only brings back a "yes" or "no." Because it's a reservation service, we needed the patron's name, their e-mail, their age, their zip code, that type of information.
>
> That was the first challenge. Which libraries could provide what information? The other issue is the particular library's policy. How do they treat their patron's data as far as what they keep, what they'll expose? For instance, some libraries don't store the patron's age or date of birth. With Discover & Go they're getting offers to so many different types of attractions from museums to jazz clubs, so age becomes an important factor. We don't want a patron to reserve a pass to a jazz club that you have to be 18 or 21 to get to and they're 10.
>
> The other part of the authentication process was, "What constitutes a patron in good standing?" Depending on the ILS system, we have different information to make that determination, such as patron type. Do they owe fines and how much do they owe? Which systems can impart that information? Which libraries allow their systems to impart that information?

Quipu and Contra Costa worked their way through many, many particulars of ILS and policy differences to make ePASS work. The challenge suggests that library systems, perhaps with support from state libraries or cooperatives, should devote more attention to cooperative agreements on policies and data-sharing. What policies regarding patron information and standing should all libraries adhere to? When administrative policy choices are aligned, the stage is set for interoperability and cooperation on programs and services existing and yet to be created, for regional collections all around.

Looking Ahead

The maintenance work that makes up administering Discover & Go includes keeping up with modifications to venue distribution formulas and managing all the renewals. Agreements are typically renewed for one or two years. "We remind the venues what they have agreed to offer: the number of tickets, which library system that these tickets are available to, and how frequently a person can get a ticket. If they can use them daily, monthly, annually, or weekly."

The Contra Costa County Library is the sole back-end administrator for Discover & Go. The other participating library systems each pay a share of the hosting and maintenance costs, about $450 per year from each system. This doesn't contribute to staff costs at Contra Costa or to ongoing software development by Quipu. Finding a shared way to better fund continuing collection development work by librarians and software development by Quipu is a challenge. Complicating this, the CCCL has been directed by the county of Contra Costa that they cannot generate revenue with what they charge the participating libraries. Given that Discover & Go is generating so much use and value at so little cost, it's a little surprising to me that there isn't more funding to support new development.

Deng explained, "We're still looking at what options are available to let member libraries know that right now all we're doing is maintaining the collections. Unfortunately, a lot of them think that they are paying into the opening-day collection. I have to say, 'No, you don't.' Sometimes they treat me as a vendor, 'Why couldn't you do this?' The challenge for me now is to develop a funding source so that we can continue to improve the software to meet the needs of our patrons."

Southern California is being added to Discover & Go with Library Services and Technology Act grant funding administered by the California State Library. The Los Angeles County Library will be the administrative hub there. Deng has been training counterparts at that library "because we want to separate the ticket pools with northern California and southern California. We're just too far away. In order to manage, I need to have somebody there that does the back-end administration." Together with Quipu, Deng is working to create separate consortia for northern and southern California in the system, but with a number of tickets from each made available to the other.

The Discover & Go team has identified features that they hope to implement or improve in the near term. Deng prepared a $25,000 grant from the Pacific Library Partnership, the consolidated regional cooperative to which CCCL and BALIS belong, which was recently awarded. The grant covers software enhancements with the Quipu Group and testing in cooperation with the San Francisco Public Library. The improvements are to include the following:

- a Spanish-language interface
- better mobile device support, which needs ongoing development
- geolocation capability, so users can find offers near their current location
- repooling of unclaimed tickets. Some participating library systems typically distribute their full fixed allotment of tickets quickly while others leave tickets unclaimed. Deng would like the option to return tickets to a pool for all members the day before an event or performance in order to best utilize those resources.
- transferring of tickets between accounts, between members, and for replaced library cards
- administrative enhancements for managing offers of performances
- filters for front-end browsing of offers
- e-mail and text notifications for confirmations, reminders, and surveys on an opt-in basis

This menu of improvements underlines just how far ticketed systems have come and are headed from circulating physical passes, and how sophisticated they might become in another ten or twenty years.

From a Collection to a Platform

Yolo County is working on partnering with some venues that haven't operated visitor programs of their own. Farm tours are one example being discussed. This prospect deserves highlighting. Ticketing programs like Discover & Go are also *a platform* that local institutions can piggyback on to administer visits. Farms, businesses, schools, community centers, and *(continued on page 34)*

The Playbook

The Contra Costa County Library developed a how-to guide for library systems joining Discover & Go. The guide draws on CCCL's experience in cultivating new partner institutions. I've edited it slightly here.

STEP ONE: IDENTIFY CULTURAL INSTITUTIONS

- What are the interests of groups that the library serves? Which organizations would benefit from library-based exposure?
- Existing relationships are a natural place to start.
- Be prepared with background on pass programs at nearby library systems.

STEP TWO: MAKE THE ASK

Speak with someone in the venue's membership department and share the following:

- We are interested in partnering with your institution to provide day-passes to library customers for checkout, similar to the way they would check out a book. The program helps us encourage library customers to discover one-of-a-kind cultural venues in [the area].
- Cultural pass programs are currently in place across the country and are extremely successful for cultural institutions and libraries. [Include local information if available.]
- [Number of card holders] would have the opportunity to participate in this program. This is an easy way to increase exposure for your institution, expand access to local culture, increase opportunities for education, and turn library cardholders into museumgoers.
- Software manages what passes are available. The software is highly customizable and can be managed by the venue. It allows organizations to target specific populations and track pass usage.

Note that funding is often available to support collaboration between libraries and cultural institutions, for example, Sparks! Ignition Grants from the IMLS.

STEP THREE: INITIAL FOLLOW-UP

Sample E-Mail:

> Thank you for the opportunity to discuss [our program]. I am excited about the opportunity for [name of library] to partner with [name of cultural institution] to provide access to your fabulous exhibits and educational opportunities. Together we can expand access to local culture,

increase opportunities for education, and turn library cardholders into museumgoers. Here are the details. . .

[Library/program name] will make day-passes available to library cardholders through an easy-to-use online collection of area venues. Library customers simply browse the venues they want to visit, select the dates, reserve passes, and, optionally, print them! (Passes can also be loaded on to a mobile phone.) The passes are secure and include the library cardholder's name and the date on which the pass is valid. Your staff simply verifies the library cardholder's ID. The number of passes to your institution can be limited in a variety of ways.

[Cultural institution] has a fantastic opportunity to increase your visibility throughout our community. We aggregate where pass users come from, provide you detailed information on where you have developed new audiences, and can help you target specific populations/demographics.

We hope that you will help us expand access to educational and cultural resources, and turn library cardholders into users of cultural institutions! Please let us know what we can do to help make a partnership possible.

STEP FOUR: FOLLOW UP/SECURE PARTNERSHIP

Within a week or ten days follow up again via phone.

- Did they utilize the demo site? Do they have questions about the customer experience?
- Is expanding awareness and usage of their institution a current priority?
- Have they considered how many passes they could allocate for this program?
- Be prepared to remind them that participation drives traffic to their institution at a minimal cost.
- Participation exposes nonusers (of their institution) to the exciting exhibits and resources that they offer.
- Participation demonstrates to the community that they are dedicated to exploration, discovery, and lifelong learning.
- Participation aligns them with an organization [your library] that is loved by [number of cardholders] customers.

Be prepared to share with them other institutions you are/have partnered with and their commitment.

Continued on page 34

Continued from page 33

STEP FIVE: FINALIZE COMMITMENT

Outline via e-mail or a formal document the following:

- Contact information (point person, address, phone number, e-mail address)
- Brief description of venue
- Number of passes per month for the library, number per month/year per customer
- Restrictions (e.g., limited to users within a specific zip code)?
- Allowances: number of adults and children admitted, define ages for children
- Dates: all dates that the institution is open and passes are to be available
- Length of commitment (two years is preferred)

STEP SIX: REPEAT! USE NEW PARTNERSHIPS TO FOSTER ADDITIONAL PARTNERSHIPS

Include in talking points:

- Institutions participating and benefits gained by each
- Value of joining an existing and successful partnership program
- Value of aligning with other participating cultural institutions

other organizations like these may want visitor programs but not have or want the public event infrastructure of their own to support open houses, tours, performances, and the like. Where it is an appropriate fit, city pass programs are platforms that librarians can help smaller organizations use to their own benefit, in addition to that of the public. Organizations can schedule public events and take advantage of the library's administered platform to manage the ticketing process. They also benefit from visibility on the library's platform, a place library members go to see "What's available to explore today?" And they add to the collective value of the collection all around.

These benefits and the general success of Discover & Go have also meant that participating libraries don't always have to seek out new partner attractions. The Contra Costa County Library has been contacted directly by many venues that want to join, making its work easier. Given that, the library has an important responsibility to perform collection development. The selection and deselection of offers should be evaluated for consistency with the library's mission and collection development policy.

So Tell Everyone

When it launched the Discover & Go program in 2011, the Contra Costa County Library dedicated the month of October to promoting Discover & Go. The library continued to promote in October in years following, and started the "October Is Discover & Go!" promotion for all participating library systems beginning in 2014. A partnership with the local food bank developed and was integrated into the October promotion. CCCL solicits additional tickets and annual memberships from popular partner venues for a raffle. For each bag of food a patron brings in for the food bank, they're entered into the raffle for a free ticket or annual membership. To increase its use in underserved communities, CCCL also pursued and was awarded a $15,000 grant in 2012 to market the Discover & Go network.

As a further part of the marketing effort, the library developed a partnership with 511 Contra Costa, a transportation support and advocacy network. Each year 511 Contra Costa provides $10,000 in Bay Area Rapid Transit (BART) commuter train tickets to Discover & Go users. When a ticket has been reserved for a BART-accessible venue, Discover & Go provides an online form to request up to three BART tickets per household to be mailed to them. In 2016 the program was expanded to include day-passes for the bus systems. City pass programs, like other collection all-around projects, lend themselves to ties like this: tickets to area venues become prizes in a food bank raffle or hooks for pairing to mass transit tickets.

Rachel Hudson described some of the Yolo County Library's promotional work:

> When we do our outreach we talk about Discover & Go. A flyer goes home to
> all the kids in all the backpacks at the beginning of the school year. It's part

of our spiel, one of the things that we talk about. People are just blown away. Like, "Wait a minute! I can do what? For free? With my library card? Really? Huh! Oh my goodness! Wow! I didn't know about that!"

You get a lot of very positive interest and you see the numbers go up after we've done a big outreach push. We've redone press releases and seen them picked up again in a couple papers. When we have school visits or when we have class tours, we definitely talk about it as what you can do at the library. It's out on our floor with all our other flyers of activities and things to do. We tell people, "You know, if you get stuck on the website the first time, give us a call. Because sometimes it can be tricky." Some of our senior citizens are not online. They'll come in, tell us what they want to do, and we'll do it for them right there. We try and make it easy for folks.

People get really excited when they have out-of-town company coming or when it's school break. "What am I going to do with my kids now?!" Get in the car, drive an hour, go to a museum for free. Have a picnic and come home. It's just reminding people that this is a resource for you, it is free, and here's how you can make it work for you and your family.

Sarah Houghton, director of the San Rafael Public Library, shared the same response. "It's a huge service. It's the one where we visit schools or talk to families, the parents are like, 'What? This is amazing!' It's one of those things that has a low cost for us but a huge impact for the community."

A Rich Pageant

The Discover & Go program is the most extensive, but not the only, ticketed day-pass library program. The Multnomah County Library (Portland, OR) uses the same ePASS software from Quipu that Discover & Go uses for their own program. The Seattle Public Library uses mp.Insight software from LibraryInsight. The Boston Public Library uses TixKeeper from Plymouth Rocket.

I spoke to Jennifer Inglis, chief of public services at the Boston Public Library, about their program, one of the first museum pass programs. A difference in their program is that the direct purchase of tickets is their main mode of acquisition. The cost is greater, but it is reasonable and is consistent with typical collection development practice. Libraries buy books, media, and all kinds of new resources to share, and purchasing access to cultural institutions and performances is of a piece with that. "Our passes are paid for by our various Friends of the Library groups. The Central Library has a Friends group, and some of the branches have a Friends group, and those organizations decide whether or not they want to fund the museum pass program."

The purchase model gives them flexibility in selecting venues, creates fewer restrictions to accommodate, and frees staff from much of the work of negotiating agreements. It also allows user requests for venues, mimicking title-purchase requests, to play a greater role. Inglis continued:

> In my last library, we didn't have a Friends group so the library had to come up with funding through other fund-raisers. We could only purchase $500 or $600 a year of museum passes, but one museum might be $500 or $600. So we're fortunate to have that funding. We take recommendations from patrons, decide whether or not it's something we would want to offer, and then present it to the Friends and see if it's something they would like to purchase. It's a super-popular program and one of the busiest pages on our website. Our museum passes are regularly booked up.

As more libraries find a place in their strategic focus for local access librarians and ticketed pass programs, we should see the breadth of offerings expand even further. Offerings could include sporting events (Contra Costa has begun discussions on this), workshops, tours of all kinds, play spaces, studio spaces, farms, tee times, theme parks, and much more that might surprise us now. I came across one instance of a library using its ticketing program to reserve GoPro video cameras for checkout. I can imagine this needing some contingency arrangements, but scheduled reservations for fixed resources (practice spaces, science labs, passport processing, etc.) might work well.

For most people, access to the wealth of resources all around is difficult. Through expertise in outreach and partnership, the habits of collection development, and engagement with their patrons, librarians are changing that. Whether part of a large consortium or a single library effort, city pass programs create tremendous value for the public, for the library, and for local institutions. Different benefits pertain to each, but in all cases the result is that our resources and cultural inheritance are better shared. They are made a greater, more accessible part of our communities than they had been: less siloed in institutions of varying accessibility. Our common wealth finds a home in the community library collection through the work of librarians.

CHAPTER THREE

Guides Make It Clear

CURATING COMMUNITY INFORMATION HAS BEEN A PART OF public library work for ages. Local history rooms, scrapbook files (now LibGuides), and bulletin boards are virtually standard in libraries. Special collections have archived local histories, maps, phone books, and small press publications. Local subject expertise may be the most familiar way that libraries have made their cities and towns more accessible.

Today, neighborhood pathfinding is aided in a number of ways. Online services like Google, Yelp, and TripAdvisor crowdsource directories to popular needs. Government and local agencies make information about their work available online to varying degrees. Collecting historical maps and postcards, school yearbooks, and neighborhood ephemera is made easier with eBay alerts. And the wide Web generally has local ephemera of all kinds strewn every which way.

Librarians have developed a number of recent programs taking local reference and pathfinding in new directions. Like the other programs we're looking at, these are discrete efforts, usually not a part of an explicit strategy or platform of access to cities and towns. And like the other programs we're looking at, they draw on the particular skills of librarianship and the position of the library in the community. Curation and explication make our communities more understandable and better connected. Librarian guides bridge barriers of language and expertise. They make the life of our communities easier to find and use. They make our cities and towns more accessible to all.

Engaging with Context

The Sacramento (CA) Public Library had been digitizing historical photos and other material from its special collections and creating detailed annotations of them for many years. When their work was being put online in 2013, Sacramento Room archivist Amanda DeWilde and digital librarian Megan Wong considered if there were other ways they might present the material. They took inspiration from the Scan José project from the San José (CA) Public Library. San José had created a walking tour of their downtown by pairing historical photos with geolocation data. The project is available through both a mobile site and an augmented reality application.

In 1880 Marshall Hale's sons Evert and Prentis opened an establishment dealing in dry goods, clothing and miscellany at 812 K Street called the Criterion, the family's fourth store in Northern California. **Read More...**

▶ 0:00 / 0:40 ●—————— ◀) ——●

FIGURE 3.1

A SacQR Entry with Photo, Text, and Audio Narration

In Sacramento, DeWilde and the Sacramento Room staff built on their work to create SacQR: a narrated walking tour of nearby K Street. The tour includes twenty sites along a single street that can be accessed in any order. A page for each site contains historical images, description, and audio narration. (See figure 3.1.) Furthermore, storefronts of the locations themselves advertise the tour and feature QR codes bringing mobile devices directly to the appropriate content. "We knew we had a great photo collection with images focused on the downtown area, specifically K Street, which runs through the heart of downtown. We had already written rich descriptions for each image, making it easier to make them available. We did additional research using city directories, maps, and a variety of other resources. What we found interesting was that people could select a location, say Estelle's Patisserie, and then pull up an image and audio showing the location when it was Jim Patterson's hat store in the 1930s."

Each Sacramento Room staff member did additional research and participated in recording the audio. Outreach to the businesses on the tour was an important element and was done in collaboration with the Downtown Sacramento Partnership and the Turn Downtown Around initiative. Those partners also helped promote the tour. In the end, not all businesses on the tour placed SacQR posters in their windows, but others were very enthusiastic, including key spots on the tour.

DeWilde explained that they'd begun with being motivated to make their digitization work more accessible, but that community partnerships took on a growing role for the project.

> Once launched, we presented it to the Gold Country archivist group made up of people from local archives and special collection libraries. They took the tour and were very excited to share it with others. It opened up opportunities with the Downtown Sacramento Partnership and others to do tours with various partners—and not just the K Street tour. We've expanded into other downtown areas, including the historic Old Sacramento area, that have allowed us to incorporate other library programs. That's been a big success. We have good relationships with a lot of the people that are doing downtown tours, like the Sacramento Art Deco Society and others, that are very aware of what we are working on.

The project saw traffic of over 12,000 views after the launch. Since then, activity has remained solid at about 2,000 views per year. Most use is self-guided, but librarian-led tours have been conducted a handful of times. Group tours and individuals simply reading or listening to the narrative on-site further contributes to the life of the street. Efforts like these—built on core library competencies—make the historical layers of the places around us more easily accessible to the public. They inform and connect and add context. Particularly in places where local identity is dilute, bringing context to the surface is assertive of a sense of place and connection.

Librarians have local expertise, resources, and connections. Turning those into projects like walking tours enhances comprehension of their neighborhoods and invites the public and librarians to engage one another. "We've had quite a few people who learned about our Sacramento Room and the collections of the library through SacQR. They'd contact us and say, 'I took this tour, found this building, and it was fascinating.' Then they'd come and visit us. That was very exciting."

The Joy of Branching Out

Neighborhood walking tours give us new ways of seeing and understanding familiar buildings and streets. The Bike the Branches program from the Brooklyn Public Library makes a similar contribution with a borough-wide community event. The library held its fourth annual Bike the Branches in 2016. At all sixty branches of the Brooklyn Public Library, library staff and volunteers work canopied tables, handing out water, stamping "passports," and welcoming riders to the branch. The passports are a motivation and keepsake for riders visiting a few branches or ambitiously trying to reach them all. Prizes are awarded to those riders who reach the most branches.

The event is a fund-raiser, with riders paying $20 to be full participants. Chief Development Officer Lexy Mayers created the program. She explained that the library's fund-raising had traditionally been focused on their Central Library, but she saw an opportunity to take advantage of the library's extensive branch network.

> There are a lot of people who support their local branch. We are in every neighborhood in Brooklyn. We are truly a local institution. This seemed like fun. Biking is something that in Brooklyn is just getting more and more popular. It seemed like a nice way to bring those things together.
>
> We had our other fund-raiser that we do with a very expensive ticket price, so this provided a way for us to do a fund-raising event that is quite accessible. It lives in development and it does raise money, but we also think about

it more as a community-building event and the staff really loves it. They've embraced it and been incredible. We have a lot of volunteers who work that day, over 200 volunteers. Every branch has a station where the participants get their passport stamped. The staff has been incredibly gracious and open to the volunteers and I think all the volunteers have a really great experience, which is another nice benefit.

The library does many months' work planning for the annual event. All sixty branches need resources, shirts for staff and volunteers, and coordination of volunteers. Special events are planned throughout the system for the day—kids' and family programs especially—and existing programs are re-themed: biking books for storytime, for example.

Eight recommended tour routes have been developed. They range from one to six hours long, take in a part of the borough, and are paired with a matching book list. This year a Prospect Park tour over a car-free route was featured for families. Partnerships with the Prospect Park Alliance and Nickelodeon lent the route a Dora theme with an activity sheet, discovery kits at the Audubon Center, a free carousel ride, and other giveaways. A Curious George–themed ride was featured in years past. (See figure 3.2.)

FIGURE 3.2
Some of the 2015 Bike the Branches Tours

The program converts the library's local expertise into a community experience centered on libraries, books, city biking, and mobility, all enlivened by a spirit of staycation tourism. "I think people are excited. It's really fun! The local branches are excited to get people from other neighborhoods to their branch and show off their branch a little bit. That's one of the things that's been fun, getting folks from one neighborhood into another neighborhood." The day shows off the library system, raises funds, and connects people to the library. It guides, informs, and gives people support and encouragement to bike and explore neighborhoods that might be new to them. The librarian-made day of city access leaves the extent of the borough less intimidating and more familiar, connected, and neighborly. And ultimately, more accessible.

The Locally Sourced Information Bulk-Goods Market

Our neighborhoods are full of quotidian things and activities that are only partly visible to us: emergency calls, infrastructure repairs, traffic stops, utility boxes, landscape maintenance. There's information collected somewhere on all of this, but it's typically siloed and lacks metadata and explanation. Librarians are working to make cities and towns more accessible by uncovering, providing, and describing this information. Open data projects have been taking root across the country and, appropriately, librarians have taken important roles in these projects as advocates, guides, and producers.

One of the first libraries to stake a role for themselves in city open data initiatives was the Chattanooga Public Library. Open Chattanooga and Chattanooga's Open Data Portal are a collaboration of the Open Chattanooga Brigade (a Code for America chapter), the city of Chattanooga, and the library. The data products are the work of the city's Office of Performance Management but are accessed through a library-affiliated portal. Richard Beeland, the library's chief administrative officer, explained: "We wanted the open data portal associated with the library because that's a natural place where people would go to gather more information. It provides the integrity, transparency, reliability, and trustworthiness that the public would need when they were looking for that information. We thought it was a natural fit to be involved."

The project started in 2012 and has been partnered with the library since its launch. It began under the direction of then assistant director of the library

Nate Hill and with support from the Benwood Foundation, an area community development organization, and the Knight Foundation. As Hill wrote for the 2014 Code for America Summit:

> Public libraries have hosted municipal collections on their shelves for years. We buy books that offer a variety of different perspectives so citizens can make their own informed decisions. This means that a data portal living at data.yourlibrary.gov rather than data.gov is maintained and curated by a crew of people invested in collecting all kinds of locally sourced data, not just local government data. The library can grab relevant sets from local nonprofits, from other government entities, or from citizen science projects, because collecting resources from these entities fits squarely within the scope of our mission. When an open data project is hosted at a library, the scope of the collection is expanded. This provides more opportunities for citizens to engage with the collections.[1]

Bearing this out, the portal includes datasets from the Chattanooga Chamber of Commerce and the city-owned Electric Power Board company, among others. Beeland continues: "We want to make sure the public knows that that information is there and they can find it there. That they can ultimately help the city solve problems." Top datasets in July 2016 included 911 calls, 311 service requests, building permits, Bike Chattanooga, and traffic citations. (See figure 3.3.) Browser page views exceeded 1,370,000 for the year and a "suggest a dataset" form on the portal solicits new suggestions from the public.

The Chattanooga Public Library is seeking new ways to employ the resource, and a collaboration with the University of Tennessee at Chattanooga is showing promise. "The Master of Public Service program in the Department of Political Science & Public Service—we can use those students to help us make decisions. In turn, those students have resources to complete their degrees." Beeland emphasized how the partnership strengthens the library's relationship to the local university, something it and many public libraries have sought but not always found an outlet for. Tim Moreland, the city of Chattanooga's director of the Office of Performance Management and Open Data, provided additional background on the open data project's outreach efforts:

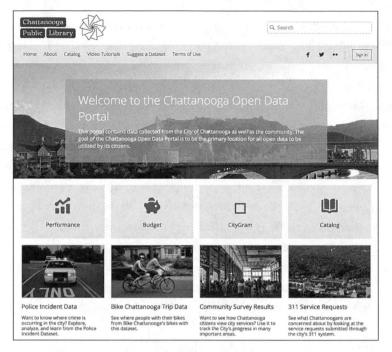

FIGURE 3.3
The Chattanooga Open Data Portal

We do targeted outreach. We've done that to the university, to neighborhood groups, and local civic technology groups. For example, last night there was a neighborhood round table meeting for all the neighborhood associations. Presidents and leadership attend these monthly round tables and we did a presentation on the data and information that's available on the portal and how they can leverage it for better understanding about what's going on in their communities.

The city also publishes our budget information on the portal and has a visualization tool built off the data on the portal for citizens to get a sense for what proportion is public safety versus transportation, how much is in capital projects. The number of people who are actually going to go and play around with a dataset is not the same as the number who would use a visualization or similar tool. We're always looking for new and interesting ways to leverage the data assets we have on the portal and make them more accessible and engaging for our citizens.

Others are creating specialized interfaces to the data as well. The Open Chattanooga Brigade took data on the portal to populate an application called "Find Your Officer." Users enter their own address to find their neighborhood policing officer contact, complete with photo, e-mail address, and patrol zone.

The library takes a primarily public-facing role and curates nongovernmental data, while support for internal municipal government use is led by the city's performance management program. Moreland continues: "We're building internal dashboards for departments so they can keep track of their major goals for the year. We leverage the datasets and provide a current view of what's going on so they can get a sense of how their department is doing."

Advocates and Go-Betweens

Sarah Houghton, director of the San Rafael (CA) Public Library, helped establish a local Code for America (CFA) Brigade. The nonprofit Code for America was founded in 2009 to help governments at all levels advance their use of information technology and design. Local brigades are volunteer efforts to apply the CFA's work. San Rafael's local brigade held planning events and selected the Adopt-a-Drain program to implement.

Adopt-a-Drain programs exist in a few places already. With them, community members volunteer to periodically check on a storm drain they've selected, particularly before a storm, and check for trash and debris in the way or nearby. Oakland writes for their program: "By helping to keep storm drains clear, you decrease flooding from storms, protect water quality and keep trash from storm drains and connected creeks and water bodies."

An online interface supports the selection and reporting process. Houghton explains:

> We are working with the GIS data analysts at both the county level and individual city and town level to pull all of that storm drain data out which they each have mapped. It's just a question of exporting it, combining it all together, and then plugging it into the existing Code for America programming which is out there.
>
> What I am finding as a librarian is that I end up being the information architect for a lot of the projects that we've worked (continued on page 50)

What Is Open Data?

Almis Udrys, director of San Diego's Performance & Analytics Department, was interviewed by Scott Lewis and Andrew Keatts on the Voice of San Diego Podcast.* The interview neatly described the benefits and many considerations for the city's open data efforts. The mission and work involved will resonate with librarians. Open data is organized information for people to understand their locale. I've edited and reproduced the interview with permission.

Our open data portal is a bunch of data that the city owns, organized in a centralized location where folks like software developers or computer engineers or members of the public can access information about the city. From, how many parking meters do we have and how much money do they make? To solar permits, street-sweeping schedules, water quality testing results, and many, many more. And this is just the beginning.

When you collect data you collect it in many different ways. What often happens when you collect data is you're collecting it in a system that's proprietary, that's owned by a particular vendor. If you're a software developer or a resident that wants to take a look at that data, you need to have and pay for that program in order to be able to access, play with, and build tools with the data. What this portal provides is data in machine-readable and accessible formats so that you don't need a particular proprietary software program to open it. You can use any number of different tools.

Not only is it more accessible but we provide more information in the way of metadata, describing how often it's updated, as well as data dictionaries. When you open up a big spreadsheet, you're often seeing a bunch of things that are acronyms or abbreviations, and you don't know what any of it means. We provide the dictionary that defines all those fields for you, so that you can go in and understand what you're looking at.

We got to an open data policy that had wide buy-in—which you need—because you need the attorneys in the room, the IT people in the room, council representatives, the public, so that everybody's on the same page. We got a policy adopted at the city council in early 2015. Just before that we had hired a chief data officer, which was one of the conditions for approving the policy. You don't want to have a policy in place and then nobody to implement it. And we scoured the city for data. That

meant identifying people in every single department that know something about the data that the department owns and can provide us with insights.

Take words that you might hear a lot decision-makers say: accountability, efficiency, transparency. You figure out how to make those real. Transparency is obviously a huge component. People want to know what their government's doing. Of course, you're going to have situations where there's confidential information or privacy issues. You want to be very careful. But there's a lot of data out there that you don't even have to get into those questions, that you can put out there.

On efficiency, say you're in one city department and you're looking for information that you typically have to pick up the phone and call your friend in another department to get and they're either not available or maybe they took a week off. You're going to wait for that Excel spreadsheet or whatever it is that you've been waiting to get for the better part of the week if that's your main source. The portal is useful for our own employees to have a more efficient way to access information and to leverage datasets that they might not have known existed at the city.

There's a couple of factors that we had to consider to decide what to put on the portal. One is quality. We want to be sure if we put something out there for the public to use, or for app developers to rely on, or for university students to do research, that it's quality. That there's not holes in it, there's not missing information, that it's not inaccurate. We can't claim that there's nothing possibly wrong, but to the degree that we can identify major gaps, holes, missing information, wrong information, we need to look and scrub the data for that.

Second, how easy is it to automate? Can we create a process where the data is getting to the portal automatically during certain intervals—whether it's quarterly, monthly, weekly—or do we have to ask one of our employees or one of our colleagues to manually re-input or resend us something, creating more inefficiency as opposed to efficiency. That's a very complicated process to go through, to get that automation set up when you've got so many databases at the city, so many different products.

We want to understand all the data that we're publishing. We don't just want to put it out there and say, "Ok, free for all." It could be all wrong if

Continued on page 50

we don't try to understand what it is. If somebody has a question about any of the data, my team can answer most of those questions right now.

Last, and certainly not least, is input: from the public or decision-makers about what's interesting. We have a lot of dialogue about what's coming in through public records act requests, because one of the benefits of something like an open data portal is if certain data is being frequently requested, you can put it into your portal and proactively provide information as opposed to reactively. We have a data inventory that we posted a couple months back and we asked folks to vote on which datasets they were most interested in. The three that were the most interesting to our voters were traffic counts, special events, and drinking water quality.

I think as raw as you can provide the data is the way to go, so long as you can provide explanations as to what it is. There is data on the portal that doesn't require a whole lot to understand. Anything that can be mapped, you can map on the portal itself.

There's a little bit of a learning that everybody needs to go through. We've never collected data in a way that folks expected that it would proactively go out into the public space. That can create a little bit of consternation, but at the same time you need to think about, "Okay, how are we going to do data collection better? How do we manage it? Maintain it? Disseminate it? Is there data that everybody thinks we have that we don't but maybe we should?"

* Kinsee Morlan, "VOSD Podcast: The Running of the Data," 2016, www.voiceofsandiego.org/topics/news/vosd-podcast-the-running-of-the-data/.

on. But also the go-between: between the programmers and techies and the government officials, because librarians can speak both languages. We understand what the data is that government departments have access to. We understand why they might be a little tentative or scared of releasing it publicly. And why they *should* release it publicly. It's like an interpreter between the people who say, "Give us all your data. We are going to do awesome stuff with it," and the people who say, "That's cool. It's public data, but I don't want you to misuse it. I am afraid of you." A lot of the Code for America Brigades throughout the country have library or individual librarian involvement. It's a role libraries kind of naturally slot into. We're about information. We're government departments. And so it makes sense to kind of utilize both of those roles.

Outreach, facilitation, and information management are well-developed skills for librarians. Applying these skills in the service of open and accessible local information is an excellent fit. Local agencies can be understandably hesitant about opening their resources to the public. It's not their specialty. But it is librarians'. Houghton suggests that we can best reassure our partners by demonstrating successful projects from other jurisdictions. Bring in representatives from those projects to speak and answer questions.

The San Rafael Public Library has been hosting many of the brigade meetings and has facilitated public outreach meetings to understand what its community would like to see. "One of the towns in our county has a huge open data program for their budget and their whole finance system. You can go online and see to a very granular degree every dollar that's being spent. So, we've had them talking with our finance director here at San Rafael. We are poised to launch that here very shortly! I think it's just getting reassurance and comfort from one of your peers that, 'No, it really is okay. It works. Here, let me show you.' It's one thing for a citizen activist group or volunteer group to say it. It's another thing for a peer to reassure you that 'This is okay. It's really fine.'"

Educating and supporting open data partners draws on work that librarians know how to do: producing programs, doing outreach, bridging cultures, and producing access to information. The library also uses its community connections and strong social media presence to play an important role as the public face for open government and as a publicity arm. "Libraries are a trusted public entity whereas maybe the planning department isn't, you know?"

The library's trusted entity role extends to helping make city services more accessible to the public. Houghton was the lead for the city of San Rafael's community engagement plan. Their goal was to expand transparency to more city operations, in greater depth, and for it to reach more of the community. "We've really changed how we seek input to make sure that we are getting representative participation and not just the same ten *(continued on page 54)*

The ILS That We're Missing

Librarians can use their event calendars and information management skills to make the cities and towns around us more accessible. Tangential to this, but worth discussing, libraries' event calendar applications could do a lot more to support all of the work and resources that librarians pour into library programs.

U.S. library systems average over 400 programs per month. At the largest systems, there are well over 1,000 programs per month. Programs have become as integral, numerous, and important to libraries as our collections. Storytimes, bilingual storytimes, baby sign storytimes, pajama storytimes, homework help, concerts, crafts, hobbies, fitness, gaming, chess, magic shows, puppet shows, Lego hours, lectures, author talks, movies, classes, clinics, community group meetings, book clubs, exhibits, displays . . . One could go on and on and on.

Putting on that many programs and exhibits—hundreds, thousands—is a lot of work and expense. Unfortunately, libraries haven't paid it much attention on the technology and automation side. We haven't paid much attention to our event calendar applications. For contrast, think about the attention and resources libraries devote to automation for their collections: the integrated library system. There's the high cost of the software itself, plus vendor support, training, maintenance, library support staff, catalogers, and more. The ILS is a constant subject of library research and review. There are countless books and articles and conference sessions—whole conferences, in fact—on nearly all manner of library technologies. Except one: event calendars. It's a glaring oversight for a system that sits at the center of much of what libraries and their patrons do now.

When we think of an event calendar, we're probably thinking of the front-end interface that we see in a desktop web browser. That interface is important, but it is only a start. Libraries typically feature a few events on the library's home page, where they belong. Again, great, but again, it is just a start. Given the time and expense devoted to programs and the fact that they're a reason for patrons to regularly turn to the library site online, the event calendar should be the hub of that site, with other elements built off of it. It should not be the other way around, as is almost universally the case now. The desktop website serves a shrinking audience, of course. What matters is that library online services are mobile-friendly, and in particular, that our timely program information is. Can our patrons, out with

young kids on a Tuesday morning, quickly and easily find a nearby storytime using their smartphone? If not, why not? My phone knows where I am and the time: it can show me by default what library programs start near me soon.

The information provided on mobile devices and the website and everything else depends on the calendar back-end: the engine that manages the content and its intersection with specific places and times, rules, recurrences, and identities. That's fairly different from a catalog, a discovery system, or a CMS and libraries should be aware of limits as they push those types of systems to perform more calendaring functions.

Inattention to event calendars has a cost on the staff side too. Event information and images originate with one person and get reentered many places. Is the event's travel—from the librarian to the calendar, multiple web front ends, mobile applications, language interfaces, social media, newsletters, community papers, flyers, printed calendars, digital displays, self-checkout screens, and receipts—easy or arduous? Information and images entered or imported once into the calendar should be able to migrate to all of these from a single source.

The calendar may be able to manage other schedule-type stuff, too: room and equipment reservations, office hours, reference appointments, sign-ups, ticketing, passes, staff scheduling, and interaction with other personal and agency calendars in the wild. For staff, the event calendar can manage workflows including program planning, logging, record keeping, contacts, evaluation, reporting, and associated media.

Event calendars are automation tools at the center of a large part of what librarians and our public do now. They are, or can be, the ILS that we're missing. Event planning software that is used by conference planners, entertainment venues, and universities, addresses some of the library's needs but is generally designed for a different set of users and outputs. Libraries have devoted too few resources to their calendars, have demanded too little of them, and have developed too little expertise with the problem set. The profession is overdue for regular and deeper coverage of event calendar product offerings, installations, performance, and road maps. Technology can advance library programming and contemporary services if adequate time, resources, and attention are devoted to it.

to twenty people who can show up for a public meeting at four o'clock on a Wednesday."

The library has had a staff person on the city's community engagement team continuously since then. "A big part of that for us is making sure that everything is bilingual because about 35 percent of our population primarily speaks Spanish. That's been one of those immediate 'we have to do this now' pushes." To that end, the library is the city's primary translator. Library staff translate many city notices and newsletters for predominantly Hispanic neighborhoods. (Houghton cautions that they don't expect that they can sustain staffing for this, but they've felt the service is too important to abandon. They are looking at contracting with professional translation services.)

The library also serves as a public alert voice for the city. The library has a large, engaged social media following that it uses as a channel for public alerts. Houghton explained, "If we get emergency alerts from the police or fire department or the county sheriff's department, we will try to push that information out if it's relevant to the local area. If there's a downed power pole on a major thoroughfare in the town, we let people know. If we are predicting flooding: 'make sure the storm drains are clear.' We'll push that out. We have a good partnership with the other city departments, particularly police and fire."

Librarians at the San Rafael Public Library are working in a number of ways to bridge cultures and idioms. They are represented on the city's community engagement team. They advocate for and bring together different actors and communities. They make local government and infrastructure—our data, communications, and services—more accessible to the public. It's a role that librarians are well suited for.

The Community Bulletin

Like our libraries, cities and towns and neighborhoods of all sizes continuously have events, performances, programs, meetings, classes, and activities of all kinds. It's not possible to keep up with all of them. What's happening at the recreation center? At the museum? Is there a health screening somewhere? Which community groups meet when and where? Who can help me organize and access all of this valuable information?

Put this way, the answer seems obvious.

At the Logan (Utah) Library, maintaining a calendar of local events is something they've done for a long time. What began with an index card directory of community organizations eventually migrated to a local database and then online. The still-active community directory of hundreds of local organizations gave rise more than ten years ago to a community events calendar, maintained and primarily generated by associate librarian Katrina Farrow.

> We try to keep the community events calendar current and offer a monthly print version on our bulletin board outside the main library doors. The online version is updated whenever we get more information. A lot of the information posted comes from posters and flyers that people drop by, hoping to hang them on our bulletin board. We also have an online submission form for events to be considered on the events calendar. Since we've been around for a while, this usually helps fill the calendar out pretty well.
>
> I try to catch recurring events (races, festivals, theater productions, gardeners' market) ahead of time, often through the event's website. I visit the websites of our local community arts center, folk music society, nature center, newspaper events calendars, and sometimes the downtown calendar. Sometimes there's a ton!

The community calendar is well used in this city of 50,000. Every month librarians list over 200 community events plus over 40 library events. The library maintains a library events calendar apart from the community calendar, although most library events are also listed on the latter. In May 2016 the online community calendar saw a busy 14,710 sessions.

The event-listing process is not substantially automated. Farrow gathers information from internal e-mails and e-mail generated by a web form, from flyers, other websites, and from phone calls. She cleans up and improves listings and descriptions—sometimes after additional research, sometimes catching inconsistencies of dates and times which need follow-up—and then enters them into the calendar database. Though this is a substantial amount of work, it's squarely in librarians' core professional skills and mission and is a tremendous service to the local organizations and the wider community.

I think both our community events calendar and community directory are very valuable. We act as information brokers. We are a place where people come to find answers to questions. As part of a vital community, knowing what is going on—whether that be arts and entertainment, clubs, education options, recreation options, government information, or sources of support— is an essential element. As libraries, we are positioned perfectly to include that as part of our regular services. I'm used to having this information available. It's always made sense.

In a direct and immediate way, knowing what's going on makes our cities and towns more accessible, more available to us. If our members need special knowledge of where to look and what to look for to attend a community meeting, that's a barrier. It particularly impacts underserved communities. Where does one find the MAD/BID/CPG, town council, round table, coffee klatch, interest group, panel, or recital and which is which? What free family events are nearby or offered when the library is closed? Many local organizations do maintain clear, findable listings, though not all do. For those that don't, it's not necessarily a case of insularity or disinterest in more participation. They may not have the skills to create good listings and put them in a shared system. They may not be comfortable administering online resources. Whatever the reasons, librarians can help those organizations and our members by taking up the cause.

There's an important and familiar collection development aspect to this. In a city or town of any size, the volume of all events very quickly becomes unwieldy for staff to post and for users to comprehend. There's too much stuff. (Not the worst problem to have.) But that's okay. There's no requirement or benefit to being comprehensive. A set of policies should show contours that are right for each library and community as to what listings to include. Community engagement in the process may help. Get input and feedback and study how the community calendar is used. Recognize that the life of the community is a resource that the library can in small ways help clarify and make more equitable. Clear, consistent, usable announcements of what's going on nearby—on a platform produced and provided by the library—improve access and strengthen community.

Bringing Friends Along

The Vancouver (BC) Public Library has taken similar steps toward making local events more accessible. Rather than a community calendar, Vancouver integrates a select number of nonlibrary programs from a subset of library partners into its library event calendar. The effort began with the library's participation in the Vancouver Learning City series and is expanding incrementally from there. The Vancouver Learning City is a consortium that includes the library, the city of Vancouver, the Board of Education, four universities, Ashoka Canada (part of the international nongovernmental organization), and the Mozilla Foundation. The consortium supports access to education with a focus on free, nonformal, lifelong learning programs throughout Vancouver. It is a natural fit for the library.

I spoke to Anne O'Shea, programming and learning manager at the Vancouver library. Building an event calendar for Vancouver Learning City was an initiative of the library. "It's meant to be a crowd-sourced calendar of free nonformal learning opportunities." The library administers the calendar platform for the consortium and is the agent for the calendar contract and purchasing. Consortium members and participating organizations are provided authoring (but not administrative) accounts on the calendar system to directly add event listings to the Learning City events database. "We don't moderate that. If something really problematic went up we'd pull it down." Admission costs have been one factor on which the library has had to limit listings on rare occasion. Programs with modest materials costs, for art supplies, for example, are accepted but those with substantial ticket fees are not.

The Learning City and library events calendars share the same software platform, BiblioEvents from BiblioCommons, with separate database files for additional security. Data from the two files is integrated in the library events calendar public interface, displaying as a single source with Learning City events identified as such. For example, alongside library programs, the Vancouver Public Library events calendar recently listed Learning City programs held around the city at Langara College, the Vancouver General Hospital, the Children's Hospital, various community centers, the Vancouver Art Gallery, and others. The library has also opened event-authoring access to other organizations with which they partner closely. O'Shea continues:

We have been talking to organizations we partner with about using the calendar. For example, we have a relationship with an immigrant settlement group called S.U.C.C.E.S.S. and we've given them access to the calendar. When they do an event at the library we take care of the entry, but whenever they're doing events out in the community or another site they can use the library calendar to amplify their reach. We have been adding more and more organizations.

Last year we organized a "Summer of Learning" and we were able to use the library calendar as a resource listing all the different learning opportunities. The program gave people the ability to participate in learning challenges and fun exercises and self-report their learning. The calendar supported that very well. We had to design the registration and reporting process associated with the learning challenges, but we already had the infrastructure and the content to support it.

We can tell that people are using it. Our partners have reported that they see greater attendance at their events. There's value in the fact that it's all pulled together in one place, so you don't have to go separately to all of these different institutions and organizational websites, you just go to this one place.

Some features of the BiblioEvents software expand on the cross-promotional aspect. Event listings contain pointers to other events near the listing's venue. Library catalog searches can turn up related events. "You might look up a book in the catalog, see it's being featured in an author talk, and be able to click through to the event listing." Connections between catalog searches and Learning City events are something the library hopes to improve going forward. What the Vancouver Public Library is not doing is pulling partner events from external calendars into their own via calendaring protocols. All listings are entered directly into the BiblioEvents software. This isn't a problem, but there may be efficiencies being missed where partners have calendar applications of their own.

Librarians managing the Vancouver Public Library event calendar are doing work on behalf of the public and area lifelong learning organizations to make each more accessible to the other. They're providing and supporting a resource

that is more capable than what many organizations would otherwise offer. And they're coordinating the work between these organizations to make the calendar more valuable to the public. The work draws on librarians' particular skills and expertise and is why libraries are competitive in this space. It's a strategic fit.

Contributing to the Ecosystem

The Seattle Public Library is an example of calendaring protocols being used to share event information from one source with another. It doesn't list non-library events in its calendar, but the library actively coordinates with the city of Seattle and with other organizations so that library listings automatically feed into those calendars.

The city of Seattle's calendar, for example, lists library events alongside programs like an electric bike expo, "Forest Restoration at Longfellow Creek," and a meeting of the Seattle Human Rights Commission. In this case, a common software vendor was purposefully sought out. The library worked with other city departments to select the vendor, Trumba. In addition to the city, the library has reached out to many local publications to encourage and assist them with "subscribing" their own calendars to library events. Examples include *Seattle's Child* magazine, *The Stranger* weekly, and neighborhood publications like the *Ravenna Blog*. A filtered selection of library events appears in each of these publications.

I asked the library's web developer, Lisa Zicherman, about its calendar feed coordination with *Seattle's Child*. "We work really closely with their staff on a lot of projects already, so it was a natural tie-in. We have so many events that we almost overwhelmed their calendar when we first started putting everything in. We've fine-tuned it several times."

Not surprisingly, simply exposing the library's events in feeds is usually not enough to get other organizations to create combined community calendars. It takes proactive work and collaboration. Are feeds importing and appearing properly? Are they automatically filtered for the desired selection of events? What event metadata does the library need to supply to meet its partners' needs? What do the library's partners need in the way of assistance and expertise? Attention to all of these is needed to ensure good and lasting results.

Devoting work to this process enhances the public's access to community events by improving other agencies' offerings, not necessarily the library's. The *Seattle's Child* calendar of area family events is an example. Librarians' work with the magazine helps promote library programs while also improving the utility of the magazine's calendar—to the benefit of public access to family activities around town, the library's events included. (Care regarding work that improves commercial products is appropriate. Consider what the businesses' interests are. That said, and particularly with nonprofit partners, it's not essential that librarians' work always directly advances library products. Lending help and expertise to other local projects can advance the library's mission and that is sometimes enough. Down the road, the relationships and goodwill created often redound to the library.) Again, to be successful this takes an active process that calls on librarians' outreach experience and expertise in information management.

The Seattle Public Library's event calendar also lists a handful of off-site events where the library is a partner. An example is the History Café, a local history lecture and salon series organized by the library, the Museum of History and Industry, and HistoryLink, an organization supporting work on an online encyclopedia of Washington State. The monthly History Café events are held around the Seattle community. As public libraries' community role is increasingly emphasized, the line between "library" and "nonlibrary" events becomes less important and library calendars become more porous.

Sharing the Way In

Each of these libraries is advancing access to community life in somewhat different ways. The Logan (Utah) Library is itself gathering, curating, and organizing information about events and meetings. Vancouver opens its platform to an increasing number of partners. The Seattle Public Library is helping other publishers automate the integration of library events in those calendars. And the city of Seattle is working with affiliated departments, agencies, and open submissions to build a common citywide calendar.

The Sacramento Public Library, while not automating listings between its calendar and others, makes concerted use of a citywide culture calendar, Sacramento365, to promote library events. The Sacramento365 calendar in turn has automated feeds into other area calendars, such as Capitol Public Radio's. Amy Calhoun, communications and virtual services manager at the Sacramento library, produces an event posting best practices guide for staff and encourages staff to use the Sacramento365 calendar. "The Franklin Branch Library had great success. They post in Sacramento365 at the same time that they're posting to the library's website and they've seen attendance increase. Media coverage of their events has also increased because they posted on Sacramento365. It has traction." The extra effort to post to Sacramento365 makes that citywide resource itself a more valuable destination for the public and enriches it as a source for other agencies in the area.

Somewhat to my surprise, I didn't find a library that is importing partner event information into its calendar using feeds or subscriptions (the flip side of how the Seattle Public Library exports theirs to others). So, for example, a library calendar could list park and recreation events—automatically or semiautomatically—by "subscribing" to an existing park and recreation or children's museum calendar over RSS, iCalendar, CalDAV, or another protocol or application program interface (API). This doesn't require that the partner agency be on the same software, only that both the library and partner's software support one of these common protocols. Many small agencies use Google Calendar for their listings, for example, which supports iCalendar.

Richer calendar efforts help library members by putting announcements into a format that is easy for the personal calendars of our phones and computers to work with. Adding a children's theater performance to one's personal calendar is a simple one-click operation from an event listing on a contemporary calendar. Marketing town council meetings and service agency open houses alongside library programs adds to the demand on our event calendars and contributes to a virtuous circle of use.

Using library event calendars to improve access to community life is a fair amount of work. It's doesn't have a lot of cachet or buzz about it. Mostly, it's traditional work, though technology is increasing its reach and relevance in new ways. It recognizes the activities around us as part of a collection (and an object for collection development) and builds on librarians' strengths as information professionals and partners.

Librarian-facilitated community events calendars have DNA in common with walking tours, Bike the Branches, local government interfaces, and open data. They're all making the places around us more comprehensible, familiar, useful, and accessible. These and similar programs have roots in traditional library work and have been meaningfully updated. A re-appreciation and reframing in terms of access to cities and towns is in order. Library-led guidance to the life and information of our communities—illuminating that messy collection, making it slightly more apparent and comprehensible—makes our communities and places, the collection all around, more accessible to all.

NOTE

1. Nate Hill, "Chattanooga Public Library and Open Data," 2014, medium.com/
@natenatenate/chattanooga-public-library-and-open-data-a6e3724afaba.

CHAPTER FOUR

Placemakers
Bring It Home

IBRARIES SERVE PEOPLE, OF COURSE. PATRONS, MEMBERS,
customers, the public, kids, adults, seniors, all kinds come to
the library or connect with librarians online or are reached at
schools, senior centers, and beyond. So librarians give a lot of
thought to who those people are, what they want, and how to
help them share in all that libraries offer. For the whole of cities and towns,
the yin to the human yang is the places themselves. Our common streets, plazas, sidewalks, parks, buildings, and infrastructure are foundational parts of
our lives in cities and towns. They're relevant to our well-being. But for most
of us they don't feel accessible or malleable in a personal way. They're the
province of city hall, property owners, and concrete fact. To varying degrees,
our places may not feel like they belong to us. It doesn't have to be this way.
Libraries can help.

Shaping our shared public and private spaces to be more welcoming, safe,
active, sociable, desirable, affirming, and accessible is called "placemaking."
Libraries have (usually) been thoughtful about placemaking with regard to our
own buildings. And "creative placemaking"—using art to enhance places and
the sense of place—is starting to receive attention in library literature. Nuts-
and-bolts neighborhood land use, meanwhile, has gotten little attention.

What business is it of libraries, after all, what happens with the intersection two blocks away or what a developer builds down the road? What does one patron's vision for their neighborhood have to do with library service? How wide should our streets be, anyway? Helping the public engage with the buildings and blocks and lanes around us is relevant to libraries. The joint-use cards, city passes, calendars, and other programs that we've looked at place libraries in the role of agents on behalf of the public to city and town resources. That role extends comfortably to addressing the places around us themselves. The skills and position of librarians in their communities make them capable and appropriate neighborhood land-use advocates.

So, why are the intersections and buildings three blocks down the road any business of libraries?

First, libraries are residents and property owners in the neighborhood. It is as simple as that. Libraries are involved on their own behalf and have a legitimate place in the community planning process. They have a simple self-interest in moving the neighborhood's center of gravity in the library's direction. Vibrant activity around the library puts the library in the center of things materially and figuratively. That centrality, to whatever degree, doesn't happen by accident. The library shouldn't be shy about advocating for itself when neighborhood plans impact the library's position.

Libraries also have a self-interest in making the connections to library facilities good ones. For example, thirteen-year-olds don't drive. We want them in our libraries and they're old enough to enjoy the library on their own. Do they? What barriers exist? Can thirteen-year-olds safely and pleasantly get to and from the library on their own? If not, libraries have a legitimate interest in and responsibility for changing that. Planning meetings, committees, and design charrettes happen frequently, if very quietly and with little attention, in most communities. Interested librarian participation in these is library work on behalf of public access to neighborhood resources.

Second, we represent our communities. The time, expertise, and social capital to engage with neighborhood land use is just not available to most of our patrons. Librarians can help and advocate for their constituents. As the public realm has been squeezed in recent decades, the library is one of the few remaining institutional voices for public spaces in neighborhoods. Few participants in the land-use planning process represent the public realm—youth interests least of all—but libraries qualify.

Finally, libraries have expertise in and an institutional bias toward improving the public's access to resources. That mission, as we've been exploring, doesn't stop when it comes to the places beyond our walls, to the collection all around. Mobility, safe streets, community planning, and public spaces are forms of access in cities and towns. Neighborhood placemaking is library work and the skills of librarians are an asset. Research, service design, user experience, community outreach, the reference interview: experience with these contributes to the work done by librarians in the examples that follow in this chapter. The public library tradition of outreach further lends us credibility and provides local connections to draw on. There is great goodwill that libraries have earned. Just being able to say "I'm with the library" opens doors.

Happily, making our neighborhoods better places brings city access librarians more goodwill. It integrates libraries further into their communities. And the improvements that are most relevant to libraries tend to improve their standing and centrality. Libraries and neighborhood placemaking form a virtuous circle.

The Room Where It Happens (Door's Open)

Librarians don't typically have much background in neighborhood land use. It's a big, specialized field and is the domain of planners, architects, engineers, and designers. Like any specialized field, it has a daunting atmosphere of opaque language and casually employed acronyms. Ministerial review, easement, level of service, form-based code, BIDs, FARs, EIRs, and VMT, anyone?

It won't be an area of expertise for most librarians but needn't be and, in any case, some comfort with the subject is easy to achieve. A first step is getting some exposure to the field. If you're lucky, there may be advocacy groups in your area that train on the process. The organization Circulate San Diego, for example, produces training material on the planning process and how to get involved in local government. It has led "Join Your Community Planning Group" training workshops for citizens interested in participating, including one hosted at the Linda Vista branch of San Diego Public Library in 2017.

See if you can find a similar one to attend or bring to your library. Kathleen Ferrier, director of advocacy for Circulate San Diego, described the workshop:

> The idea was just to encourage more people to get involved in the process. We did them at community spaces downtown and in southeastern San Diego, trying to draw more people from those communities. We had several people who currently serve on community planning groups sit on a panel. We talk to them about their experience and getting over the hump of, "Is this something that I can really do? Do I have to know more? Do I have to be smarter? Do I have to be more of this, that, or the other?" The answer is no. You just have to be interested. And if you are interested then these are the things you can do to start participating. You can have coffee with somebody. You can go to a planning group meeting.
>
> We outlined all these steps, because a lot of people feel intimidated that they have to know more about city government or planning, and that's not really the case. There can be a learning curve. Half the effort is just interest and being willing to show up. I always talk to people about the fact that these decisions are made all the time and they have an opportunity to get involved.

As the Join Your Community Planning Group (CPG) workshop suggests, one of the best places to start engaging with neighborhood decisions is with advisory agencies like community planning groups. They go under different names in different places, including neighborhood councils, neighborhood development associations, community advisory groups, round tables, and so on. Related agencies include business improvement districts (BIDs), maintenance assessment districts (MADs), community development corporations (CDCs), parking districts, town councils, and commissions of every kind. In some places neighborhood issues like policing and schools are part of the same group, in others land use and services are reviewed by separate associations. Attendance at neighborhood councils is common in library outreach work, usually from the stance of listening and promoting the library. More assertively, libraries can represent their interests and advocate for their communities in the decision-making process.

Land use is not an obvious part of local decision-making for librarians to get involved with, but it's easier and more ubiquitous than one might guess. There are small and large decisions being made all the time. Government agencies, developers, and others in the field often hold community workshops to get feedback and insight into local wants and needs. Usually there are requirements to hold these and they're generally not well attended or are attended by a narrow demographic. Show up. Let them know: "Speaking for the library, I know that our members often get to the library along this route. This corner, though, is a problem. Cars whip around it too fast and visibility isn't great. I know it would help folks coming to the library if they felt safer crossing there. Fixing that is a priority for us."

That goes a long way. Often there's money for improvements, with only a question of where the improvements will go. I've attended regional planning agency design charrettes like this and been able to express the library's interest as it relates to our members. As librarians sit in with these agencies and gain experience with ongoing projects, they'll be more comfortable participating in the decision-making. As anchor institutions, libraries and librarians have an important place at the table, including on these agencies' boards. Familiarity with the land-use process and people means, next, that they can bring others in the community along. Bring a teacher or a teen. Who better than libraries to facilitate that access? Or formally represent community members. It's not uncommon for these meetings to be held during regular working hours. Librarians may be able to go as proxies for members who can't attend.

Our streets, our sidewalks, the fence, the bus shelter, the cell tower, the apartment addition, the empty storefront, all that stuff that we mix with every day? They're being permitted, studied, endorsed, mitigated, prioritized, and designed. They're part of the collection all around.

No Library Is an Island

Parklets, pocket parks, pavement parks, street plazas: these conversions of parking and other paved areas into mini public spaces are quintessential place-making forms. In recent years they've been widely and successfully employed in cities around the country, benefiting from their simplicity and low cost. New York City's more than sixty new pedestrian plazas—created out of surplus street width, turning lanes, and parking—are popular, successful, and better-known examples. Times Square was made mostly *(continued on page 69)*

Unlearning the Way Around

The twentieth-century conventional wisdom about place and street design has been undergoing a big change, a generational reversal, or return. That's made for some challenges and volatility in community group and other planning circles. Basic precepts are up in the air. Is free parking a help or a hindrance to local business? Are streets safer when chaotic or orderly? Does the big box store support the neighborhood pizza parlor or the reverse? Some background with these debates can help librarians take their place in neighborhood land use discussions.

I mentioned streets and, yes, yikes! They're daunting, but essential and unavoidable. They're by far the biggest piece of the public realm. Streets are not just vectors for transportation. They're places, with many roles to fill. Interestingly, traffic engineering policy has in most places kept up with the shift to a more holistic understanding of streets.

"TO MAKE STREETS SAFE YOU MUST FIRST MAKE THEM DANGEROUS"

This line come from Hans Monderman, a Dutch traffic engineer. The idea is that as we've segregated uses of street space, made lanes wider, added shoulders, controlled traffic with lights, kept trees and activity set farther away, and restricted foot traffic, perversely this has not made us safer. Instead, it's given drivers cues to feel yielded to and to be less vigilant. The result seen everywhere is that drivers drive faster and less carefully. Speed, in itself, compounds the problem of inattentiveness. With higher speed, drivers' cone of vision narrows, they see less detail, and stopping distances expand. And last, tragically, injuries from collisions increase geometrically with speed: a pedestrian struck at 20 miles per hour has a 95 percent survival rate, but a pedestrian struck at 40 mph has only a 15 percent survival rate.

Slower streets are safer. Narrower and more chaotic streets are slower. Streets with trees adjacent to the roadway make speed more perceptible, and as a result slower. "If you need a sign to tell people to slow down, you've designed your street wrong," is how Charles Marohn, president of the advocacy group Strong Towns, summarizes it. But if those narrow, chaotic streets are slower, couldn't they still be less safe on account of being less segregated from traffic? The evidence suggests they're safer after all.

Jaywalking is illustrative. Pedestrian culture (and policing practice) varies from place to place. In some places, folks jaywalk and in others they don't. And when comparable streets and neighborhoods are looked at, the ones with the jaywalkers have fewer collisions. Where pedestrians instead always wait for a light and cross only where expected, drivers draw the predictable conclusion that they can

be less attentive. They drive faster, and collisions increase. Note to law enforcement: careful jaywalking saves lives.

Old assumptions are also receding about road design for travel efficiency. Our arterial roads have high peak speeds but require stoplights with long delays, which have an outsized impact on net travel time and traffic volume. The net travel times of slower but more continuous streets are competitive with those of fast arterials. Ben Hamilton-Baille's reconfiguration of a Poynton (England) interchange is a case in point. A busy, multilane interchange at the hub of a village center served 26,000 vehicles per day but was continually backed up and was inhospitable to pedestrians. The adjacent

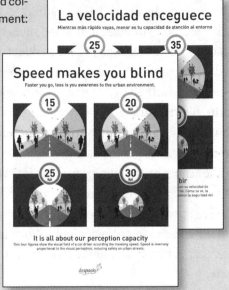

Illustration of Driver's Field of Vision by Claudio Olivares Medina, Despacio.org
Bill Lindeke, "The Critical Ten," *Streets.mn*, April 2, 2015, http://streets.mn/2015/04/02/the-critical-ten.

shopping streets suffered from the harsh environment. To remedy this, traffic lights, lanes, and highway fixtures were removed or reduced. The interchange was reconfigured for continuous, slow traffic and pedestrians. The redesign nevertheless reduced traffic delays and increased activity in the surrounding shops. There's no one right approach to street and place design, of course. Libraries and others should simply approach their neighborhoods with assumptions about speed, complexity, parking, and development that are not taken for granted.

car-free virtually overnight with traffic cones and hundreds of beach chairs. Net traffic speed through Times Square improved, incidentally, as a result.

Libraries are starting to look at their own adjacent pavement and parking surfaces as well. While we've given attention to placemaking with our buildings, the pavement that surrounds many of them, and its relation to the neighborhood, has been less considered. Stephanie Loney, public services manager at the Chula Vista (CA) Public Library, told me about the parking lot surrounding her library in a medium-density urban location. "This is a building that was built in the 1970s. It was all just driveways and for vehicles. A pedestrian walking in didn't have anything dedicated for themselves. They had to look over their shoulder and make sure that a car didn't knock them down."

Loney started thinking about parklets and bike and pedestrian connections to the streets nearby, particularly a street where the city had been working to improve walkability. "I guess you'd say my motivation for doing the thing in the library parking lot was to connect us to Third Avenue, so that people would think of coming from Third Avenue to the library easily. You shouldn't have to navigate parked cars and stuff."

The "thing in the library parking lot" was the creation of a new pedestrian path with handrails through corner landscaping, the conversion of thirteen parking spaces into an open, painted route with parklet islands along the way, and the extension of flower beds. Worn landscaping at the corner had shown that patrons were already cutting from the street through to the parking lot there.

> Pedestrians would walk through this piece of landscaping. The gardeners got annoyed because the landscaping got trampled down. At one stage somebody put one fence panel, just one random metal fence panel to stop the people from walking in, so what do the people do? They walk around the panel and they make two bits of worn landscaping. I remember looking at that two years ago, and I said to my library director, "This is ridiculous. It's telling you that people want to come in this way. They want to take the short route in and why shouldn't they?"

Loney took her cue from the public to design a new path and public space. The route connects the street corner to the library through the parking lot. Three small parklet islands were created along the route from what had been parking spaces and were painted and furnished with benches and planters. (See figure 4.1.) When I visited, two of the three were being used, one by a couple talking, the other by somebody reading.

The path and islands through Chula Vista's parking lot were "built" using just durable road-quality paint on the lot's surface, in light green and khaki,

FIGURE 4.1
Parklet in Chula Vista Public Library Parking Lot
Photo by Stephanie Loney

and were outfitted with benches and planters. "I was pleasantly surprised at how easy it was," said Loney.

> The parking lot held 150 cars . . . A couple of weeks I ran up there and I took a sample, 10:00 or 11:00 in the morning and 3:00 in the afternoon. How many are actually in the parking spaces? I discovered that between 65 to 85 spaces were occupied. The rest were sitting empty.
>
> We have some groups that escort special needs people. You'd watch them go through the parking lot. Vehicles are backing out, people are driving around looking for parking spaces, they're not looking around at who's walking. If you're a pedestrian and you parked on the southeast corner, you have to cross over two driveways to get to our east door. The car was the predominant element there and yet when you look at who comes to the library, there's a lot of activity with families and the retired. They're the very ones who need a little help getting across a parking lot with strollers, wheelchairs, or walkers.
>
> I'll be honest, when I painted out the parking spaces I thought, wait till somebody doesn't get a parking space someday . . . They're going to call someone in the mayor's office and complain about this (continued on page 73)

We Can Do This

The concrete stuff of our cities and towns can seem beyond the reach of most of us to change. Improvements that we might imagine around us seem to require Herculean lobbying efforts, public investment, and more patience and time than most of us can sustain. New approaches going under labels like "tactical urbanism," "lean urbanism," and "urban acupuncture" are variations on the idea that small, lightweight, low-cost public space improvements are easy to try and can have outsized effects. They leverage our responsiveness to simple cues and demonstrate the value of further improvement. They invite us to see the malleability of our surroundings and to imagine what we might want for our neighborhoods. In spite of the "urban" nomenclature, these techniques are finding application in cities and towns of all sizes. Some examples:

- Corner bulb-outs made of paint and planters or straw wattles in Los Angeles and Hallam (NE)
- Bike lanes created using traffic cones in Atlanta and Lawrence (KS)
- Curbside parks created using just benches and bistro sets (and sometimes, coins in the parking meter), from San Francisco to Covington (KY)

The interventions are sometimes made with permission, and sometimes without. Traditionally they've been the work of grassroots organizations, but more and more frequently they're the product of local government, business districts, and service agencies that are eager to try things quickly and cheaply.

Tactical urbanist techniques are the province of libraries too. Librarians lead these projects themselves or lend support to community partners. Librarians have the facilitation skills and position in their communities to help make them happen. The projects generate confidence that small changes are possible and that they can address big problems. Many of the projects in this chapter fit this description. For more on tactical urbanism (and there's much, much more) see, for example, the books *Tactical Urbanism for Librarians: Quick, Low-Cost Ways to Make Big Changes* and *Tactical Urbanism: Short-Term Action for Long-Term Change.**

---

* Karen Munro, *Tactical Urbanism for Librarians: Quick, Low-Cost Ways to Make Big Changes* (Chicago: American Library Association, forthcoming); Mike Lydon, Anthony Garcia, and Andres Duany, *Tactical Urbanism: Short-Term Action for Long-Term Change* (Washington, D.C.: Island Press, 2015).

crazy librarian who took away parking spaces. But I'm standing there two or three days after the paint had all gone down. I looked over and this woman came in up the dedicated entrance and she had three kids on bicycles and they all just cycled right across the space over to the door. And the woman shouts out to me: "This is awesome! I've been waiting years for this." I felt, you know, that's great! I think I mentally had this little conversation. My mantra was going to be if someone complained: my job here is to improve access for everyone, not just people who drive cars. This improves access for pedestrians and for people who want to cycle. I have to think about that. That was what I was armed and ready to say. I've never had to say it. Nobody has complained.

Loney found grant money for the project and had the work done by a contractor for $17,000. (One source gives that as a typical cost.[1]) Some similar projects have instead gone the route of a "community build," using local volunteer labor. This was the case at the Linda Vista Branch Library in San Diego, where volunteers worked to convert eight spaces and a thruway. Free of cars, that space joined together two existing landscaped areas to form a substantially sized plaza. The library worked with a municipal agency, the Civic Innovation Lab, and community groups including the neighborhood community development corporation, community planning group, and a community center. Together the team secured approval from the city police, fire, planning, real estate, and streets divisions to do a temporary pavement plaza. The community build process also had a neighborhood organizing outcome. Neighbors from different groups and of all ages worked together on pieces of the project. They worked side-by-side painting the lot's surface. The benefits of that collaboration are intangible but built local identity, confidence, and ownership.

The Linda Vista project was designed to be temporary and was: the plaza was in place for about two years. Designing for temporary improvements can be an effective way to get administrative buy-in. Costs are lower, the commitment is less, and the project exists as an experiment that the library and community can both learn from.

At Chula Vista, Loney had a facilities manager that she approached about her idea.

I said, "Is there anything that stops me from painting a parking lot? Is there any sort of code thing?" We had an informal meeting with the traffic engineers and our landscape gardener. "You can do what you want with your parking lot" was the message I got. So, a green light! I applied for the grant.

The thrust of the grant was "We're going to do information boards and model good behaviors using native plants. We're going to create a space where something like a blood drive could take place or a book sale." We'd had a few bloodmobiles in here and they usually park in an inconvenient area. This would move some of those events where they could be seen. I would do an information board to talk about native plants and the benefits and the insect life they support.

We were successful with the grant. We ended up being able to get a contract which included a pedestrian walkway down to the corner and painting of the parking lot for $17,000. Which was amazing. They put Botts' dots [raised roadway buttons] in. The only thing traffic engineers said to me was, you have to do a blue stripe row for pedestrian access for ADA [the Americans with Disabilities Act]. By October we were working with the Native Plants Society. Our facilities manager was able to go through the public works yard and discover planters that had been over-purchased. He commandeered a couple of extra planters and we redid old trash cans that were concrete—took the liner out of them, painted them a bright color—filled them with soil and plants and they're all doing okay. He found some park benches. We installed those, we notched them to stop skateboarders from jumping on them, and it all seems to work! I was just past it yesterday and there was someone sitting right in the halfway mark, what would have been in the middle of a parking lot. It's worked quite well.

Interventions like this have value for the library and its members. They contribute to the neighborhood, creating safe common spaces that open our cities and towns to more public use. Loney continued: "The next stage is to work on a policy for how we're going to lease out the space for larger events, if someone approaches us and says, 'Hey, we'd like to have a farmers' market or we're thinking of having a battle of the bands. Could we use your parking lot?' I'm dying to get a food truck here. I have the staff breathing down my neck about that . . . I'd like when kids are doing their reviews for final exams to have food trucks out there. Encourage the kids to come to the library, get something to eat. Also it's a win-win for us, we're able to provide food without the hassle and the cleanup." Public uses like these (we'll discuss food trucks again later in this chapter)—like the simple enjoyment of the parklet benches—along with improved connections between these spaces and our public streets, reinforces convivial neighborhood activity. Loney explained:

> The Third Avenue corridor is always trying to improve the economy of the area. I hope that we're seen as a useful resource. People want to do multiple things and the library can be an attractant: bring people in who also go and eat dinner on Third Avenue or something. It can be so helpful when you've just got somebody in the parking lot. If the library is sitting there like a temple on its own and it's a wasteland all around it, it's no wonder you're going to have issues—you've turned it into this island. Have you ever seen how a school visit comes to a park? The kids go out there and run around and scream at the top of their voice and have their lunch. Suddenly the park's safe. I'm a big believer that the more you normalize the activities happening around a building, the easier it is for you in the long term.

The use of the library's adjacent spaces outside of library operating hours is a powerful lever. Food trucks that precede the library's opening or remain after closing, for example, are a low-cost way to extend use of the library site, improve area activity and safety, and further the library as a neighborhood center of gravity. Whether or not these projects are guided by library staff and contractors or by neighborhood partnerships, they improve local public spaces and connections. Library members brought into the process, or who simply use these spaces, take part in their cities and towns in a concrete way that they hadn't before. The library's cities and towns are moved forward in small but cumulative ways into being more available, malleable, and accessible to the community.

Make Way for Everybody

Safe Routes to School programs have been around for many years at the national level. The programs aim simply to increase the number of children who walk or bike to school with the greater goal of improving the safety, health, and community strength of neighborhoods and the kids in them. They provide funding and organizational support to promote walking, improve corridors, and address barriers such as poor walkways, difficult crossings, limited adult supervision, and crime. A Safe Routes to School program typically begins with an audit around the school. Local parents and kids branch out from the school for a quarter mile, noting issues in detail: this crosswalk isn't visible enough, on this corner we're concerned about crime and safety, on this road folks are driving too fast. The audit becomes an inventory of improvements that can be made.

Where a dedicated organization can't be created, the programs have often been sponsored by a community health agency in partnership with a school. The mission and community role of libraries make them a good fit for the work as well. Libraries have participated and should look to do more, to make "Safe Routes to the Library" a component. The map shown in figure 4.2 is of Chagrin Falls, Ohio, the 2012 national Safe Routes award winner. The Chagrin Falls Branch of the Cuyahoga County Public Library is at the center of the map and in the inset, just north of Chagrin Falls Intermediate School (CFIS).

The Safe Routes Chagrin organization has completed and runs an impressive number of projects and programs. The following is adapted from its website (www.saferouteschagrin.com):

- Added clearly defined walk/bike paths on school property separated from vehicle traffic
- Added new sidewalks and paths and fixed continuity problems at prioritized locations, connecting large populations of students to their schools
- Improved snow removal on school routes with a community outreach campaign and worked with local law enforcement to reinforce the local snow removal ordinance so that students can walk/bike in the winter
- Added bike racks, signage, pavement markings, and driver feedback signs
- Provided school assemblies, bike safety education, bike club support, educational materials and handouts (route maps, safety tips), and teen driving outreach
- Organized Walk to School–Walk to Town Day, Bike to School Day, Bike Rodeos, Bike-a-Palooza, Walk and Roll Wednesdays, and Mileage Club contests

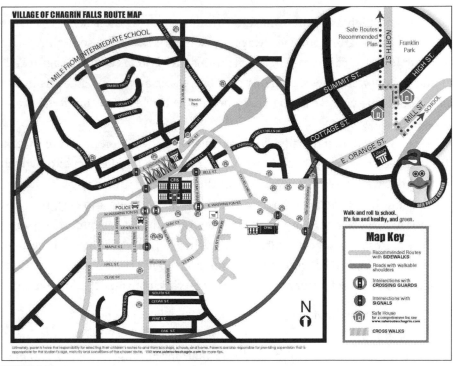

FIGURE 4.2
Map of safe routes, Chagrin Falls, Ohio
Map designed by Jill Markey for Safe Routes Chagrin

- Coordinated volunteer crossing guards, Safe House Program, police patrols, and community outreach on sidewalk shoveling

The organization was awarded federal funds for a separated sidewalk for one route. The Safe House Program coordinates volunteer homes along the school walking route that are certified safe places for students to go if they need assistance. Safe House volunteers are given a background check and houses are clearly marked with a garden flag and indicated on the School Routes Map.

Though not a part of the route planning process, the Chagrin Falls Branch Library has participated in Safe Routes Chagrin's community work. Katherine Malmquist, branch manager for the Cuyahoga County Public Library's Chagrin Falls and Gates Mills branches, described their participation in the annual community-wide Walk to School–Walk to Town Day. "The library has participated each year. The library parking lot is a stage for one of the schools in the morning (three of the four schools participate in Chagrin Falls: intermediate, middle, and high). Children move off from our lot to their school walking together. In the afternoon we always have a booth that does something with the theme. I also participate in the planning. The Friends of the Chagrin Falls Branch Library supplies and helps pass out water at various stations in the afternoon. This year we had children make 3-D turtles with the 'go slow and look both ways' theme."

A safe routes program is in the early stages of development where I work. It's being led by the local children's hospital and the middle school on which it's currently centered. I participated in the audit and inventory, which have since been completed. The program is now in the planning and design stages. Librarians' experience doing outreach provides valuable background on community patterns to inform feedback and evaluation. Libraries are well situated to lend skills and to be an organizing hub for neighborhood access programs like safe routes. When starting a program like this, consider the following:

- Reach out and include the community. Speak to neighbors and community groups. Let anyone with an interest know what's being considered. You'll find advocates and good information. Finding out early if there's any resistance gives the community time to address concerns and find common ground.
- Find examples of similar projects in your region. Someone who can present "we did this, it worked, and here's how" is very effective public relations.
- Speake to city or county officials and engineers to get their early participation in the process.
- Look for temporary improvements that can be proof of concept. Safety cones or planters can be used to create lightweight safety improvements. Seeing that, neighbors become comfortable with and then demand permanent improvements.

As suggested earlier, safe routes make our neighborhoods more accessible to the public, particularly the young and old. They make libraries more accessible too. City access librarians have the background to be leaders in this work. In doing so, they make the resources of neighborhoods, cities, and towns more open and equitable.

You Are Here Writ Large

Intersection murals—big, painted murals filling the asphalt of an intersection and connecting streets—have been employed in many neighborhoods for traffic calming, route making, community building, and the enhancement of neighborhood identity. Great examples can be found in Portland (OR) with over twenty completed, and in Montclair (NJ) and San Diego. Libraries are relatively free to improve their own properties, but sometimes the most relevant sites are found elsewhere. Saint Paul (MN) has completed a handful of murals under the project name "Paint the Pavement," with some located near schools or libraries. The street murals are created with volunteer labor, paint, and a city permit for temporary street closure. The designs are often the product of collaboration between an artist and residents working with a nearby school.

The example shown in figure 4.3 is one of two murals adjacent to the Pacific Beach Middle School in San Diego. The project was led by a community organization, beautifulPB, and was painted by 120 volunteers. They describe the value of crosswalk murals as a "gesture to alert motorists to slow down, be more alert and yield to pedestrians and bicyclists. The process of selecting artwork and painting the mural fosters collaboration and strengthens the community bonds by providing opportunities to bring the community together to promote health and safety." BeautifulPB provides a how-to and advice for others to follow, adapted here with permission.[2]

FIGURE 4.3

Volunteers Completing a Beautiful PB Intersection Mural

1. Identify a location that would improve safety for children traveling to/from school.
2. Gather support from neighbors and the local school.
3. Select a design. (They used a student competition. Other community input processes can also be successful.)
4. Gather permits. (More below.)
5. Coordinate a community block party to paint the mural.
6. Promote the event!
7. Organize an early shift to arrive prior to the event start, to block off the street and post signs to reroute vehicular traffic. Use brooms to clean the area to be painted. Ideally, the area is power-washed the day before and allowed to dry. Road condition is extremely important. A newly resurfaced road will require less paint, look better, and last longer.
8. The artist and a small team familiar with the artwork lay out a grid over the crosswalk, outline the artwork using chalk, and mark colors to guide volunteers.
9. Divide the mural into sections, and have teams of volunteers paint sections of the mural under supervision. Paint from the center out. Cinder blocks and planks can be used to pass over freshly painted areas.
10. One coat of paint may take two to four hours to apply depending on the complexity of the artwork and the number of volunteers. Depending on the paint selected, the number of coats and drying time varies.
11. Be sure to have photographers on hand to document the day!

Your streets department may be able to supply road-quality paint with anti-skid additive in standard colors. Chalk lines can be used to lay out a grid. Bring painting and cleaning tools, a ladder, and road barriers. Chris Olson with beautifulPB adds, "The simplest way to minimize costly road closure costs and assure easy maintenance and touch-up is to combine the mural painting with a regularly scheduled event like an annual block party or other event at the same location."

In the Linda Vista neighborhood of San Diego, a community center, county health agency, neighborhood library, and middle school are working together on intersection mural projects to adjoin a middle school and elementary school. The regional transportation planning agency provided a small grant to partly cover supplies and permits. The library's Friends group helped pay the artist's stipend. The team's hope is that the projects will be the first of a handful in the neighborhood, including a mural adjacent to the library. The team is also working with city representatives to craft policies and recommendations to make these projects easier to complete in other neighborhoods in the future.

The permits required vary widely in number, cost, and time to issue from one jurisdiction to another. Possible permits and fees required include the plan check, right-of-way permit, encroachment maintenance and removal agreement, traffic control plan, and road closure/block party/special events permit. Example permit costs studied ranged in total from $50 in Rochester (NY) to $232 in Seattle to $1,691 in San Diego. Street mural project guidelines are available from a number of cities, including Seattle and Milwaukie (OR).

Local Enrichment

Safe routes fill mobility gaps to create very real and critical access in our communities. A related enhancement is appearing at a number of neighborhood sites along public routes. "Born learning trails" is a package of outdoor early learning stations developed by the United Way. The trails are a bit like a parcourse fitness circuit. They consist of ten stations with signs depicting an activity that kids and their caregivers can do at that spot. Usually installed in parks, a number of born learning trails have been installed at library sites, developed in partnership with libraries along their sidewalks or on library property. The activity signage is currently available in English, Spanish, and Vietnamese.

The Brown County Library (Green Bay, WI) partnered with its local United Way Emerging Leaders group on a Born Learning Trail at two library sites. The connection to the United Way's program had been made for the library by the Community Partnership for Children, a local kindergarten readiness network that works with the library and is supported by the United Way. The Emerging Leaders raised funds and provided labor. Together with the library they installed born learning trails at Brown County's Central Library and its Southwest Branch Library. (See figure 4.4.) Sandy Kallunki, youth services coordinator for the Brown County Central Library, shared their experience.

When I heard about [born learning trails] I asked if they would consider putting one in at the library because it ties in so well with what we do. They were really excited about that. We became their first installation and then the Southwest Branch Library became their second.

We have two copies of each sign, in Spanish and English. They are early literacy activities that can be done in that particular spot, intended for parents or other adults to do with their kids that don't require them to bring any extra toys. They're self-contained. Some of them have something painted on the sidewalk. There's one station that has three circles of different colors and then there's another one that's like a hopscotch. It's on library property and is accessible twenty-four hours a day. On the signs are the kinds of activities that we're encouraging parents and day care teachers to do with their kids. It ties in nicely with our mission.

The library has seen the greatest successes with the trails when they're combined with kids' programming:

If we have a costumed character here for a storytime, we'll have the character go out on the trail with the kids and do the activities along with them and that really gets a crowd. We've had Olivia and we've had the Very Hungry

Enjoy the Born Learning Trails
at the Central Library and Southwest Branch Library!

Ten outdoor stations, with signs in English and Spanish, encourage simple activities that parents and other adults can do with young children to help build language and reading skills.

FIGURE 4.4
Promotion for Born Learning Trails at the Brown County Library

Caterpillar and we have a local program, Cowboy Dusty. That's been really successful.

There are a couple of organizations in town that work with disadvantaged kids that bring their groups. They'll meet at the library and then the teacher or the group leader leads the kids and the parents through the trail. I didn't know that we had these groups [using the born learning trail] until I was at a meeting and they were talking about it. It's not like you need to sign up or anything. They said that they found it a really good way to introduce parents to some of these really simple things that they can do with their kids to help build foundational skills.

Through structured and unstructured use, the trails become both an extension of the library and a part of the neighborhood. At the Brown County Library branch location, it's "a feature that makes the library special. The trail goes all the way around the library. You can't miss it. It's very visible." The library has promoted the born learning trails with ribbon-cutting events with county executives and special guests, turning the openings into neighborhood celebrations. "When we're doing presentations to day care providers or literacy programs for parents, it's one of those things that we mention. We don't have an advertising budget; we don't do much media. It's very much grassroots."

Though principally a "passive programming" element for early learning, the trails make a real contribution to the neighborhood. The area around a library may otherwise be a space to simply get through. Adding a born learning trail or similar tactical element identifies the area as "kid-friendly" community space and activates its use. Experience using the trails connects kids and adults to the space. The neighborhood gains a unique public space and is made more accessible and active.

We Belong Here

Identity is important to all of us. This needs little explanation. Who we are, where we're from, and where we live are sources of pride, contest, and connection. The identity of the places we call home is likewise something we each aspire to shape. We do that with the stories we tell about those places and what we put into them. The placemaking examples discussed so far all have neighborhood identity implicit in them. "Creative placemaking" is a sub-field of placemaking that is explicitly about the use of art to build place-based meaning and identity. It's an active focus of many public arts organizations, including libraries and library arts programs. Often this is undertaken as a piece of a major project, like an artist brought in to add public art elements to a new building. Other times the project may be more community-based and unconnected to other construction. There's a rich spectrum, of course, spanning public murals, mosaics, sculpture, and more.

An example of the more grassroots-type variety is the intersection murals discussed above which contribute both to neighborhood mobility and community identity. Another variety that is well established and which has been led by many libraries is "yarn bombing." Often a library-based knitting club will lead the effort, which requires the preparation of a large number of knitted panels followed by a day of knitting the panels together to wrap trees, posts, railings, and more in colorful knitwork. Libraries usually conduct these on library grounds, but wider city interventions are possible. The decorations last six to nine months and are then dismantled.

Christina Wainwright, a branch manager with the San Diego Public Library (SDPL), had been active in organizing yarn bombings at a number of SDPL locations. She'd planned a yarn bombing at her own branch that took on special meaning. "My dad passed away the day before the yarn-bombing at my library. I was knitting pieces at the hospital for the yarn-bombing when he fell ill and I continued to knit when we brought him home to die. My family decorated a tree in his memory. My sister and her kids helped to make knitted fish and jellyfish adorning the tree. I made a tree sweater and turtle. The knitting gave us something beautiful to make together while we cared for him, and was a happy reason to get out of the house that day and celebrate life at the library. It meant a lot to us."

When we can see our stories visible in the world around us, we make those places ours, our families', and our communities'. Librarians can help their cities and towns to be more open to this; providing the organization and opportunity and maybe the yarn.

Librarians have made efforts in recent decades to consider representation in all aspects of librarianship. We need diverse books. For marginalized communities, there are limited outlets to make an impression in and to see themselves reflected in the city- and town-scape. Librarians are helping their communities to write identity and representation into their surroundings, to author the collection all around.

The Place Is Where the People Are

Making the places around us more social and engaging often requires little more than an invitation. In 2013 the Duluth (MN) Public Library invited food trucks to set up on Fridays at the covered streetside entry plaza of their Central Library. The program runs from June through August in Duluth. Your seasonal mileage may vary. Library Manager Carla Powers spoke with me about the annual series. "Right out of the gate people were showing up. I can remember the first Food Truck Friday that we put on. The food trucks weren't really prepared for the number of people that they would get and it took a long time to get your food that first week. I think the food trucks actually beefed up their staffing once they saw the amount of customers they'd be getting at the library."

The program came about right after the city of Duluth began to license food trucks. "The city council representative who was involved in that also happened to be our city council representative on the library board. She was very involved in library activities and was the one who suggested it." Permitting varies from city to city, but typically the requirement for food trucks is only that they're licensed and have the permission of the property owner. A site permit is usually not required. Additional local codes govern food truck use of street parking, which wasn't the case for the Duluth Public Library.

> We made sure that the food trucks were licensed. We set out tables—folding tables from our meeting rooms—and put them in the plaza so people would have a place to sit. We put out trash cans and recycling. And that's about it. The only problem was just being prepared for the crowd.
>
> The first year, the director of our Library Foundation was in charge of it and she brought in some music. It wasn't really a fund-raiser for the foun-

dation, so it didn't make sense for her to continue doing it. It switched over to being staff-driven and we didn't quite take it to that level just because of staffing resources. At some point we want to bring in some music or maybe other little vendors, make it a farmer's market type of thing.

Inviting the food trucks, promoting the event, and providing tables, chairs, and electricity has been enough to make Food Truck Fridays a popular destination and "activation" of the space. (The jargon use of "activation" is from community planning for providing the push, in the form of planned events and activities, that some places need to pass a threshold toward becoming more continuously safe, welcoming, and desirable.) Powers continued: "The community really likes it. I don't know how many of the people who come to Food Truck Fridays actually come into the library and check out books or do anything else here. But just the fact that they are at the library, they're talking about the library. The food trucks are putting this on their Facebook page that they are going to be at the library. It generates a buzz that's great. They've got a lot of followers who just go on Facebook to see where the food truck's going to be. They ended up doing a lot of publicity."

An informal "go ahead, try it" attitude is useful in placemaking and can be seen here. I asked about formal arrangements for electricity. "No. We have the outlets out in that area and it wasn't a problem. They didn't blow any circuit breakers or anything. So, yeah, we just had them plug in and do it." Though the program at Duluth doesn't do this, similar programs have operated outside of regular library hours, for example at the Linda Vista Branch Library in San Diego. There, a dinnertime taco truck in the library parking lot activated an urban space that could otherwise feel unsafe after hours. The service extended the sphere of safety that activity creates later into the evenings, to the neighborhood's benefit and, less directly, to to the library's benefit as well.

Activating city and town spaces in various convivial ways (and food is an easy one) unlocks the places around us to be more public, more valuable, and more open and accessible. This is as true in poor neighborhoods as in wealthy ones. Librarians have the skills, resources, and contacts at their disposal to help bring public space activations about. Powers said about Duluth's Food Truck Fridays success: "We've been really happy with it. There is a synergy there."

Public Library as a Verb

Downtown Knoxville (TN) has been undergoing a renaissance. The area is again bustling with restaurants, shops, and new residents. Some credit for the renewal belongs to the Knox County Public Library, which twelve years ago began programming a six-week-long movie series at downtown's Market Square, three blocks from their Lawson McGhee (main) Library. The family movie nights now attract many thousands of people from downtown, nearby, and even from beyond Knox County. The motivation to conduct a programming series off-site was driven in part by space limitations. But equally, "the initial impetus was to be part of this downtown revitalization process, to upgrade the brand of the library, and to utilize some of these great outdoor spaces that we have."

Mary Pom Claiborne, director of marketing, development, and communications at the Knox County Public Library, created the program. She took the same city activation approach with another program, the Children's Festival of Reading, which is also in its twelfth year. The library's children's book festival is held at Knoxville's World's Fair Park, five blocks west of the main library.

The central business improvement district (CBID) and numerous corporate sponsors help with funding for both the movie series and the children's book festival. The funding pays for licensing, projection, Porta-Potties, street closures, permits, cleanup, and pre-movie performers. Pre-show performers have included bands, magic shows before kids' movies, and a presentation on sharks led by Ripley's Aquarium complete with a shark mascot (before a screening of *Jaws*, of course). Claiborne explained that the CBID budgets for Movies in Market Square every year, "which to me says they really do like it, because it brings in a different group. It's very family-oriented. Families come out and have picnics on the square. It's lovely. It contributes to the overall culture. I know of one woman who came down to the movies, and she looked around and she saw the crowd. She decided to open a business on the square because of it." (Rita's on Market Square has now been there over a decade serving Italian ices, gelati, and custards.)

The program has spurred other investment in Market Square, including a top-quality sound system purchased by the city. "There's a lot of entertainment that happens on the square, but Movies on Market Square is one of the things that really helped them make the decision." The library takes advantage of the event to promote the library and conduct marketing surveys. When the sun drops low enough, a slideshow begins that interleaves sponsor credits with library promotions and "Did you know?" graphics about library services. "It's a really good way to promote library services to audiences that aren't necessarily library users." The library extends its community engagement weeks ahead with public voting on the movies to be shown, making the series a marketing vehicle for eight weeks or more.

Producing the off-site program has depended from the beginning on coordination with the city's Office of Special Events. The city doesn't charge the library for use of the space. The electric utility turns off street lamps near the screen at no cost. The series' success is now itself creating some challenges. The plaza is thriving so much that the movies compete with invigorated patio dining and other activities.

> The square itself is filled with stores and restaurants, so we don't deal with vendors because it's all right there. It's a benefit to the merchants to have us bring those crowds in. It's gained so much popularity that it's almost hard to have the movies there now. There's a lot of ambient noise. You have to compete with conversation.

By design, the library's Movies on Market Square program has helped activate Knoxville's downtown. The library has benefited and made great use of the events. But most saliently, librarians' work and expertise have contributed to making the city more vibrant, public, and accessible. "I'm really pleased that some of our most loyal folks that come out are like the Sertoma club, a housing program for adults with physical challenges. It just makes a heart soar to see these guys come in week after week and set up their chairs and it's like their big outing. It's an amazing setting."

Sharing the Wheel

Though not traditional activation, a partnership between the Brooklyn Public Library and Zipcar is interesting. Zipcar is a membership program for short-term car rentals, with automated pickup in locations distributed widely within cities. The library reached out to Zipcar to be a sponsor of the library's Bike the Branches program. In addition to becoming a sponsor, Zipcar proposed a partnership. Branch libraries in Brooklyn have small staff parking lots that weren't being used to capacity. Would the library allow its lots to be used as Zipcar locations in exchange for revenue sharing? Lexy Mayers, chief development officer at the Brooklyn Public Library, worked on the project.

> There was a lot of anxiety internally around putting Zipcars at our branches and doing something very different. Would librarians be expected to answer questions that they weren't equipped to answer? But it's really been super smooth. The really nice part of it is that the revenue that we get from Zipcar for using those spots goes to that local branch. That way the staff at that library feels that whatever additional work they may have to do—because the occasional person does come in and say, "The Zipcar won't start" or whatever—they feel like they're getting something out of it. We do feel like there's some overlap in terms of the message: you don't need to own a car; you don't need to own a book.

Zipcar's advertising for the locations mirrored this. From Zipcar's ads: "We bow to the inventors of this whole sharing thing. The library. They got it way before the rest of us. Borrow it. Use it. Return it. Then it's someone else's turn." (See figure 4.5.)

Zipcar named the cars at the Brooklyn Public Library branches after authors and characters. Margaret Wise Brown at Bedford, Richard Wright at Bay Ridge, and Knuffle Bunny at the Walt Whitman branch, to name a few. "That seemed like a really cute way of making a connection with the 'borrowing' culture."

FIGURE 4.5
Promotional Graphic for Zipcar's Service at Brooklyn Public Library Locations

The program was piloted at three branches and has since expanded to nine, with staff from the first three helping with the expansion. They've "been great ambassadors to the staff at the new branches in terms of being able to say it's been good for the funding. But also they've reported that they have gotten some folks who've come in to their library because they were getting their car. They like that they're getting a little bit of traffic, no pun intended, that they wouldn't be getting otherwise."

The partnership with Zipcar is small but intriguing for the way it makes the library a site for access to transportation and the city, for borrowing one mode of mobility. Of course, Zipcar is a commercial service and it's worth debating how that aligns with the library's values. It's worth noting, though, that the cost for occasional users is far below that of car ownership. (A promotion also gives Brooklyn Public Library card holders a free $30 credit at sign-up.) Would libraries start loaning vehicles out on their own? It's not inconceivable.

Team Effort

When done well, placemaking is a low-cost, high-return enrichment of community assets: it produces wealth that communities continuously benefit from for years and years after. A lot of placemaking can be done relatively cheaply, from a couple hundred to a few thousand dollars. Funding for Linda Vista's parklet came mostly from their city council office, with other community partners donating materials and volunteer labor. Community planning groups, town councils, Friends groups, community centers, urban corps, boys and girls clubs, schools, and hospitals are all examples of organizations that may be interested and able to contribute to placemaking projects. Public health agencies have been notably active in placemaking. Other unique sources of funding for special projects are covered, for example, in *40+ New Revenue Sources for Libraries and Nonprofits*.[3] Community crowd-funding may fit library-based placemaking well. The neighborhood development, crowd-funding, and organizing site www.ioby.org (for "In Our Back-yards") is worth noting as a potential support hub for these projects.

Placemaking depends on broad participation. Engage the community and the library system early in the process. Make them equal partners in planning and execution. Support their work through the library's particular strengths: making community connections, organizing, researching, and event programming. There's a lesson of tactical urbanism that librarians understand in other contexts that they should take to heart for placemaking projects: seeing projects through quickly has a multiplier effect. Neighborhood improvements generally take years (or more) to go from discussion to finish. That's an enormous discouragement to people. Why put time into getting a corner park for your kid when they'll be in high school or past when it's done? Why try to get street trees added? Or a playful bus shelter? Changing that experience—seeing things completed in under a year—has a big impact on people's expectations and engagement.

There are barriers, too. Expectations about one's claims to public space are often shaped by class, race, and gender. Libraries can play an affirmatively egalitarian role. A lot of the ostensibly public realm is privately owned. Improving those spaces requires the participation of the land owners, for whom it may not be an interest or priority. Try them anyway. If they can see benefits and that they won't have to bear all the work or cost themselves, a partnership may be possible. For community members, the case for investing time into improving a neighborhood corner is not always easy to make. We're busy. The benefits are diffuse. And the design of the places around us is easy to take as given. There's ammunition for saying "we can't." Questions of liability can stop conversations, but needn't. If there is a relevant insurer, ask them how they see the site. Insurers don't expect infallible safety, only that safety was considered when decisions were reached.

Librarians can help make their cities and towns more receptive to community-led improvements. Advocate for simpler approval processes, faster turnaround times, and fees appropriate to community projects. Build a network of experienced placemakers to draw on.

As an explicit consideration of libraries, community placemaking is a relatively new topic. But many librarians have been doing this work for a long time, self-consciously or not. Libraries are appropriate and capable facilitators for our members to improve their cities and towns, to make their streets safer and more convivial, to put public spaces where they're needed, and to inscribe their own stories and meaning in those places. The streets, sidewalks, plazas, and other places around us are part of the collection all around. Accessing those—being able to pursue one's own vision for those—can easily seem daunting and out of reach. With the help of city access librarians, communities can find their surroundings to be malleable, available, and accessible to all.

NOTES

1. Zach Patton, "Parklets: The Next Big Tiny Idea in Urban Planning," 2012, www.governing.com/topics/energy-env/gov-parklets-next-big-idea-in-urban-planning.html.

2. Chris Olson, "PB Murals," 2016, beautifulpb.com/projects/pbmurals.

3. Edmund A. Rossman, *40+ New Revenue Sources for Libraries and Nonprofits*, (Chicago: American Library Association, 2016).

CHAPTER FIVE

Rangers Tend the Trails

CITIES AND TOWNS ARE RICH WITH CULTURAL RESOURCES, entertainment, education, recreation, connection, and all manner of places and activities. Completing the picture of what our locales are to us and offer us, the places we live are rich with nature too.

It's easy to think of the natural places around us as already accessible. Whether in small towns, suburbs, or cities, most communities have a park or preserve or undeveloped open space not far away. With some exceptions, these treasures aren't behind admission gates. For most of us, though, we spend less time in contact with the wild—the big and the small of it—than ever before. There are many contributing reasons for this, but accessibility of different kinds plays a role. Librarians have taken up the cause of making connections to nature easier for their communities. Their efforts take place at the library, through circulated resources, in nearby parks, and through interventions, information, and passes. Like other programs we've looked at, these are mostly discrete and not part of a systematic focus on access. But they put in relief less visible barriers to access that many people encounter. The work of these librarians puts the natural world around us in better reach.

Building Literacy with Sticks and Mud

Reducing barriers to access is a library value, and that in itself is relevant to libraries' approach to the natural world. But there's an additional and traditional reason for libraries to take an interest in bringing the natural world closer to hand. Time spent in nature makes important contributions to learning. Libraries' attention to early, preliterate learning in particular has grown in recent years as recognition of the crucial foundation that children's first five years play in later literacy has increased. Early learning shares with libraries two essential, standout qualities: both are uncredited and exploratory. The currency of early learning is play. These qualities also describe time and learning in nature.

Recent years have seen a renewed movement for making time for connections to nature. It's driven in part by a new body of research confirming the benefits of time spent in natural settings and the deleterious effect of time increasingly spent without them. The positive and negative effects are particularly visible in child development. Richard Louv is credited with popularizing the issue with his 2005 book *Last Child in the Woods: Saving Our Children from Nature-Deficit Disorder* and through his founding of and work with the Children & Nature Network.

Some findings of the research, adapted here from "Natural England Access to Evidence Information Note EIN017, Links between Natural Environments and Learning,"* are as follow:

1. Greater access to public spaces with natural elements is associated with a range of positive behavioral indicators and with cognitive development in schoolchildren.
2. Greener school environments are linked to better motor skills, psychological restoration, and rates of physical activity.
3. Children from poorer families and minority ethnic groups are less likely to have the opportunity to engage in learning in natural environments, potentially widening inequalities.
4. In both adults and children there is evidence that learning in natural environments fosters pride, belonging, and involvement in the community.

Many schools have responded to this research and movement by developing green school yards and nature trails. Libraries are responding too.

* "Natural England Access to Evidence Information Note EIN017, Links between Natural Environments and Learning: Evidence Briefing," Natural England, 2016, publications.natural england.org.uk/file/6292437136310272.

Welcome Outside, Look Around

A flagship for "nature-smart library" efforts is the Sun Ray branch of the Saint Paul (MN) Public Library. In 2013 the branch was starting to plan for a major renovation. The architectural firm that was selected included the architect Mohammed Lawal, who is a board member on the national Children & Nature Network, an advocacy group for connecting children and families to nature. Lawal proposed the idea of taking advantage of the branch's setting in an urban park to demonstrate ideas about libraries as gateways to nature. Rebecca Ryan, a branch manager at the Saint Paul Public Library, was Sun Ray's manager at the time.

> The Sun Ray building was originally built in 1970. It was a nice brutalist concrete structure that had a lot of windows and brick. Some of the windows had been boarded up. The library was in a park which I constantly forgot about because I couldn't see the park from the library. Mohammed saw opening back our connection to the park. We needed to comply with elements of LEED certification that the city council identified as most important. It was an interesting opportunity to think, "Hey, we're looking at this building in a new way, we're looking at its connection to the neighborhood and the park in a new way. We're doing these environmentally friendly things to it. Now what happens if we go a step further and see if, through programming and a mindset shift, the library can help better connect families and people in the neighborhood with nature."
>
> I will say, at the beginning I was like, "Well, I think my patrons care about jobs and they care about their kids' educations. This nature thing seems like something that white middle-class people care about. I'm not sure that the majority of my patrons, who are not white and middle class, are going to resonate with it." I'm happy to say I was wrong.

The Sun Ray library sits along one side of Conway Park. The gateway to nature efforts started simply, with planting more trees in the park. "Honestly, Conway Park isn't the world's greatest park, but that's kind of what makes it perfect. You can see across it. It's not big and intimidating and scary for people." Sun Ray staff started thinking regularly about the areas surrounding the library and what the library's role was with those areas. The community experienced those spaces when going to the library, so it made sense to think beyond "Are the sidewalks clear? Is the parking lot plowed?" as Ryan put it.

> It's hard to describe the mindset shift that we were experiencing. In Minnesota we're used to our libraries being this indoor place that we program. We have space for people. We have publicity, we have relationships, we have expertise in early literacy and helping people find jobs. These are very indoor things. We might have a reading garden but as in, "Go out on the reading garden. You can fly your paper airplane out there."

Ryan got help from Saint Paul's Parks and Recreation Department. While she'd partnered with Parks and Recreation often, it had been with the recreation center parts of the department. "I never would have called up the forestry folks. But it was interesting to meet them and to have this discussion about the space around libraries that my patrons experience all the time. The forestry folks were like, 'Yeah! We totally want to come and plant trees in this neighborhood, because we see shade as an equity issue. If you're a low-income neighborhood you tend to walk more and you tend to walk in places that are more unpleasant for walking in the summer because it's not as shady.' That was really interesting."

The Children & Nature Network got a grant from the U.S. Fish and Wildlife Service and Wells Fargo provided a team of volunteers to plant trees. "Some of the project partners had been working on green school yards. This was like a green library yard." The green school yard movement is being advanced by many schools independently and by a number of organizations, including Green Schoolyards America. As the spaces for natural exploration have shrunk for kids over recent decades, the school yard and the library yard have taken on greater importance as opportunities for time spent in nature. Recognizing this and in reaction to the asphalt and concrete-dominated school yard designs that had become common, schools have been devoting larger portions of their yards to natural elements and areas for exploration. The Sun Ray Library improvements do the same with a public space for all ages.

A formal reading garden was the centerpiece of the Sun Ray renovation. The large parking areas were re-landscaped and, needing to find more work for the Wells Fargo volunteers, "we thought, 'You know, it'd be pretty cool if we could have a garden that's a little bit less formal and that we can use to educate people about the [pollinator] issue and do programming with all ages of patrons.'" Ryan continued:

> I had so many conversations with my patrons about the garden and how they approach the library and how they think about the outside of the library. It's obviously part of their visit. I had people asking, "What's this plant?" and "I have this plant in my garden," and then "What is a pollinator?"
>
> There's obviously some patrons who know all of the issues and are very educated about it, some who have no idea, and others who are in the middle. And then others whose kids bring them out there, because they're like, "Hey, mom! We let the monarch go in our class! This is where it could wind up!" That was the beginning: this focus on the space around the library and what we could do with it and how we could think about it in a different way now that we had this renewed connection to it.

They started the demonstration pollinator garden in their parking lot with help from the Wells Fargo team, and it was being expanded in 2016 from 28 × 53 feet to 53 × 100 feet. Ryan said at the time, "It's going to be a hefty pollinator garden. And this time we're getting smart and we're including a little circular area so we can more easily take people out there and talk about the plants and the root systems and pollinator issues in general." Their further plans include beehives and programming matched with them.

The changes at Sun Ray appear in new thinking and new programming. After the full renovation of the building and a kickoff party, they began developing programming pieces with the Children & Nature Network, Americorps, and Urban Roots. Urban Roots is a Saint Paul-area organization focusing on food systems, the environment, and youth empowerment. The partner organizations brought specialized experience and background with nature education (and building snow forts) that the library didn't have. Storytimes and activities in the pollinator garden, for example, include families exploring the garden and getting help doing seed identification and learning about root systems.

A "longest night of the year" program included a geocache (GPS-based) treasure hunt in the park followed by a bonfire with marshmallows. A favorite program was "Winter Survival Camp and Book Club." They selected *Disaster Strikes: Blizzard Night*, by Marlane Kennedy, something exciting and easy to read. Ryan explained:

> We have a lot of kids that come to us in different ways. We recruited kids in the tutoring program. We recruited kids in the homework center. We recruited kids whose parents bring them to the library because they're big readers. We recruited kids who just come to the library on their own more or less every day as a place to hang out. They were really excited about the books and the idea of a club. Out of the 25 books that we gave out, 23 kids showed up for the program.
>
> Urban Roots did some activities: "Okay, how do you dress for when it's wintertime? How do you save someone from hypothermia?" There was an indoor component and then we took them all outside and they built snow forts. So, "If you're stuck in a blizzard, how do you get shelter? You can build a snow fort!" The best thing, this kid turned to me—I know him pretty well, and I had called up his grandma to get her permission—he was really excited about it and he goes, "So what are we reading next?!" Alright! We're going to keep going with this.
>
> We had all these kids that kind of knew each other but not really and they were out there for a good hour just digging in the snow, totally having a blast. We had to raid the lost-and-found so everyone had appropriate clothing. Some of them so clearly never had unstructured time outdoors. Some of them clearly had had plenty of unstructured time outdoors, but nobody to guide them and say "Hey, this is something that you could do. . ."
>
> That's one of the nature focuses that I find really interesting. It appeals to these different demographics of children. Some families have lots of time and not so many resources to scaffold their children's outdoor time. Then there are others who have lots of activities but no kind of unstructured time where they can go outside and play, build snow forts, and be kids.

Other programs that Sun Ray offers include the ongoing circulation of nature backpacks. Varieties of nature backpack programs are in place in many libraries, including Colorado's Anythink Libraries, discussed later in this chapter.

Sun Ray's backpacks were developed with the Children & Nature Network and Sun Ray's children's specialist. The library has eighteen backpacks, each holding a collection of items for activities on a theme. Examples include reptiles, urban birds, camping, and winter fun. Two age groups are targeted by the kits: ages 2 to 6 and 7 to 11. There are four "group adventure" backpacks that are designed for taking a group of children to a park or preserve. The backpacks' kits include field guides, activity cards, magnifying glasses, bug catchers, and a first aid kit. "They've been super popular and we use them for different kinds of programming." The "urban birds" backpack includes binoculars, a CD of bird sounds, and activity cards. "Urban animals of the day" and "urban animals of the night" are other themes with a "nearby nature" orientation.

> We were intentional about wanting it to be things that anybody could walk out their door and find evidence of. So there's trees, frogs, bugs and spiders, clouds and weather. It could be your own backyard. It could be this particular tree that you think is really cool that you happen to notice on your walk to the bus. Whatever it is. We tried to make them generic and not that specific. Although I did like the idea of "Here's a backpack to take to this park". . .

The backpacks and nature programming support experiential styles of learning. This is in contrast to libraries' traditional literate mode and is an aspect of the collection all around to consider. Libraries that share access to the world around are reaching some audiences for whom learning is most accessible when rooted in places, activities, and relationships. In this case, in nature.

Welcome Outside, Everyone

While the parks and nature preserves around us are ostensibly available to all, Ryan was interested in the ways a lack of experience, assistance, and welcome keeps many families—those in urban areas, especially—from accessing them. Access is often about social and cultural capital and claiming entitlement to something that is only superficially available. Making the world approachable, understandable, and safe is a service libraries can and do provide. "We had a lot of ideas for how we scaffold people's outdoor access, particularly if they're scared, if they feel like they're not welcome, if they don't know what to do when they get to the park, or they don't know where the park is."

Ryan took advantage of a neighborhood teen leadership group that meets in the library and does community work. Though not a library-sponsored program, Ryan had recruited the Young Mentors Group to move their meetings to the library when Sun Ray reopened. With an eye toward outdoor learning and green jobs opportunities, Ryan started connecting the group to the Children & Nature Network. A library staff person who is also a leader with Young Mentors organized a campout for teens and tweens in Conway Park, next to the library and in the city. REI donated camping gear, and the library and the Children & Nature Network helped with staffing.

> That was one of the pieces that convinced me. It was mostly African American kids and lots of single moms who were like, "Heck yeah, I want my kid to go camping! I'm never going to be able to do that." Or, "I don't have the access," or "I don't know how to do it," or "I don't know where to go."

Expectations about use of the outdoors, with racial undertones, surfaced quickly.

> They had not one, not two, not three, but four police calls to the park because people are like, "There's kids in the park! It's late at night, what are they doing?" Fortunately, they didn't have any trouble. If you're a black kid and you go to the park and somebody expects to not see you there, that's a different kind of barrier to park access.

Importantly, as "hosts," the library and its partners lend authority and permission that shouldn't be needed, but often is. Social barriers to access—local access, especially—deserve more attention as a target of librarians' work and investigation. Disparities in access to nature along socioeconomic and racial lines are well documented. The trend among cities toward open data and trying to measure outcomes may be of some help in identifying and understanding specific gaps. Social barriers exist for public resources as well as private ones. And as Ryan notes, "Our public resources are dwindling, so we better really make use of what we have."

The campout was a nice demonstration of a library improving access simply by providing a familiar "interface" (the library itself) and adding a small amount of experience and facilitation; in this case, with camping how-to and park permits. Other agencies and city departments are likewise starting to see in the library an interface to the public that fills in for what is a weakness of their own. (This was the case for the San Rafael Public Library in chapter 3.) The campout was a success. The teens "all wanted it and they were all interested in it. And they all had a great time. Except for the leaders who were like, 'Oh my God, I didn't sleep all night.'" Since then the Young Mentors Group has maintained a "natural leaders" focus. They've gone on urban birding expeditions. They've hiked a larger, wilder park nearby that neighbors do not generally use. Ryan continued:

> The Children & Nature Network brought in different groups to talk to them, like Wilderness Inquiry and the Department of Natural Resources, and exposed them to different areas around the city that they could go to that they didn't know about. They're going out on their own. It's been really cool to see the teens take on the idea and make it their own and see what they're interested in about it. Some of them had had a little bit of previous experience, but most of them had absolutely no outdoor experience of any kind. Lots of them hadn't even really been past the soccer fields or the playground of this big park. The idea of "taking a hike" was novel. Now they're interested in camping and canoeing. They go on some group hikes. Some of the kids go on their own and take their siblings. They're definitely interested in bringing their parents.

While Sun Ray has led the way for the Saint Paul Public Library, other branches and the system are beginning to integrate access to nature into their work. One branch library has a partnership with an urban gardening organization and others have gardens. Some branches that are in parks are adopting the nature adventure backpacks for circulation and programming. "It's definitely on the agenda of other libraries, making it something that we think about system-wide. It's not a hard sell, and not a hard thing to replicate."

The National League of Cities launched a three-year Cities Connecting Children to Nature initiative in November 2014. It is explicitly focused on access and disparities in access. Saint Paul, one of seven cities selected for the planning cohort, is a leader, and relatively alone in demonstrating the centrality of libraries to this conversation which is otherwise conducted by parks, nature centers, and public health agencies. Librarians have the community relationships and skills to build access and connections from the ground up. As Ryan concluded, "It's always interesting to me, how little it can really take and how big that little bit can be."

Naturing Miscellaneously

At Anythink Libraries, the public library system for Adams County in Colorado, just north of Denver, Explore Outdoors is a multibranch effort to extend the learning happening inside of the libraries into the outdoor spaces. It is contributing to the library having a local role in enhancing access to nature. Suzanne McGowan, manager at the Anythink Wright Farms branch, explains that the library grounds provide opportunities for learning and time in nature that can be scarce for many kids and adults.

The library's Explore Outdoors "nature classroom" adjacent to Anythink Wright Farms opened in September 2012 and includes areas using natural materials for building, music, art, and creative play. The nature classroom was inspired and is certified by Nature Explore, a collaborative program of the Arbor Day Foundation and the Dimensions Educational Research Foundation, which has certified over 320 outdoor classrooms in the United States and Canada. Nature Explore, working mainly with schools, researches and designs outdoor classrooms and offers educator workshops and resources. Library administrators were familiar with a Nature Explore garden at a nearby daycare center and worked with the Adams County Open Space Department and the Anythink Foundation to secure grant funding for the two-year project.

The library's outdoor classroom is part of a one-acre park and is designed to encourage curiosity, learning, and connection with the natural world. "Watching children of all ages interact with nature is the perfect extension of library learning spaces," Anythink Director Pam Sandlian Smith said. Suzanne McGowan described the nature classroom:

There's such a variety of outdoor experiences, from bubbles to water features and other water play. At Anythink Wright Farms, there is an old-fashioned handheld pump. We have [outdoor] instruments in all of the Explore Outdoors spaces, and the kids play on those. Each branch has something a little different. We just installed a nature loom, the newest addition to our branch, which we're really excited about. People include cut grasses and weeds they find, and they weave them in.

In these spaces, we wanted to provide a connection to the outdoors and less-structured playtime. We put different items out for kids to explore. From time to time, the children's guides will find shells. We've put out an empty beehive. On the climbing areas, we put out scarves thinking the kids would make forts and tents, but they've learned to tie them into hammocks. On any given day, we have 10 to 12 kids out there in hammocks either swinging or resting, or a lot of times just reading. They'll grab books and go out and read in the outdoors, which is really nice to see.

In addition to the nature classroom, the adjacent park includes outdoor seating and reading nooks. There is also a community garden at the Anythink Wright Farms library, as well as two other Anythink locations. "We have planters in the Explore Outdoor space beyond just the community garden with flowers and other kinds of plants," says McGowan. "We've put out watering cans, and children have fun watering all the plants. We host a program called AnyAbility, where groups of adults with disabilities come into the library for regular programming, and they'll sometimes do the watering. At the Anythink Brighton location, we grow vegetables and watermelons and other fruit."

The staff at Anythink Brighton have partnered with Brighton Shares the Harvest, a local organization which helped fund that location's Explore Outdoors classroom and continues to provide food to the community through the local food bank. At the Anythink locations with community gardens—Anythink Wright Farms, Perl Mack, and Commerce City—community members can rent a garden plot for $30 a year. This money helps to maintain common areas, community plantings and shared tools. The libraries provide seeds at low or no cost. Like the partnership at Brighton, harvests are shared with local food banks. Support for the community gardens program has also come from the Denver Urban Garden and the Tri-County Health Department.

Access to local resources—a garden plot, community work, and shared skills and expertise—is facilitated by the library. The library provides the space, but the community oversees the gardens' maintenance and resources.

One other way that Anythink connects its members with nature is through a state park pass program launched by the Colorado State Library and Colorado Parks and Wildlife. Eight Colorado library systems were selected to prototype the program, including Anythink. Members can check out a state parks pass, as well as a backpack with information and tools. Anythink had already been active in its Explore Outdoors program and was selected to help pilot the state parks program from the outset. They tested out the lending workflow and policies and worked out changes. After close to a year piloting the program, it launched statewide on June 20, 2016.

"Our summer program is called mySummer: Read, Think, Do. We put a lot of emphasis on getting out and doing things, moving around, learning about what you're moving around in," says Gretchen Crowe, creative lead for special projects at Anythink. "The state parks program made sense to us. We reached out to Barr Lake State Park, which is the closest one to our branches. The park ranger there is absolutely amazing. She has come to the library and done programs, and we've met with their staff there. It really became a co-teaching model, which was really fun."

Every public library location in Colorado, plus some college and military base libraries, received two activity backpacks. The backpacks include a pass good for entry into any Colorado state park for up to seven days plus a collection of outdoors items. The selection of items benefited from the testing period. "They had bird-watching books, magnifying glasses, bug boxes, all these different things. When you have that many little teeny things, it's hard to check them in and out," says Crowe.

The libraries pooled their experiences and pared the selection to include binoculars, a wildlife viewing guide, a tree and wildflower identification guide, a park brochure, and a suggested activities list. Some variation in circulation policy is permitted. For example, some libraries allow holds and some do not. Feedback about the program has been "overwhelmingly positive. There were people that said they had never been to a state park, and they could now afford to take their family."

The pass covers entry and parking, which can run over $8 per person per visit. The state library reached out to the governor's office, which highlighted the program on Facebook and Twitter when the library program first started. This led to local news coverage throughout the state "the exact day we got the backpacks in hand. That was just amazing," says Crowe.

The backpack and park pass programs are not unique to Anythink. Other good examples are found in small and large library systems, including the following:

- My Own BackYard backpacks in southeastern Massachusetts, "individualized for each of three regions and their local ecosystems. One of the backpacks . . . helps children explore local saltwater areas by including a net for catching fish and other ocean life, as well as a plant press. At Plumb Memorial Library, students can check out a stargazing kit with binoculars, star charts, and books that identify the phases of the moon. Mattapoisett patrons can use a snow-themed backpack to help identify different types of snowflakes."[1]
- The North Olympic Library System (WA) cooperative partnered with Olympic National Park on a nature walk program, park poetry walks, and Explore Olympic! backpacks. The backpacks include passes for the national park plus trail and field guides, a magnifying glass, and binoculars. Additional funding was provided by Washington's National Park Fund and Discover Your Northwest.
- Nature Backpacks at 135 Virginia libraries feature state park passes; pocket guides to bugs, animal tracks, Virginia birds, mammals, and Virginia trees and wildflowers; a bug cage, magnifying glass, and dip net; and suggested activities.
- Circulating State Park and Historic Site passes are available at all Georgia public libraries.
- The Indiana State Parks system provided state park passes for circulation to all Indiana public libraries, which inspired some of those libraries to purchase additional passes for their collections. "I'm just amazed at the popularity of this initiative," said Mike Williams, area resource manager at the Indianapolis Public Library. "Clearly there's a huge demand for this type of service."[2]

- I noted similar backpacks at the Mill Valley (CA) Public Library, Wheaton (IL) Public Library, York (ME) Public Library, and seventeen Wisconsin library systems, among others.

Yet another way Anythink has helped connect its members with nature is by promoting the National Parks' "Every Kid in a Park" program for fourth-graders. Every Kid in a Park allows fourth-graders to print a national parks pass which admits a group of three adults with any number of children. The library helps with registration and printing and also promotes the program. Through personal assistance and marketing efforts, the library also helps patrons differentiate the state and national parks and which types of passes can be used.

Through a handful of approaches—outdoor learning features on the library grounds, community gardens, explorer backpacks and park passes—Anythink's Explore Outdoors program supports the Adams County, Colorado community's access to and connection with the wealth of nature in their area.

Neighborhood Expeditionary Party

Safe Routes to Nature is a variation on the Safe Routes to School program discussed in chapter 4. It's not been implemented as a library program that I've found, but it is one for libraries to consider. Circulate San Diego, a mobility advocacy organization, teamed with the Chula Vista (CA) Elementary School District. They led weekly walks from schools and senior centers through a nearby canyon and created assistive signage and routes. They branded the walks "Safe Routes to Nature" and were supported by a grant from the San Diego Foundation to promote health and fitness.

For school walks, classes are accompanied by a staff person from the YMCA, which runs the after-school program, and sometimes by Parks and Recreation Department staff or by "Canyoneers," volunteer guides from the Natural History Museum. According to reporting by Christine Huard in the *San Diego Union Tribune*, the students walk and "identify bird calls, collect bugs, discover how flowers are pollinated, and learn about becoming good stewards of the park. As they make their way from their school to the open space, they also take note of how they get there for a report on improving safety and accessibility that will be given to school and city officials."[3]

They evaluate the walking environment as part of the program and the students are quick to notice changes. As in many urban areas, the students have limited access to nature. Program coordinator Michelle Luellen told Huard that "the walks have been so popular that kids are already taking their parents to the park to spend time together." I spoke to Kathleen Ferrier, director of advocacy at Circulate San Diego:

> We had been talking with the director of Parks and Recreation for the city of Chula Vista. We solicited some grant funds from the San Diego Foundation and we were successful in getting them. I don't know how many walks we ultimately led, but we did it every Friday for a while. We took kids and we worked with the rangers. The rangers were a really important part of it because they can speak knowledgeably about the flora and the fauna.
>
> We had hundreds of students participate and it was just a really positive thing. It was a grant-funded project, so it's not happening anymore. That's always one of the challenges. Ideally the city would think, "Wow, this is a great project and we're just going to build this into our budget so that we can keep taking kids."

Circulate San Diego developed way-finding signage, including proposed locations, and created suggested route maps from the four school sites to the park entrance. "We are not only doing the education for the walking, we are trying to improve the actual walking experience."

We talked about the potential for libraries to produce "safe routes to nature" programs. Regular group walks from school to the library going through open-space areas fit the geography surrounding some libraries. Librarians know their communities and have the connections to schools and city partners to develop the walks and increase access to nature for those groups. Ferrier agreed: "I think it's really great! Libraries and schools are always the center of our community."

You Can Get There from Here

The Linda Vista Branch Library in San Diego is in an immigrant, working-class neighborhood with little park space. There is substantial canyon open-space along one side of the neighborhood, but unlike some other canyons in San

Diego, it is little used by Linda Vista residents. There are few official trail-heads here and they aren't well known. I began asking library users about their awareness of park and nature spaces in the area. As anticipated, use of the canyon was low and knowledge of the neighborhood parks was limited.

Early learning is a principal focus of the library. Motivated by the impor-tance of time spent in nature for child development, I was interested in find-ing ways the library could respond to the low level of neighborhood nature resources and use. Our fairly simple response was to develop a "Next Door Nature" map: a map of the neighborhood highlighting the accessible local nature places that do exist. The library, of course, is set at the center of the map.

A mix of interview, car, and shoe-leather research was required to gather information. Where were the canyon access points, official and unofficial? Many trailheads aren't mapped elsewhere. Most are only visible on-site and can only be distinguished from private side yards in person. There are public easements between some lots that we discovered as well. This information hadn't been collected in a map or other form before. Making the map required simplifying the full street network and considering what routes made sense for pedestrians. (A side benefit of the research was much greater fine-grained knowledge of the neighborhood, particularly those parts farther from the library.) Like the other examples discussed, this is work librarians excel in: research, outreach, organizing information, and producing pathfinders. Lit-eral pathfinders in this case.

Having plotted the parks, pathways, and canyon access points, I drew up the map using Google Maps for a base map and traced roads and features on layers in the open-source vector illustration program Inkwell. We printed the map on quality paper with a natural look and have distributed it at the branch and at a number of neighborhood land use meetings. In both cases, responses have been very positive and the maps are received enthusiastically. (See fig-ure 5.1.) It's anticipated that they'll be used in a nature backpack program that's in development.

I've been able to reuse the work on the map for three projects: A walk-ing tour, a preschool locator, and to aid a partner doing planning work for a Born Learning Trails program, another of which is discussed in chapter 4.

All of these are of a piece with making the world around us, the collection all around, more accessible through applied librarian skills and expertise.

Grab Your Phone, Sun Hat, and Genomic Sequencer

A naturalist's eye and tools play a role in many of the library programs aimed at making nature more accessible, familiar, and comprehensible. At the La Jolla (CA) Branch Library, this extends into the realm of original research, into citizen science. The branch is part of the San Diego Public Library and sits within a few miles of science and engineering powerhouses

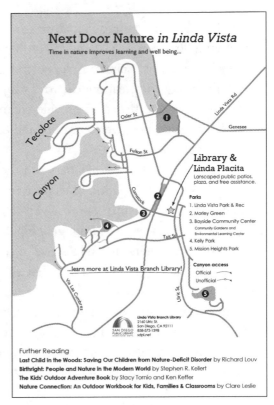

FIGURE 5.1

Library-Produced Map of Neighborhood Access to Nature

like the University of California at San Diego, the Salk Institute, Qualcomm, Illumina, and one of the world's largest biotechnology centers. The first library biotechnology lab is at the La Jolla branch and science lectures are a routine part of the library's schedule. Branch Manager Shaun Briley is turning those strengths and innovations into a theme, connecting the community to and through citizen science.

Citizen science is simply nonscientists assisting in the conduct of scientific research, usually field-based. Briley gives the example of the Urban Tides Initiative, which has participated in library programs. "Urban Tides wants help recording the tide levels here at La Jolla Shores. They can't send somebody every day. They rely on the public to take snapshots with their cellphones.

People just walking the beach and measuring the tide levels." Though consistent with library maker labs and STEAM programming, citizen science has a different emphasis. Librarians supporting the former share tools and services for learning and creation. Librarians supporting citizen science focus on connecting communities; they provide channels for their members and the scientific community to work together and to engage the natural world from a particular perspective.

Connecting the library's members and the local scientific community has been a focus of Briley's work. "There are too many things out there for the limited number of scientists to research them all. The public can provide a workforce for the scientists. And for the public it's a chance to participate, a chance to learn something, and a sense of community involvement. It's very win-win." We talked about the role that the library inhabits in this regard, that of a familiar, trusted, and unintimidating gateway. "A lot of the biotech companies have outreach where they'll invite people up to a big corporate building and say, 'We are going to tell you something!' And people don't want to go. 'What's their agenda? What are they selling?' Whereas if you do it here at the library, it's a trusted public venue. We have no agenda other than the education."

The collection all around includes these local resources—corporate outreach, participation in the world of science—that, whether ostensibly accessible or not, are not well utilized. Librarians facilitate entry and connection. That role is available to libraries whatever the local resource. Citizen science can be relevant to communities far from scientific centers.

The first National Citizen Science Day was held on April 16, 2016. The day was organized by the Citizen Science Association with support from a large number of organizations, including the National Science Foundation. At the La Jolla Branch Library, Briley prepared a Citizen Science Day Expo, with eighteen exhibitors and eight short seminars. Exhibitors included some types of projects unique to La Jolla and others one might find in most places. Representatives from the National Park Service, a wildlife survey organization, marine science programs, a genomics initiative, a watershed conservancy, the California Department of Fish and Wildlife, the local Audubon chapter, and many more attended. Briley explained:

It was fantastic to get all these people together in a room. Even just to net-work with each other. The idea was, "If you need the public to help you, come to our expo. We are going give everyone a booth for nothing at the library." We'll create a critical mass. It's an opportunity for all these organizations to connect with the public. At the same time, if you are a member of the public and you think that it would be cool to get engaged, you go.

The expo was a success, receiving local media attention and a sponsor for the next year. "There's lots of interest in it and all the groups are, 'Yeah, let's do that again!'"

Very recently a new, ongoing citizen science program was launched at the library. The Barcode of Life is an international effort to collect and catalog genetic information on all species on the planet. The project sequences a short, standardized section of the DNA from a sample organism to create a "barcode" identifying the species and recording where it was found. The DNA barcode and metadata about the sample are then added to a Database of Life. The database is a record of biodiversity, much of it vanishing in the current period of mass extinction. The La Jolla Branch Library is providing the frame-work for local citizen scientists to participate in an attempt to add all of San Diego's insects to the Barcode/Database project. Briley continued:

> San Diego is the most biodiverse county in the contiguous states, which is a surprising fact for a lot of people who live here. It's because we are on the migratory routes; we have the ocean, we have the deserts, we have the moun-tains. We don't have a lot of numbers but the diversity is incredible. At the public library you check out a little kit that's no bigger than a paperback book. You take it home and collect a sample [insect] from your yard or the local park. You return it to the library. We get it sequenced by a local firm. And then it's added to the catalog of the Database of Life.

Using the Life Scanner mobile application, citizen scientists record a geo-tagged photo of the insect they find, place the specimen in a bar-coded test tube that the library provides, and then scan the test tube, associating the two. The test tube is mailed to a lab, paid under contract by the library, analyzed, and added to the Barcode of Life project. Volunteers working with a MiniSeq or other desktop genetic-sequencing machine were considered as an alternative to a lab contract. Briley elaborated:

> We get all kinds of data regarding where life exists in an urban environment because we're doing it all across the city. Even if you're collecting duplicates—you found a wood louse and your neighbor found a wood louse—we are learning there are a lot of wood lice in this type of urban setting and not in that type. We are learning it clusters around here or there.
>
> From the patron's point of view, they have the engagement of going out and getting involved hands-on in research. Once your sample has been sequenced, on your app it will say, "Congratulations, you found a wood louse," and there will be some information about wood lice that you can read, so it's educational. But there is a very good chance that it will say, "Congratulations, you found something that isn't in the Barcode of Life yet," because so few things are. When you get down into the smaller things, a lot of them are not cataloged. When we did a trial run of it here, we found things that weren't in the catalog.

The library is also collecting specimens at library sites using Malaise traps, small tents that are left on the roof or other protected area that trap flying insects. "It's something about bugs that they accumulate at the top of a tent-like structure. You put some kind of sweet fluid up there and they fly into that and get trapped. I have one on the roof here [at La Jolla Branch Library]. I put one at Central Library. We managed to find some interesting stuff."

Briley notes the parallels between the Barcode of Life citizen science project and traditional librarian skills: cataloging, online databases, (bio)literacy, community engagement and participation, and connecting the public to expertise. "People still need to connect to each other, and the library gives people a chance to get together and do that." The role for the library in this case is as a connector and producer of the relationship and opportunity. Librarians act as facilitators between the public and scientists, but librarians also need to dive into the process and the science. "You've got to roll up your sleeves and figure it out, otherwise it's not going to happen."

Citizen science adds a unique mode of access to the places around us. It contributes to our personal awareness and understanding of the natural environment. It contributes to human knowledge. It creates new collaborations between communities. And it lowers barriers to an important mode of being with nature, to being a naturalist. Librarians facilitating citizen science in their communities are making the world around accessible through an uncommon lens.

Ranger-Librarians

It's understandable to see time in nature as already accessible, or of low priority, or tangential to the mission of libraries. The work of the librarians covered here hopefully shows why that's not the case. Barriers of cost, background, support, and relationship exist and can be bridged in the same ways that access to city and town resources is bridged. The assistance that librarians provide to make time in nature more accessible enriches the lives of our members and the strength of our communities. It contributes to early learning, to literacy, and to well-being. It nourishes new connections among our communities. It enhances the public's participation in our surroundings. And it responds to important and challenging issues of equity.

From our library grounds, to the corner park, to the canyons, and from our backyards to the state and national parks, librarians lend, share, scaffold, create, partner, program, research, and do outreach to make the collection all around available to all.

NOTES

1. Lauren Barack, "STEM-Themed Library Backpacks Encourage Outdoor Exploration," *School Library Journal*, 2015, www.slj.com/2015/06/programs/stem-themed-library-backpacks-encourage-outdoor-exploration/.

2. Carrie O'Maley Voliva, "Check Out a State Parks Pass at Indiana Libraries," Public Libraries Online, 2016, http://publiclibrariesonline.org/2016/02/check-out-a-state-parks-pass-at-indiana-libraries/.

3. Christine Huard, "After-School Program Connects Kids with Nature," *San Diego Union Tribune*, September 15, 2016, www.sandiegouniontribune.com/news/education/sdut-after-school-program-connects-kids-with-nature-2015sep16-story.html.

All Together Now

THE COLLECTION ALL AROUND DESCRIBES CITY, TOWN, AND nature access projects that are already active and successful in large and small libraries around the country. We've seen how the next generation of circulating pass programs provides admission to hundreds of thousands of library members in just one region. Programs like these open local treasures to a remarkable degree, with potential to expand the model in countless ways. Traditional information services—grounded and updated as walking tours, community-building events, open data, municipal liaisons, and community calendars—are making the places around us more comprehensible, familiar, and accessible. Place-making partnerships are giving communities new opportunities to shape the neighborhoods around them, contributing to safety, mobility, activity, and local character. These practices extend to libraries' surrounding natural places, helping communities engage with those riches and with one another. Library membership is the gateway and through line to these and other new, local uses and benefits, from identification to venue admissions and discounts to mass transit and more. All of these advance libraries' communities' access to their world, to the collection all around.

The efforts so far have been discrete. There are some here, some there. None are yet part of a strategic platform that I've been able to find. As such, their effect is diffuse and easy to miss. As remarkable as each of these programs is, they've received little attention. Ticketed pass programs, and Discover & Go especially, for all their embrace by the public, have been underappreciated by the library profession. Yoking just a few local access programs together would help their visibility and build momentum. There are two, maybe more, practical steps to be taken in this direction.

One step is branding. An umbrella brand for a library's ticketed passes, community calendars, and safe routes support, such as "Awesomeville PL All Access" (but something better than that) would make the library's ambition and value proposition clear. "Awesomeville PL All Access" can brand and refer to a combination of open data, food trucks, and nature backpacks; or to citizen science, school/municipal ID, and planning group representation. It can brand as many or as few appropriate projects as are right for each library.

The second step is systemic commitment. A library with a City Access Division staffed by "city access librarians" will over time build connections, skills, and expertise to advance these projects in ways that they couldn't be advanced without a place in the library's organizational chart. That's the case even for a division composed of only one person. In the introduction I discussed some of the strategic strengths of a focus on access to the collection all around. Working on related projects like these will help develop resources and harness strengths that various collection all around projects share in common. More on this later in this conclusion.

Branding, organizational commitment, and cross-development for collection all around projects remain in the future for libraries. More discussion of, recognition for, attention to, and sharing of experiences with local access efforts will lay the groundwork and create momentum for those next steps. Talk to your communities and library staff about the potential you see in this direction. Explain what you're doing already. Explore the technological and administrative context in which movement in this direction takes place.

Then, try out some All Access-like branding on a mix of local access projects. Get responses from members and partners. Use the marketing effort to pull together staff working separately on projects that together move in the common direction of improved local access. What duplicative work are

Job Description:
City Access Librarian, Awesomeville Public Library

About the Job

The City Access Librarian develops, supervises, and evaluates Awesomeville Public Library projects to improve its members' access to the life and resources of the Awesomeville region. Under the general direction of the Director, this responsibility is carried out largely in partnership with local organizations.

You've demonstrated passion for outreach and community-based work; the ability to organize and implement new programs and services in partnership with other agencies; excellent customer service, judgment, and initiative; and interest in and aptitude for learning about fields outside of your expertise.

Areas of Experience Preferred
- Project management;
- Culturally competent, equitable, and inclusionary service;
- Library online systems and services, and the library technology marketplace;
- Training and end-user support of library staff, volunteers, and the public;
- Collection development and program assessment and reporting.

Perform related work as assigned.

they doing? What platforms and resources can they share? Can staff hours be assigned to seek and develop local access opportunities? Who among library stakeholders can be cultivated as allies for this approach? Much of the work of providing access to the collection all around is already in place. Making a cohesive push out of those components is just around the corner.

The Member-Centric Universe

Robert Anderson of the Quipu Group which developed the ePASS ticketed pass software for Discover & Go had an interesting observation that harkens back to local access's foundation in membership. Library automation systems (ILSs) originated to manage the circulation of library-owned physical items, a catalog-centric view. Today those systems are being pushed to support libraries' new frame of reference: "It's a patron-centric world now." The programs, services, and collections that libraries share all orbit *library members* at the center. Members each use many different library services to varying degrees and at different times. Libraries' physical lending, digital access, programs, tickets, calendars, facilities, and other uses have library members in common, but often little else.

As a result, library automation structured with members at the center better supports the work of libraries today. Standards for ILS vendors to meet with regard to the richness and control of member records are one step in that direction. Implementations vary and typically come up short of allowing real interaction between member records and other online services. Anderson explained, "With the SIP2 connections that we have, we need a separate one for Koha vs. Evergreen vs. Carl vs Polaris, because they implemented it differently and they return maybe the same information but in different tags. The ILS vendors have gotten pretty close to being able to expose the information they need to expose. They've got a lot of read-only type APIs and processes. Where they're behind is the other side: interacting and modifying information about the patron record."

For library automation systems to truly become member-centric, they will need to anticipate third-party services, like ticketing, and be built around a repository for those, of which traditional circulation might be just one service among many. Anderson hypothesized:

> Patrons log in to their account, and on their account page not only can they see what items they've checked out from the library, but they can also see their reservations they've made to Discover & Go, their room reservations. That would require the ILS systems to set up some kind of repository so third-party systems could report back to it, that they made this reservation. More of a central area, instead of them bouncing around to Overdrive to see what e-books they have, and Discover & Go to see what reservations they have.

Security and privacy are a related concern. Quipu stores encrypted information about library patrons. They keep those records "as limited as possible, then reassign them an internal ID to keep up with their reservation." Connections between Quipu and the library ILSs are mediated by firewalls and authentication keys and passwords. Consistent with improving member-centric infrastructure, library automation benefits from better authentication handoffs, so that members can move from one online library service to another with third-party sites like ePASS able to verify when a user has already securely logged in, their status and privileges, etc. Some libraries may want to offer single-sign-on—"Would you like to allow sign on with Facebook/Google?" over the OAuth protocol—for example. Anderson continued:

> Trying to integrate these services so that they stay within the library's website is the other thing that we've been trying to do. Communication is happening somewhere else in the world while the patron is staying on the same web page. The technologies for that, like AJAX-type technology, but also SSL connections and encrypted communication, encrypted data storage . . . letting the patron not have twenty million different passwords and log-ins to different services. We're getting closer to allowing you [to] go to your library's website and having access to all these services in one shot. I've had other friends and colleagues say, "Your online registration form that's on the library website should have 'powered by.'" Our viewpoint is, "No. This is a library service. The patron should not be confused with other things; it should look like it belongs to the library."

Interoperability is also essential for membership programs like joint school IDs and library cards or the MyDenver card. ILSs need to support batch upload and the creation of new patrons from school registration data, for example. Here too libraries would benefit from member-centric ILSs designed to anticipate third-party services. These are technological issues calling for improved cooperation and groundwork. Library consortia are candidates to address this. Access to cities, towns, and natural places is made stronger and easier through regional cooperation. Anderson explains: "We'll get an inquiry from a single library: 'We'd like to try this service.' Especially with ePASS our response first is, 'Are there other libraries in your area that could benefit that would be willing to join?'" The good news, Anderson continues, is that "once you have a group of libraries that join forces, that's a very powerful group."

Stronger Together

We've looked at the *local* access that libraries create, but in practice the task is *regional*. It's easy to see that in many places library service is divided among neighboring systems where a regional approach might be more beneficial. Many large cities are agglomerations of municipalities and county areas, with a single "city" served by a handful of separate library systems. In a sense, regional cooperation reflects recognition of the move to member-centric library work: users shouldn't have to navigate multiple library jurisdictions to access the world around them; libraries can do that work instead.

On the other hand, the idea of "local control" is popular and—well-intended or not—a fact for libraries. Funding and oversight are drawn along political boundaries, placing limits on the resources available for regional approaches. And *most* library service is genuinely local. The storytime down the street is far and away the relevant one, not the storytime in the next town over. Last, for many library services there are diminishing returns to scale. Operating 60 branches may not require twice the resources as operating 30, but it's close enough that beyond a certain point the impetus for scale is low. If library services scaled up more we might see stronger network effects—serving more people hypothetically could make the offerings more valuable—but the effect seems to be mixed. Excellence comes as often from small or midsized library systems as from large ones.

State libraries and consortia balance against this to varying degrees, supporting resource-sharing, interlibrary loan, cooperative programs, and other centralized services. Regional cooperation was a requirement of the grant that funded the creation of the Discover & Go program. While a number of adjacent, discrete city pass programs would still have great value, a strength of Discover & Go is that participating library systems don't need to duplicate the work of negotiating with venues and administering the platform. There's great value for patrons too in having venues available regionally without the friction of needing to register with a patchwork of library systems. We noted earlier, meanwhile, how variation among ILSs and library policies was a challenge. Ticketing software needs information about patrons and their standing in order to present appropriate offers. There's an important role, therefore, for state libraries and consortia to play in pushing for consistency among automation protocols and library systems' policies, making interoperability and regional services easier to implement.

Partner to Partner

Collaboration between library systems enhances some aspects of librarians' work to improve access to local resources. In a case like Discover & Go, collaboration between libraries makes implementation easier and the product more valuable. Other projects are essentially self-contained. In either case, though, programs of local access are additive. They make the next project of city or town or nature access stronger and easier to implement. Together they create a platform. Work on that platform aligns with libraries' skills, strengths, and mission.

Turning that platform into a strategy can be an aim of the strategic planning process. For that process see in-depth titles like *Strategic Planning for Results*.[1] Strategic orientation to the collection all around belongs in these planning documents. I spoke with Brett Bonfield, director of the Princeton (NJ) Public Library and a contributor to *Planning Our Future Libraries: Blueprints for 2025*[2]. He situated the strategic role of local access in these terms:

> More and more public library directors... understand that we are just one of the nodes that communities rely on in order to understand how to navigate their own neighborhood and their own community, and that we're a very important node. The library is a resource that enables you to access information or access activities or access other aspects of social capital that people either may not be able to afford or may not know about otherwise.

We are empowered by having connections to the people and cultural resources around us. Scaffolding social participation and access to the cultural resources of our cities and towns can be an explicit aim of libraries, consistent with their role of facilitating the sharing of knowledge and cultural goods. Guidance to neighborhood planning group meetings is one example. Understanding the role that social capital plays in library members' access to resources is important to thoughtful direction setting for library strategic-planning efforts. Communication with library boards and other stakeholders should make clear the relevance of social and cultural capital to community needs; the library's mission; and the fit between a collection all around strategy and those aims.

The issue is visible in poor communities and wealthy ones. Bonfield shared an example from Darien, Connecticut:

> The Museum of Modern Art in New York has a partnership that it's been exploring with Darien Public Library. MOMA did research and found that people who attended MOMA tended to really, really like the exhibits and give them very favorable reviews but tended to give MOMA as a whole very negative reviews. What they found out is that people felt very, very intimidated by museums in general, by art museums in particular, and most especially by modern art museums.
>
> This is a social capital thing. Where they didn't have a lot of experience, they felt either judged or stupid or whatever. So MOMA made an effort to reach out to the community, first of all to make museum passes available. But they went farther with that and started working on getting their catalog of published materials into the Darien collection, sending lecturers out to give presentations, giving online classes to Darien cardholders, and taking feedback in terms of how to structure programs and their collections and other things in ways that would be appealing to Darien's cardholders.
>
> Darien, in terms of social capital, practically breaks the bell curve. It's way way way on one end. And even still, people didn't necessarily feel comfortable going to MOMA. That was why MOMA went there. It wasn't because they were trying to raise money. It was because they really wanted people to feel good. It's a nice example of how you can be bidirectional. You can help these institutions—these peer agencies—learn from us and offer better services to our cardholders. There's an art museum at Princeton University and an arts council in Princeton and we can say, "You know, MOMA is doing this and they want to work with us in this way. Do you want to also?" It opens up additional avenues for conversation. "What do libraries know that can make you better?" Ideally it's bidirectional. We can then ask, "What do they know that can make the library better?"

We've talked about the centrality of partnerships and outreach to the collection all around. Partnerships and outreach have been a touchstone of library work for a long time, but have not always had expansive goals or outcomes.

Access to the world around us provides an organizing principle for bidirectional partnership that previously had often been either about simple sponsorship and support, or about offering library services at partner facilities. The bidirectionality of Discover & Go, for example, can be taken in this direction. On the one hand, what do partners gain from joining library platforms? And, on the other, how can they help libraries serve the community better?

Pathbreaking

Building institutional support for a new strategic direction isn't easy. More than once, librarians mentioned the leverage that their communities have lent to their efforts. Community engagement programs are typical building blocks of the strategic planning process. They can include facilitated sessions and other ways to leave and capture ideas and interests. They can be undertaken any time and provide useful feedback and persuasive ballast for collection all around efforts.

The collection all around can be given strategic focus at the level of the library system or at a single branch. Projects that demonstrate that direction to a smaller community and to partner institutions introduce the idea to the public. Engagement sessions build on that. As Amy Calhoun at the Sacramento Public Library explained, "the way you get administration behind it is to say, 'We have these community partners and individuals in the community who are saying that this is important to them.'"

The Fayetteville Free Library (FFL) in upstate New York is a community library, part of the larger Onondaga County Library System. It's the site of the first library makerspace in the United States and it's been a *Library Journal* Five Star Library for eight years. FFL Executive Director Sue Considine talked about how the FFL has been a leader in the profession from within a larger library system and how it has leveraged community engagement to achieve community goals:

> We approached [the makerspace project] with a keen eye focused on the community engagement piece first. Meaning, we understood that this would be considered by most a nontraditional type of direction we were proposing

to take the library in. We also understood that in order to get the best support possible in the early stages, the need was to position ourselves such that the community itself was moving our agenda forward.

We decided to fling our doors open on a series of Saturdays and let the public know that they could come in and put their hands on some of this technology, but even more importantly to bring people together to informally interact with each other around these technologies. That approach really paid off. We had staff in the room, we had board members in the room, we had stakeholders in the room, and we invited people in and saw some amazing things happen very quickly. We did a series of about five or six of them. By the time we were done we had a community of people within our community who were so on board with the idea that we knew that we could turn to them to carry the message forward.

An open house for local access services might make comparable sense. "Here are the pass programs available. Here's the community calendar, the transit benefits, the walking tour, the outdoor gear, a parklet, and a safe route program. What do you want to do or enjoy in our town that you can't afford? Or don't know how? Or want someone to be there with you for support? How do we make the world around more available to you?" If not a literal open house, engage library members with the same menu of projects and questions elsewhere. Many, many library members already use the collection all around through existing discrete programs. Connecting with those members and making them advocates for a local-access strategic approach are essential.

Marketing and branding are important to this. I've struggled some with the language to describe these programs. These are not "Come to the library!" or "Get your library anywhere!" programs. They are, "Another important piece of where you live is here for you, made more available and public with help from your library creating and brokering better access on your behalf." Someone will figure out a simpler way to say this.

Helping the public and library staff and stakeholders find an image of the collection all around—the children's museums, gardens, neighborhoods, concerts, buses, state parks, all the community riches around us—opened to one with the wave of a library card, that's something to work toward.

For the FFL, educating the larger system that they are a part of about their vision was a similarly important step. "We were out here as a community library with a great big idea that we knew whose time had come. We knew we really couldn't wait. We couldn't wait for our leadership at the time to get on board with the idea and move it forward."

Considine looked to the system to help secure grant funding to renovate a space to be a venue for their maker activities. "Through that process we were able to educate our system leadership on what this is all about. What is this maker culture and what is a fabrication lab and why is it in alignment with a public libraries mission? We had the opportunity very early on to have that discussion and it was successful. Our system was enthusiastic about our proposal and we did receive that grant from the state. That was gratifying."

Considine also talked about the effect that being leaders of a new strategic direction had at the FFL; of being the one to do something first.

We were inundated with library folks and educators, all kinds of people. My phone was ringing constantly and my staff's phones were ringing constantly. We were getting e-mails every day. We wanted to share. We wanted people to learn from what we were doing. We wanted to hear from other people too. We wanted to get feedback if people were iterating on this idea and what was working in their communities and what wasn't.

We decided very quickly to spend a lot of time in developing an online learning portal for our colleagues and peers and put everything there: FAQs, inventory lists, vendor contacts, program ideas, everything related to making that we had experienced and were experiencing. Every time we would receive questions or ideas that were outside of what is already on our portal, we would add that. We get over 200,000 hits a year on just that page alone. We understood very quickly that because we are first here we have a responsibility to do as much sharing as we can. So we spent a lot of our professional time, all of us, over the last several years, virtually and physically running around and talking to our colleagues about our experience and encouraging them to take some risks in their thinking and actions to bring informal, participatory learning, in the form of makerspaces, to their communities.

The Fayetteville Free Library in upstate New York has had visitors come from as far away as Australia, Sarajevo, Italy, Sweden, Korea, and Spain, all over, come and visit with us and learn with us.

The work that we've done here is contributing to the idea that central New York is a hot spot for innovation and technology; we are an economic engine, a small business resource, an entrepreneurship incubator, an invention and discovery catalyst in central New York. We feel very grateful that we've had that opportunity to have that kind of impact in our larger community.

In contrast to what was then the relative newness of makerspaces, local access librarianship is already well established in programs big and small around the country. There won't be a "first" library to this space in the same way. But there will be libraries that are early to making the collection all around into a principal strategic focus. They'll move the practice forward in new ways. FFL's impressive work to become a professional hub and advocate in their area of innovation is instructive. As with makerspaces, other libraries will be eager to learn from the experience of libraries that focus on the collection all around.

Sharing the Neighborhood

Leading "from where you are" is the first step to advancing local access as a strategic direction and to a library running point on this in the profession. The work of city access librarians doesn't depend on the title or on an explicit administrative endorsement of the strategy. The programs discussed here have succeeded at both system and branch levels without those. Advancement is helped along, of course, by the usual tools of being good at pursuing an agenda. Community engagement and cultivation of allies in particular are invaluable and can help get the message out and speak credibly from another perspective. Library Friends groups and community partners are ready-made for this. (There's more to the mysteries of networking, influence, allies, communication, and authority that belong to another book. See, for example, *The Machiavellian Librarian: Winning Allies, Combating Budget Cuts, and Influencing*

Stakeholders.[3]) Inform the agenda with attention to social and cultural capital and bidirectional partnerships. Address technical and policy contexts, including regional cooperation, movement toward patron-centric library automation, and interoperability. And be ready, if you're early in making the collection all around a strategic focus, to attract attention and share your experience.

Hopefully, this book will generate continued revaluation and appreciation of the local access programs being led by librarians across the country. Many are discussed here and many, many more are out there to be discovered. They are invaluable. Though rooted in core skills, they are quietly new and innovative. They have strategic advantages, including scalability and longevity. They build on the strength of libraries' position, familiarity, and goodwill in their communities. Because of their value to and visibility in so many segments of the community, they broaden support for libraries. And they operate in a space with little competition. Libraries uniquely help people access the wealth of resources all around.

Maybe you or your library already provide access to the collection all around through one program or more. If not, I hope this book inspires you to pursue one of the projects discussed here. What contacts do you have that could add a benefit to your library card? Who'd help support safe routes to the library or to nature? What surplus resources nearby can you make available to your members? What institutions in your area could serve the public better with the library's help? If you offer a service or services like these, how can they grow? Do you have a pass program that could go ticketed or a ticketed program that could add new types of resources? If you produce more than one local access program, are there ways those programs can reinforce one another and be a part of your All Access campaign? Are the librarians behind those programs working together and could they be?

Facilitating access to the wealth of resources all around is increasingly how we think about a large part of public library service. Libraries share stuff. Libraries share books and storytimes and tickets to the symphony. They collect children's museums and lighthouses and architectural tours. Libraries share the neighborhood itself, making it easier to enjoy, get around, and claim for our own. Libraries share our natural places, providing gear or passes or an overnight in the park. Libraries share the history and data and activities around us that were siloed away and unclear. Libraries share participation in scientific exploration. They provide membership in our cities and towns. All this valuable stuff around us—the local and particular, both ordinary and extraordinary—is a grand collection. It doesn't need to be in the library. We just need librarians to lend it out.

NOTES

1. Sandra Nelson, *Strategic Planning for Results* (Chicago: American Library Association, 2008).

2. Kim Leeder and Eric Frierson, *Planning Our Future Libraries: Blueprints for 2025* (Chicago: American Library Association, 2014).

3. Melissa K. Aho and Erika Bennett, *The Machiavellian Librarian: Winning Allies, Combating Budget Cuts, and Influencing Stakeholders* (Oxford: Chandos, 2013).

INDEX

PRAISE *for*
10 Steps to Take Charge of Your Emotional Life

"Learning to control emotions is both difficult and rewarding, probably one of the most important steps to attain optimum health of both mind and body. Dr. Eve Wood has authored a detailed and practical guide to help you do it. I recommend this book and am completely in agreement with the philosophy behind it."

— **Andrew Weil, M.D.,** director, University of Arizona Program in Integrative Medicine; clinical professor of medicine and public health; the author of *8 Weeks to Optimum Health* and *Healthy Aging*

"Psychiatrist Eve Wood, America's number one practitioner/educator in mental illness and integrative medicine, understands that our minds can't, don't, or won't always register the emotions that impact us so profoundly. Her long-awaited, authoritative new book is an outstanding resource for navigating the myriad mainstream and alternative options to empower the reader to make informed decisions about treatment choices. Dr. Wood has created a balanced work that health-care providers, patients with psychiatric diagnoses, and anyone interested in developing their mental wellness will find extremely useful."

— **Candace B. Pert, Ph.D.,** scientific director, RAPID Pharmaceuticals; and the author of *Molecules of Emotion* and *Everything You Need to Know to Feel Go(o)d*

"A clear, intelligent, and sensible guide to cultivating emotional health, integrating the best of holistic therapies with sound allopathic medical principles. Dr. Wood demystifies psychiatry without talking down to her readers, taking it that extra, badly needed step: She explains the cutting-edge mind-body therapies that are making such impressive inroads with what have traditionally been daunting mental-health challenges. A wonderful resource for those who want to know how to make smart, individualized choices that respect their unique needs and collaborate with their inborn abilities."

— **Belleruth Naparstek, LISW, BCD,** the author of *Invisible Heroes: Survivors of Trauma and How They Heal*

AUTHOR'S NOTE

Many of the stories in this book are true accounts in which the names and identifying details have been changed to protect confidentiality. Others are composites drawn from years of clinical work. The latter are true to the spirit of the teaching, although not to the experience of any particular person.

10 STEPS

TO TAKE CHARGE

of YOUR EMOTIONAL

LIFE

10 STEPS

TO TAKE CHARGE

of YOUR EMOTIONAL

LIFE

OVERCOMING ANXIETY, DISTRESS,
AND DEPRESSION THROUGH
WHOLE-PERSON HEALING

EVE A. WOOD, M.D.

An *In One*™ Series Book

HAY HOUSE, INC.
Carlsbad, California • New York City
London • Sydney • New Delhi

Published in the United States by: Hay House, Inc.: www.hayhouse.com
Published in Australia by: Hay House Australia Pty. Ltd.: www.hayhouse.com.au
Published in the United Kingdom by: Hay House UK, Ltd.: www.hayhouse.co.uk
Published in India by: Hay House Publishers India: www.hayhouse.co.in

Editorial supervision: Jill Kramer • *Design:* Tricia Breidenthal • Index: Richard Comfort

Library of Congress Cataloging-in-Publication Data

Wood, Eve A.
10 steps to take charge of your emotional life overcoming anxiety, distress, and depression through whole-person healing / Eve A. Wood.
    p. cm.
Includes index.
ISBN-13: 978-1-4019-1121-8 (hardcover)
ISBN-13: 978-1-4019-1122-5 (tradepaper) 1. Alternative medicine. 2. Mind and body therapies. 3. Medicine and psychology. I. Title: Ten steps to take charge of your emotional life overcoming anxiety, distress, and depression through whole-person healing. II. Title.
    R733.W645 2007
    616--dc22   2006007984

Hardcover ISBN: 978-1-4019-1121-8
Tradepaper ISBN: 978-1-4019-1122-5

1st edition, January 2007

Printed in the United States of America

*In loving memory of my dearly departed father,
Leonard Wood, a gifted storyteller who: lived on the
sunny side of life, was always thrilled to hear from
me, routinely asked, "What can I do to help?" and
never failed to end a conversation with "I love you."*

*Dad, you know this book is for you. We spoke of its
dedication as you lay dying, ecstatic that I would have
the opportunity to help so many people! You had a
wondrous way of viewing life and its many challenges.*

*I carry your wisdom, humor, love, and support in my heart.
Your presence and memory are true blessings in my life.
Thank you for all that you've given me. May you rest in peace.*

Amen.

~ CONTENTS

INTRODUCTION

Congratulations on your decision to take charge of your emotional life! I'm glad to be partnering with you. No matter what your history or challenge, you can succeed. There's always hope.

Perhaps you've been trying to take charge for a long time but find yourself confused, lost, stuck, or not quite well. Or perhaps you've only recently become aware of your internal distress and aren't sure what to do about it. Maybe you've been diagnosed with a condition such as depression, attention deficit disorder (ADD), or panic disorder and wonder what you can do to best heal.

You may be taking medication but be unsure about whether you ought to do so, or you may not have a prescription and be wondering if you need one. You might be in therapy but question whether it's right for you, or without a therapist and feeling the need for one. You may realize that even when medication and/or therapy are necessary, they're only part of the healing puzzle. You may be taking herbs or supplements; engaging in yoga, meditation, or prayer; or watching what you eat and trying to support your wellness in other ways. You're probably confused about how to bring all these practices together in your life.

We live in very challenging times and are constantly bombarded with messages that raise one intervention up as the full answer. A TV commercial says: "Try medication and move from depressed to ecstatic." A practitioner's ad declares: "Enter therapy and transform your life." A yoga-studio brochure reads: "Begin a regular practice and you'll never need to do anything more." Our radios, televisions, and magazine pages overflow with advertisements for the ultimate medications, herbs, supplements, and mind-body or spiritual interventions. Each is touted as all you'll ever need for total well-being.

These messages often appeal to us because our health-care system is in a shambles. Most of us, even if we're lucky enough to have medical insurance, lack a long-term relationship with a doctor who knows us. A physician like the old TV character Dr. Marcus Welby—a friend, partner, and guide in life—is an ancient myth. We're wandering around dazed, with information overload. We have no idea where to turn for guidance; we don't even know who to trust.

My dear reader, I have good news for you: There's someone you can believe in, and there's a solution to this dilemma. There's a path through this maze, and you're ideally suited to find it. You can trust yourself—*you* are the answer! You can take charge of your emotional life, and I intend to teach you how.

You see, in the field of emotional and mental health, all diagnoses are made on the basis of your story and no one else's. We have no diagnostic tests in psychiatry. In other fields of medicine, a lung x-ray can find pneumonia, and blood analysis can find diabetes. But in the field of emotional well-being, only your report of symptoms—such as a depressed mood, sleep disturbance, hopelessness, and impaired concentration—can reveal depression.

Therefore, if you're given adequate information about the symptoms of common conditions, *you* can begin to figure out if you need medical assessment. Additionally, if you're given *enough* data about treatment and self-empowerment interventions, you can begin to find your own personal path to wellness, wholeness, and spiritual well-being. You can do so whether or not you have a known medical condition—you can find your way.

There's a right answer about what steps to take to promote healing and wellness, but it's *always* a *personal* solution. What makes sense for you may not be the best idea for your neighbor, spouse, sibling, or friend. Given enough information, guidance, and support, however, you'll find the keys to your own health. You can learn to tap into your inner healer and put together a "Take-Charge" program that fits your unique and wondrous being. You're the captain of your own ship, and I intend to teach you how to sail it.

10 Steps to Take Charge of Your Emotional Life is just what it sounds like. Each chapter walks you through one of the 10 steps. You'll find examples, stories, self-assessment questions, and guidance on what actions to take, based on your own unique situation and responses to the exercises. I've written a series of steps for you to visit and work on over time. Don't expect yourself to read each chapter once, implement all its lessons immediately, and totally transform your life by the time you finish reading the book. Taking charge is a process, and it takes a while. Here are the 10 steps involved:

Step 1: Consider your story and its lessons: Do you have a medical condition or chemical imbalance?

Step 2: Explore your need for medication.

Step 3: Follow treatment guidelines when medication is necessary.

Step 4: Include complementary and alternative interventions.

Step 5: Make life choices that fit your nature.

Step 6: Identify the beliefs that imprison you, and reprogram the brain circuits involved.

Step 7: Learn the language of your body, and make friends with your inner healer.

Step 8: Share stories and build connections.

Step 9: Live in the power of the possible.

Step 10: Nurture your spirit.

While I don't intend this book to be a substitute for medical care, psychotherapy, or other forms of treatment, I do mean for it to guide you through the Take-Charge process. I'll teach you how to bring your medical care, complementary and alternative approaches, self-help, and spiritual practices together for wellness.

You and only you can take charge of your emotional life—and you can succeed! In all my years of clinical practice, I've never met a single person who truly wanted to heal who couldn't. Where there's a will, there's always a way. In this book, I intend to show you how.

STEP 1

Consider Your Story and Its Lessons: Do You Have a Medical Condition or a Chemical Imbalance?

Welcome to Step 1 of your Take-Charge program. Perhaps you know the song "Do-Re-Mi" from *The Sound of Music.* In it, Maria teaches the importance of starting any project at the very beginning: When we learn to read, we begin with the ABCs; and when we sing, we begin with Do-Re-Mi. The first three actions just happen to be these initial stepping-stones. The only sensible place to start any journey is at its very beginning.

You've decided to take charge of your emotional life, but where should you begin? Which steps come first, and why? What are the ABCs or Do-Re-Mi of taking charge? Well, your initial plans are grounded in the field of medicine. They involve:

Step 1:   Identifying the symptoms or problems that trouble you and figuring out which ones may be part of an illness or disorder

Step 2:   Evaluating your need for medication intervention (whether you have a disorder or not)

Step 3:   Learning how to use drugs properly, if they belong in your Take-Charge program

Oh boy, you may be thinking, *that doesn't sound like fun. And I don't want to have to take medicine. I don't like this idea one bit.* You may even be wondering why an integrative psychiatrist like me—who so values the role of love, energy, mind over matter, and spiritual pursuits—insists that you start your Take-Charge program with a medically based analysis of your symptoms and troubles. Why begin with the stuff that most of us view as a last resort?

Well, it turns out that many failed attempts at life transformation—most "stuckness," in fact—results from skipping over defining problems and implementing crucial interventions. You can read many stories that illustrate this problem in my first book, *There's Always Help; There's Always Hope.* All the mind-body tools in the world won't work if you're too depressed or anxious to use them. You'll set yourself up to fail if you try to do things that your mind isn't able to master because it's in a compromised state. So, you need to figure out if you have a diagnosis needing treatment.

You see, the process of taking charge of your emotional life is like building a house or planting a garden: You have to do a lot of things in a particular sequence in order to succeed. And although a lot of those early steps aren't particularly pretty or glitzy, you sure wouldn't want to miss them. For instance, in order to construct a sturdy home, you must dig and pour a foundation; in order to create a flowering oasis, you must fertilize and prepare your soil for seeds. When you build a house or create a garden, you have to do a lot of grunt work before you get to have fun—such as choosing carpet for your floors or cutting flowers for your table. Similarly, when taking charge of your emotional life, you'll need to do some exploring and groundwork before you can move into the steps that seem more appealing. You must start by examining your story for its lessons.

I've been a student and a doctor for many years, and I've been taught more facts than any one person could possibly remember. Occasionally, however, a teaching stands out. One such lesson is that the answer to the question *What's wrong with the patient, and what must be done to promote healing?* is contained in their original complaint and initial clinical history. When I listen carefully to my clients as they describe their challenges, and question them until I learn how they tick, I can often discover what's amiss—both diagnostically and holistically—and what they'll need to do to heal. The answers are in their stories.

In Step 1, you'll be considering your own story for diagnostic and treatment lessons. But you may not be sure what that means right now, so let's look at some examples of this process.

Expectations of Deterioration: Greg's Story

The first tale I want to tell you concerns an inappropriate diagnosis. Greg's label simply didn't fit his story. When this middle-aged veteran came to our integrative-medicine clinic as a patient, he was in a wheelchair. He was so weak that he was unable to lift a cup, for a debilitating illness had gripped him. He told us that he had Gulf War syndrome and post-traumatic stress disorder (PTSD). He'd read all about the former condition, and like the afflicted people he'd studied, he was becoming progressively weaker and more debilitated. He'd given up his job and almost everything else that gave him pleasure in life. He felt hopeless and only wanted to return to work. He wondered if we, in the integrative-medicine program, could help him.

As Greg told his story, his description of PTSD didn't sound accurate to me. I questioned him about his symptoms—and then it *definitely* didn't sound like he had that disorder, so I shared my thoughts with him: "I'm a psychiatrist, and as best as I can tell, it doesn't seem to me like you have PTSD. Maybe you aren't as ill as you think."

Several weeks later, Greg appeared for a follow-up visit. Only this time, he was walking and carrying his cup. He reported feeling better than he had for a long time, and he'd even taken on some work again. A medical student asked him what had happened to turn things around so much.

"Well," Greg said, "when that psychiatrist told me that I didn't have PTSD, I decided that maybe I shouldn't believe everything they were telling me at the VA. I decided to stop going there and to carry on as if I really were okay. It's made all the difference."

What's the lesson in this? Greg had become progressively more ill as he took on stories that didn't actually fit his own tale. He expected to worsen, so he did! But the diagnoses were incorrect. In choosing to throw out that faulty data, he was able to access his inner healer and find his own path to recovery. He was thus able to accomplish his goal of returning to work. The answers for combatting his problem were in his initial story: He didn't have what he thought he did.

The Origins of Pain: Jake's Story

Here's another example of "the answer is in the initial story"; this one concerns a missed diagnosis. Jake, also a middle-aged man, was referred to me for back pain and insomnia. On the phone, he told me that his pain was so severe that it would awaken him from sleep. He spent most days lying in bed, suffering and unable to do very much. Three years of extensive assessments and interventions had done little to improve his condition. His symptoms had been getting worse and worse over time, and when I spoke to him, he was feeling desperate.

I suggested that he read my first book, *There's Always Help; There's Always Hope,* before our initial visit two days hence. When he said: "I'd give anything for one good night's sleep," I told him that we'd start a long-acting sleep aid when he came in the following week.

When he arrived for his appointment, he told me that he'd read the book and, for the first time, realized that he had generalized anxiety disorder (GAD). He'd been a "worried guy" his whole life but never recognized that he had an anxiety-related illness. In taking his history, I discovered that he'd had a migrating series of physical symptoms over the years, such as headaches and stomach problems. This is common in GAD, and I felt that the body issues were part of his disorder.

Over the course of three visits, I was able to help Jake settle his agitated nervous system and calm his out-of-control anxiety disorder with medication. I also began to reframe his current pain. I told him to think about the sensation as psychological, not physical, since his back would hurt when he was upset about something. I urged him to wonder, *What is my body trying to tell me?* whenever the discomfort appeared. He was to stop focusing on his pain and searching for miracle remedies.

By Jake's fourth visit, he said, "I had a great week! I feel like myself again, and I was able to enjoy reading and being with my family. I haven't felt this well in months—maybe even years. I didn't have severe pain this week, so I could keep going. Thank you! I only wish I'd met you three years ago."

What's the lesson in this case? Again, the answer to the question *What's wrong?* is in the initial story. Although Jake was referred to me for insomnia and back pain, it quickly became clear to both of us—through knowing and learning his story—that his primary problem was an anxiety disorder that required appropriate treatment. The correct path became apparent once the proper identification had been made.

LINGERING GRIEF: RHONDA'S STORY

A third example of "the answer is in the initial story" also concerns an unidentified diagnosis. During her first visit with me, a 37-year-old married woman named Rhonda said, "I don't understand what's wrong with me. Ever since the day my house was broken into, I've been unable to get my work done—I just can't concentrate. And what's worse, I don't even care! I'm not sleeping, food doesn't interest me, and I often think it would be easier if I could fall asleep forever when I go to bed. I'm not suicidal, but I don't see the point in going on; all I do is cry. None of this is usual for me. What do you think is wrong?"

Upon questioning Rhonda, I learned that her most cherished family photos and jewelry had been taken in the robbery. Her sense of safety and the connection to her past had been shattered, and grief had set in. Over time, the unprocessed emotion turned into a full-blown clinical depression. She was in my office because she was at the end of her rope. The condition was so big that nothing could interrupt it. She needed professional help to shift her brain chemistry enough to enable her to resume life and process her losses.

Her initial story dictated her treatment course. Since Rhonda's energy, concentration, and even interest in life were compromised, medication was a necessary first step. I started with an antidepressant. Then with brief psychotherapy, she was able to reconnect with herself and move beyond her pain. As in my experiences with Greg and Jake, the answers to the questions *What's wrong?* and *What must be done?* were clear in her initial visit.

WHAT DOES YOUR STORY TELL YOU?

Think about the lesson in the preceding cases. The first step in each of them involved listening carefully for diagnostic clues. For Greg to take charge, he needed to throw out an incorrect diagnosis. For Jake to heal, he needed to identify and treat an anxiety problem. For Rhonda to recover, she had to name and address her clinical depression.

To take charge of your emotional life, you'll need to consider the lessons of your own story. This starts with identifying your "presenting complaint," problem, distress, questions, and concerns. As you begin, consider the following questions:

- Might you meet the criteria for a diagnosis you haven't been given?

- Have you been tagged with a label that doesn't fit?

- Is it possible you have more than one condition?

- Are you carrying around ideas about who you are or what you ought to be doing that are a mismatch for your nature or essence as a human being?

- Is your "internal taskmaster" really a slave driver?

- Is your body trying to tell you something your brain doesn't want to accept?

- Are you sad, anxious, distractible, overwhelmed, irritable, forgetful, or highly sensitive to rejection and criticism? What's that all about?

In the following sections of this chapter, you'll find a series of questions and checklists drawn from my work with patients and the diagnostic criteria for common problems such as depression and anxiety. I urge you to answer these simple self-assessment queries. They'll help you determine whether a medical condition or chemical imbalance could be part of your presenting complaint or life problem.

But before beginning, let's talk about why you are the way you are and the importance of self-acceptance in healing.

THE ROOTS OF ILLNESS

In order to lay the proper foundation for healing, we need to explore questions such as *Do genes cause depression or attention deficit disorder (ADD)? What's the role of mind over matter?* and *Can we skip over the diagnostic piece and still heal?*

It turns out that we can receive a strong genetic vulnerability to illnesses such as depression, bipolar disorder, and panic attacks. So we are the way we are because of our ancestors . . . but genes aren't the whole story! Even identical twins aren't exactly the same. Although genetically identical twins are more likely to suffer from the same illnesses than even fraternal twins, no two individuals will have the exact same experience of well-being in their lives. Each of us is unique, and each life journey will be different.

Our genes play a huge role in what happens to us. They determine our vulnerability to disease in profound and powerful ways. Many illnesses, such as manic-depression and attention deficit disorder, run heavily along lines within families. However, gene expression is complex. It turns out that our experiences—even in utero—determine what, when, and how some of our genetic material appears later in life. Hence, even identical twins aren't carbon copies! There's a complicated interplay between our genetic endowment and what befalls us going forward, and the choices we make.

THE POWER OF CHOICE

We don't choose our vulnerability, and we can't control much of what affects our gene expression in the developmental years. What we *can* decide is whether or not we honor our nature and susceptibility, and how we respond to it.

For example, if you currently meet diagnostic criteria for major depression, generalized anxiety disorder, attention deficit disorder, or obsessive-compulsive disorder, you can choose to identify it and figure out what interventions to pursue. Think about Jake and Rhonda—naming their problems was the first step to taking charge of their emotional lives. Although you don't pick your disorders, you too can take charge of your life.

You can also decide what to tell yourself about your capability to heal; this is where mind-body techniques come into play. You have the ability to transform the trauma and challenge of just about anything you discover, if you honor and respond appropriately to your own story. But first you must identify *what is* in order to effect change. In giving voice and space to what exists now, you open the door to incredible growth and health.

Let's return to Maria and *The Sound of Music* for a moment. The tale wonderfully illustrates the power of self-acceptance in transforming lives. Remember the song that asks: "How do you solve a problem like Maria?" Mother Superior sings it when she discovers that Maria is late and unprepared for prayers again. The girl desperately wants to be a good nun, but she can't seem to get it right. Mother Superior describes the dilemma beautifully when she wonders how to catch a cloud, keep a wave in one place, or grasp a moonbeam.

Maria's brain isn't wired to be a nun. The structure doesn't suit her, so Mother Superior sends her off to be a governess. Identifying and respecting the young girl's true nature opened the door to what became a wondrous love and family life for her. If you want to be inspired to trust in the wisdom of your story and nature, see this film.

DISCOVER YOUR JOURNEY

I'd like you to start exploring *your* story by answering the questions that follow. You can learn amazing things about yourself when you take the time to visit your own history. In preparing for a first-time visit with me, many patients happen upon new insights. This week a new patient said, "I didn't realize until just last night that being diagnosed with cancer kept me from having time to grieve the loss of my father." What an important breakthrough that was!

In answering these inquiries about your own presenting problem, its history, and your nature, you may very well gain new insights. Be open to that possibility as you write down what comes to mind upon reading the ten questions below, and look for the lessons in your story.

1. What's bothering me? What's my presenting problem or chief complaint? Am I too anxious, self-critical, sad, angry, lonely, distractible, irritable, or hopeless (or some other state of being)?

2. What do I hope to change, accomplish, or transform with the Take-Charge program?

3. What's the story of my distress?
    • When did it start?
    • How has it shown itself over time?
    • What sort of interventions have I pursued?
    • What's been helpful?
    • What's made my problem worse?

4. When in my life have I felt my best?
    • Where was I?
    • How old was I?
    • How was I spending my time?

5. When have I felt my worst?
    • Where was I?
    • How old was I?
    • How was I spending my time?

6. What (or who) heals me, calms me, soothes me, and lifts my spirits?

7. What (or who) unsettles me, makes me sick, or makes me want to run for the hills?

8. If I could travel backward or forward from this point in the timeline of my life story, when would I visit and why?

9. What's the role of my family history in my life and my problem?

10. What, if anything, can I learn about my issue and my path to healing from my responses to these questions?

In answering these queries, you may have included experiences with psychiatric or medical conditions. Perhaps you wrote about problems with depression, anxiety, concentration, or memory. Maybe you noted a diagnosis (or several) that you've been given, or found yourself wondering if you have a condition that's been missed. You might even have been resistant to the idea of being diagnosed but realized that you need to consider its possibility.

HOW PSYCHIATRISTS DIAGNOSE DISORDERS

You might be wondering, *What does a "psychiatric" diagnosis really mean, anyway?* You may understand other kinds of illness (such as the medical condition of pneumonia) because you know you can see evidence of infection on a lung x-ray, but you may be confused about something like identifying major depression. Since you can't see anything in x-rays, and there's no blood test for it, you may find yourself questioning whether this is even a real illness.

This is a crucial question. The way diagnoses are made in psychiatry is on the basis of your story, not any laboratory test. If a person is suffering enough from a specific series of symptoms that the individual is unable to function, or he or she is overwhelmingly distressed by them, psychiatrists and medical doctors consider the person to have a *disorder* characterized by those symptoms. For example, someone with sleep and appetite disturbance, impaired memory and concentration, a lack of interest or pleasure in usual activities, or depressed mood and hopelessness would be considered to have the disorder of major depression.

How did that particular bunch of troubles get a specific name? Well, a group of experts actually meets periodically to determine what lists of symptoms should be classified as a disorder. They share their research and clinical-practice observations to reach a consensus on what makes sense. Then they publish their decisions in the *Diagnostic and Statistical Manual of Mental Disorders (DSM)*.

A new edition comes out every few years with changes that are the result of research and observations that have been gathered since the last publication. A different number is added to the end of the title to indicate what edition of criteria that book contains. The *DSM* is the bible of diagnosis in psychiatry, but unlike the real Bible, this work changes progressively over time.

Once diagnostic criteria are created, medication and treatment-intervention studies can be performed to see how to improve the symptoms of each disorder. This allows for the possibility of finding remedies and solutions. It also enables doctors, therapists, researchers, and patients to speak a common language and understand one another.

You see, although there's nothing absolute or magic about naming a series of symptoms of a disorder, doing so allows us to figure out how to help people move from a place of pain and hopelessness to a state of well-being. Over the years, we've learned that the vulnerability to groups of symptoms or conditions such as manic-depressive disorder, panic disorder, and attention deficit disorder are strongly genetically transmitted. We've also found that specific interventions can help heal those with these groups of symptoms—and that without those measures, some people won't get better.

You may have gotten stuck on your path to health because you lack a necessary diagnosis or carry one that doesn't fit. You may have received incorrect interventions or missed out on necessary ones. Like Greg, Jake, Rhonda, and Maria, you may be feeling lousy because you're going down the wrong path.

For this reason, it's really important to identify *what is.* You might consider:

- If you're sad or blue in a way that won't quit, you may be suffering from depression.

- If you're anxious, stressed out, or jumpy, you may have an anxiety disorder.

- If you're irritable or quick-tempered, you may be depressed, anxious, addicted, or have ADD.

- If you're forgetful or have trouble with memory and concentration, you may also be depressed, anxious, addicted, or be suffering from ADD.

- If your mood is erratic, with extreme highs and lows, you may have manic-depressive illness.

In order to help you determine whether you have a medical condition or a chemical imbalance, I've provided a series of questions for some of the most common problems people face. Although you'll find checklists for eight disorders, they cover three basic types of problems. The first two, depressive illness and bipolar disorder, are mood problems. The third through seventh—panic, obsessive-compulsive disorder, post-traumatic stress disorder, social phobia, and generalized anxiety disorder—are all anxiety disorders. And the eighth—attention deficit disorder—is a problem of memory, concentration, and impulsiveness.

Many of the checklists are drawn from National Institutes of Health (NIH) publications. The full text of these publications can be found at **www.nimh.nih.gov.** You can also find some of the information on my Website, **www.DrEveWood.com**; and in my first book, *There's Always Help; There's Always Hope,* where you'll find many examples of healing that illustrate the importance and method of making proper assessments, as well as stories that demonstrate how to include your diagnoses in a healing path that works.

COULD YOU BE SUFFERING FROM A DEPRESSIVE ILLNESS?

In any given one-year period, 9.5 percent of the population (or about 18.8 million Americans) suffer from a depressive illness. So when you attend a dinner party for ten people, at least one individual at the table will meet the criteria. In the supermarket when there are lines of six shoppers at eight checkout counters, at least six people in the front of the store are afflicted with depression. And the percentage is equally high in almost every other country in the world.

There are many kinds of depression. Some examples are major depressive disorder, seasonal affective disorder (SAD), dysthymia, and postpartum depression. To determine whether you could be suffering from a depressive illness, read through the following list of symptoms. Check off all the ones that you've experienced for at least two weeks:

Depression-Symptom Checklist

- ❑ A lasting sad, anxious, or empty mood
- ❑ Feelings of hopelessness or pessimism
- ❑ Feelings of guilt, worthlessness, or helplessness
- ❑ Loss of interest or pleasure in activities once enjoyed, including sex
- ❑ Decreased energy or a feeling of fatigue or of being "slowed down"
- ❑ Difficulty concentrating, remembering, or making decisions
- ❑ Restlessness or irritability
- ❑ Sleeping too much, or can't sleep
- ❑ Change in appetite and/or unintended weight loss or gain
- ❑ Chronic pain or other persistent bodily symptoms that aren't caused by physical illness or injury
- ❑ Thoughts of death or suicide, or suicide attempts

You may have a major depressive episode if you have five or more of these symptoms most of the day, nearly every day, for a period of two weeks or longer. But there's something surprising and crucial about this diagnosis: *You don't have to feel depressed in order to be suffering from such an illness!* You must have either a depressed mood *or* a loss of interest or pleasure in usual activities for two weeks to be considered clinically depressed. Often, sufferers don't feel sad or blue at all. They just don't care about anything—their usual passions seem irrelevant to them.

If you've put checks in five or more of the symptom boxes, you may well be suffering from a major depressive illness. If you checked at least three boxes, but fewer than five, you could be suffering from dysthymia, which is a chronic low-level depression that lasts for years.

If you have mood symptoms that occur only during the darker winter months, you could have SAD. If you're a woman who has recently given birth, you may be experiencing postpartum depression. Women are very vulnerable to developing depression immediately after giving birth. The abrupt drop in hormone levels during delivery, particularly estrogen, affects the brain.

If you've marked at least three of the symptom boxes and not been evaluated for depression by a doctor recently, I recommend that you schedule an assessment; you may well benefit from therapeutic intervention. This condition is quite treatable; but left untreated, it's second only to ischemic heart disease in the degree of morbidity and mortality that it causes in most countries in the world, for those over the age of five.

To learn more about depressive illness, visit:

- My Website: **www.DrEveWood.com** (click on "Medical Guidance")

- National Institute of Mental Health (NIMH): **www.nimh.nih.gov**

- National Alliance on Mental Illness (NAMI): **www.nami.org**

- International Foundation for Research and Education on Depression: **www.ifred.org**

COULD YOU BE SUFFERING FROM BIPOLAR DISORDER OR MANIC-DEPRESSIVE ILLNESS?

Bipolar disorder, also known as manic-depressive illness, affects more than two million American adults in any given year; it's equally common in many other countries. Bipolar disorder involves rapid mood swings—from overly "high" and/or irritable to sad and hopeless, and then back again. *Most* individuals with bipolar disorder are depressed for many more days of their life than they are "high" or manic.

To determine whether you could be suffering from bipolar disorder, check off all the symptoms of mania that you've experienced for one week or longer.

MANIC-EPISODE CHECKLIST

- ❏ Increased energy, activity, and restlessness
- ❏ Excessively "high," overly euphoric mood
- ❏ Extreme irritability
- ❏ Racing thoughts and talking very fast; jumping from one idea to another
- ❏ Distractibility, can't concentrate
- ❏ Little sleep needed
- ❏ Unrealistic beliefs in one's abilities and powers
- ❏ Poor judgment
- ❏ Spending sprees
- ❏ A lasting period of behavior that's different from the norm
- ❏ Increased sexual drive
- ❏ Abuse of drugs, particularly cocaine, alcohol, and sleep medications
- ❏ Provocative, intrusive, or aggressive behavior
- ❏ Denial that there's anything wrong

You might have had a manic episode if you experienced elevated mood with three or more of the other checklist symptoms for most of the day, nearly every day, for one week or longer. If your mood was irritable, you must have had four additional checklist symptoms for the episode to qualify.

In order to meet the criteria for manic-depressive illness, you would have to experience at least one episode of depressive illness *and* an episode of mania. If you checked off three or more boxes in the depression-symptom checklist and three or more in the manic-episode checklist, you could very well have bipolar disorder or cyclothymic disorder.

If you checked off two boxes in each list, you could have sub-threshold bipolar disorder. It turns out that at least as many people suffer from this variation as meet the full criteria. These individuals have fewer checklist symptoms, but just as much impairment, in terms of the number of days a year (an average of 43) they're unable to work or perform normal daily activities.

Bipolar disorder, cyclothymic disorder, and subthreshold manic-depressive illness are all very treatable—and treatment is crucial. The risk of suicide in bipolar illness is much greater than in all other forms of depression. Even without this danger, the disease is often life crippling if sufferers don't receive adequate intervention. Medication is often necessary in the treatment of cyclical mood disorders, and it's best prescribed and monitored by a doctor familiar with these particular conditions.

If bipolar disorder, cyclothymia, or subthreshold bipolar disorder is a possibility for you, I recommend assessment by a psychiatrist, as opposed to any other medical doctor. Many primary-care physicians aren't knowledgeable enough to make these diagnoses.

For more information about bipolar and cyclical mood disorders, visit:

- My Website: **www.DrEveWood.com** (click on "Medical Guidance")

- National Institute of Mental Health (NIMH): **www.nimh.nih.gov**

- National Alliance on Mental Illness (NAMI): **www.nami.org**

- Depression and Bipolar Support Alliance: **www.DBSAlliance.org**

COULD YOU BE SUFFERING FROM A PANIC DISORDER?

In any given year, 2.4 million American adults will suffer from panic disorder; the frequency of this illness is similar in many other countries. People with this condition have feelings of terror that strike suddenly and repeatedly with no warning. They can't predict when an attack will occur, and many develop intense anxiety between episodes, worrying about when and where the next one will strike.

If you're having a panic attack, most likely your heart will pound; and you may feel sweaty, weak, faint, or dizzy. Your hands may tingle or feel numb, and you might be flushed or chilled. You may have nausea, chest pain, smothering sensations, a sense of unreality, or fear of impending doom or loss of control. You may genuinely believe that you're having a heart attack, losing your mind, or on the verge of death.

To determine whether you could be suffering from panic disorder, check off all the symptoms that you relate to in the following list. These must all occur during a sudden burst of fear that comes on for no apparent reason.

PANIC-DISORDER CHECKLIST

During sudden bursts of fear:
- ❑ I have chest pains or a racing heart.
- ❑ I have a hard time breathing or a choking feeling.
- ❑ I feel dizzy or sweat a lot.
- ❑ I have stomach problems or feel as if I need to throw up.
- ❑ I shake, tremble, or tingle.
- ❑ I feel out of control.
- ❑ I feel unreal.
- ❑ I'm afraid I'm dying or going crazy.

If you checked off three or more symptoms, you might be suffering from panic disorder. While an assessment can be done by most physicians, many can't provide the full course of treatment. Psychiatrists and many therapists, however, can do so. If medication is needed—and it often is, at least for a while—a psychiatrist or other medical doctor will need to prescribe it. A psychiatrist or other type of psychotherapist can often provide the rest of the treatment. Cognitive behavior therapy is an especially helpful approach for this condition.

My *Stop Anxiety Now Kit* (available in June 2007 through Hay House) is a good resource as well. It includes some mind-body techniques and cognitive-behavior tools, as well as a relaxation and guided-imagery CD to help you manage your anxiety.

For more information on panic disorder, visit:

- My Website: **www.DrEveWood.com** (click on "Medical Guidance")
- National Institute of Mental Health (NIMH): **www.nimh.nih.gov**
- National Alliance on Mental Illness (NAMI): **www.nami.org**
- Anxiety Disorders Association of America: **www.adaa.org**
- Freedom from Fear: **www.freedomfromfear.com**

COULD YOU BE SUFFERING FROM OBSESSIVE-COMPULSIVE DISORDER (OCD)?

In any given year, 3.3 million Americans will have OCD. If you do, you have repeated, upsetting thoughts. You do the same thing over and over again to make them go away, and you feel as if you can't control these thoughts or actions. Many people with OCD know that their behavior isn't normal, and they may to try to hide their problem from family and friends. Some sufferers may have trouble maintaining their jobs and relationships because of what they do.

If you have OCD, you feel trapped in a pattern of upsetting thoughts. To determine whether you might have this condition, check off all the symptoms that you relate to on the next page.

Obsessive-Compulsive Disorder Checklist

❑ Upsetting thoughts or images enter my mind again and again.

❑ I feel as if I can't stop these thoughts or images, even though I want to.

❑ I have a hard time stopping myself from doing things again and again, such as: counting, checking on things, washing my hands, rearranging objects, doing something until it feels right, or collecting useless objects.

❑ I worry a lot about terrible things that could happen if I'm not careful.

If you checked off two or more boxes, you could well have obsessive-compulsive disorder. Most psychologists and psychiatrists are equipped to evaluate you. Treatments include medication and cognitive behavioral therapy. For more information about OCD, visit:

- My Website: **www.DrEveWood.com** (click on "Medical Guidance")
- National Institute of Mental Health (NIMH): **www.nimh.nih.gov**
- National Alliance on Mental Illness (NAMI): **www.nami.org**
- Anxiety Disorders Association of America: **www.adaa.org**
- Obsessive Compulsive Foundation: **www.ocfoundation.org**

COULD YOU BE SUFFERING FROM POST-TRAUMATIC STRESS DISORDER?

In any given year, 5.2 million Americans have PTSD; this number is substantially higher in some countries where trauma and danger are a regular part of life. This debilitating condition can develop following a terrifying event. Often, sufferers have persistent frightening thoughts and memories of their ordeal and feel emotionally numb, especially with people they were once close to.

PTSD was first brought to public attention by war veterans, but it can result from any number of traumatic incidents. These include violent attacks such as mugging, rape, or torture; being kidnapped or held captive; child abuse; serious accidents such as car or train wrecks; and natural disasters such as floods or earthquakes. The triggering event may be something that threatened the person's life or that of someone close to him or her; or it could be something witnessed, such as massive death and destruction after a building is bombed or a plane crashes.

To determine whether you might have PTSD, consider your story. Have you lived through a scary and dangerous event? If so, review this checklist and mark all the symptoms you relate to.

POST-TRAUMATIC STRESS DISORDER CHECKLIST

- ❑ I feel as if the terrible event is happening all over again. This feeling often comes without warning.

- ❑ I have nightmares and scary memories of the terrifying event.

- ❑ I stay away from places that remind me of it.

- ❑ I jump and feel very upset when something happens without warning.

- ❑ I have a hard time trusting or feeling close to other people.

- ❑ I get mad very easily.

- ❑ I feel guilty because others died and I lived.

- ❑ I have trouble sleeping, and my muscles are tense.

If you marked three or more boxes in the PTSD checklist, you may have this condition.

Many therapists are equipped to make this diagnosis. Specific forms of psychotherapy and guided imagery are very helpful in the treatment of PTSD. A great resource for understanding trauma responses and how to heal is the book *Invisible Heroes: Survivors of Trauma and How They Heal* by Belleruth Naparstek. To learn more about this condition, visit:

- My Website: **www.DrEveWood.com** (click on "Medical Guidance")
- National Institute of Mental Health (NIMH): **www.nimh.nih.gov**
- Anxiety Disorders Association of America: **www.adaa.org**
- National Center for PTSD: **www.ncptsd.org**

COULD YOU BE SUFFERING FROM SOCIAL PHOBIA?

In any given year, at least 5.3 million Americans have this condition; the incidence is quite high in other countries as well. Social phobia, or social-anxiety disorder, involves overwhelming anxiety and excessive self-consciousness in everyday social situations. People with this illness have a persistent, intense, and chronic fear of being watched and judged by others and being embarrassed or humiliated by their own actions. Their terror may be so severe that it interferes with work, school, and other ordinary activities. While many sufferers recognize that their fear of being around others may be excessive or unreasonable, they're unable to overcome it. They often worry for days or weeks in advance of a dreaded situation.

If you feel afraid and uncomfortable when you're around other people, you could have social phobia. Please review the checklist and mark all the statements that you relate to.

Social-Phobia Checklist

❑ I have an intense fear that I'll do or say something to embarrass myself in front of other people.

❑ I'm always very afraid of making a mistake and being watched and judged.

❑ My fear of embarrassment makes me avoid doing things I want to do or speaking to others.

❑ I worry for days or weeks before I have to meet new people.

❑ I blush, sweat a lot, tremble, or feel like I have to throw up before and during an event where I am with anyone I don't know.

❑ I usually stay away from social situations such as school events and making speeches.

❑ I often drink to try to make these fears go away.

If you marked three or more boxes in the social-phobia checklist, you may have this condition. Many therapists, psychologists, and psychiatrists are equipped to make this diagnosis; generally, internists are not. Treatments can include medication, psychotherapy, and cognitive-behavioral interventions.

For more information about social phobia, visit:

• My Website: **www.DrEveWood.com** (click on "Medical Guidance")

• National Alliance on Mental Illness (NAMI): **www.nami.org**

• Anxiety Disorders Association of America: **www.adaa.org**

COULD YOU HAVE GENERALIZED ANXIETY DISORDER (GAD)?

In any given year, four million Americans will have GAD; the disorder is common in many other countries. If you have this condition, you worry all the time about your family, health, or work, even when there are no signs of trouble. Sometimes you aren't anxious about anything special, but still feel tense and nervous all day long. You also have aches and pains for no reason and feel tired a lot. Everyone gets worried sometimes, but if you have GAD, you stay that way, fear the worst will happen, and can't relax.

If you worry almost all the time, you may have GAD. To determine the likelihood, please check off the statements that are true for you:

GENERALIZED-ANXIETY-DISORDER CHECKLIST

- ❑ I never stop worrying about things big and small.
- ❑ I have headaches and other aches and pains for no reason.
- ❑ I'm tense a lot and have difficulty relaxing.
- ❑ I have trouble keeping my mind on one thing.
- ❑ I get crabby or grouchy. I have a hard time falling asleep or staying asleep.
- ❑ I sweat and have hot flashes.
- ❑ I sometimes have a lump in my throat or feel that I need to throw up when I'm worried.

If you put a check next to three or more of the above statements, you may have GAD. Most therapists, psychologists, and psychiatrists can make this diagnosis, but many internists miss it when patients come in with a series of physical complaints. Remember, this was Jake's story. Treatment often involves medication, and some additional form of therapy. My *Stop Anxiety Now Kit* (available June 2007 from Hay House) can help you manage the anxiety of GAD.

For more information, visit:

- My Website: **www.DrEveWood.com** (click on "Medical Guidance")

- National Institute of Mental Health (NIMH): **www.nimh.nih.gov**

- Anxiety Disorders Association of America: **www.adaa.org**

COULD YOU HAVE ATTENTION DEFICIT DISORDER?

At least two million adults in the United States suffer from attention deficit disorder (ADD), also known as attention-deficit/hyperactivity disorder (ADHD); it's common in other countries as well. By definition, the problem has to begin early in life, before age seven, and continue for at least six months. Although many adults who have recently been identified as having ADHD weren't diagnosed when they were young, their childhood stories have to fit the criteria. *Some* symptoms must have been present before the age of seven.

At present, ADHD is a diagnosis applied to children and adults who consistently display certain characteristic behaviors over a period of time. The most common actions fall into three categories:

1. **Inattention.** People who are inattentive have a hard time keeping their mind on any one thing and may get bored with a task after only a few minutes. They may give effortless, automatic consideration to activities and things they enjoy. But focusing deliberate, conscious attention on organizing and completing a task or learning something new is difficult.

2. **Hyperactivity.** People who are hyperactive always seem to be in motion. They can't keep still, so they may dash around or talk incessantly. Sitting through a lesson can be an impossible task. Hyperactive children squirm in their seats or roam around the room; or they might wiggle their feet, touch everything, or noisily tap their pencils. Teens and adults can feel intensely restless. They may be fidgety or try to do several things at once, bouncing around from one activity to the next.

3.   **Impulsivity.** People who are overly impulsive seem unable to curb their immediate reactions or think before they act. As a result, they may blurt out inappropriate comments. Children may run into the street without looking. Their impulsivity may make it hard for them to wait for things they want or to take their turn in games.

Not everyone who's overly hyperactive, inattentive, or impulsive has an attention disorder. Since most people sometimes blurt out things they didn't mean to say, bounce from one task to another, or become disorganized and forgetful, how can specialists tell if the problem is ADHD?

To assess this condition, we consider several critical questions:

•   Are these behaviors excessive, long-term, and pervasive? That is, do they occur more often than in other people the same age?

•   Are the issues a continual problem, not just a response to a temporary situation?

•   Do the behaviors occur in several settings or only in one specific place, such as the playground or the office?

The pattern of behavior is compared against a set of criteria and characteristics of the disorder, which appear in the DSM. According to the manual, there are three patterns of behavior that indicate ADHD: Sufferers may show several signs of being consistently inattentive, have a pattern of being hyperactive or impulsive, or they may show all three types of behavior.

In order to determine whether or not you could be suffering from ADHD, check off as many symptom statements as you relate to in the following list. Some of the characteristics must be present in more than one setting.

Attention-Deficit/Hyperactivity Disorder Checklist

Inattention

❏   I make careless mistakes in work or during other activities.

❏   It's hard for me to pay attention while reading or sitting in a meeting.

❏   I have trouble following through, completing assignments or tasks.

❏   I have difficulty getting organized.

❏   I avoid activities that require concentration for very long.

❏   I continually lose what I need, such as keys, pens, books, and tools.

❏   I'm easily distracted.

❏   I'm forgetful.

Hyperactive/Impulsive

❏   I feel restless when I have to sit still.

❏   I have trouble amusing myself quietly.

❏   I'm always on the go.

❏   I talk excessively.

❏   I interrupt often.

❏   I have a hard time waiting in line, in traffic, or for my turn in other situations.

❏   I answer questions before they're completed.

If you checked off four boxes in either the Inattention or Hyperactive/Impulsive sections, you could very well have ADD or ADHD. You may be suffering with this disorder even if you're a highly successful professional. I've treated many physicians and attorneys with this problem. In *There's Always Help; There's Always Hope*, you'll find lots of examples of gifted individuals who were held back by their undiagnosed ADD.

If this condition is a possibility for you, begin to educate yourself about the disorder. There are many great books and resources out there. One of my favorite books for this is *Driven to Distraction* by Edward M. Hallowell, M.D., and John J. Ratey, M.D. While many professionals can help you make this diagnosis, you can sort out its likelihood very well on your own first.

Interventions range from medication, coaching, and time-management techniques to psychotherapy. To learn more about ADD/ADHD visit:

- My Website: **www.DrEveWood.com** (click on "Medical Guidance")
- A.D.D WareHouse: **www.addwarehouse.com**
- Children and Adults with Attention-Deficit/Hyperactivity Disorder: **www.chadd.org**
- National Institute of Mental Health (NIMH): **www.nimh.nih.gov**

You've come to the end of the checklists for common disorders. Take a few moments to make note of what you've discovered. Did something important jump out at you or surprise you? Is there something you need to pursue?

If you related to one or more of the conditions described, you're not alone. Take the lesson seriously. According to the *Archives of General Psychiatry* (June 2005), 55 percent of Americans will suffer from a mental illness in their lifetime. The breakdown of most types is given in the chart on the next page. Please note that the general numbers (such as 28.8 percent for any anxiety disorder) indicate the percentage of the 55 percent of Americans just mentioned who experience the condition. The specific percentages (such as panic disorder, agoraphobia without panic, and so on) may add up to more than the general number because many individuals are diagnosed with more than one condition.

ANY ANXIETY DISORDER	28.8%
Panic disorder	4.7%
Agoraphobia without panic	1.4%
Specific phobia	12.5%
Social phobia	12.1%
Generalized anxiety disorder	5.7%
Post-traumatic stress disorder	6.8%
Obsessive-compulsive disorder	1.6%
Separation anxiety	5.2%
MOOD DISORDER	20.8%
Major depression	16.6%
Dysthymia	2.5%
Bipolar I or II	3.9%
IMPULSE-CONTROL DISORDER	24.8%
Oppositional-defiant disorder	8.5%
Conduct disorder	9.5%
Attention-deficit/hyperactivity disorder	8.1%
Intermittent explosive disorder	5.2%
SUBSTANCE DISORDER	14.6%
Alcohol abuse	13.6%
Alcohol dependence	5.4%
Drug abuse	7.9%
Drug dependence	3%

While I didn't provide you checklists for every disorder on the list, you'll notice that the anxiety, mood, and attention-related conditions are the most common problems. I chose not to include the other big category—alcoholism and other addictions—in this book because there are many resources that cover these problems quite well.

Given how common substance use and abuse is, you may have problems in this area. If so, please pursue appropriate treatment and support. I love the 12-step recovery programs such as AA (Alcoholics Anonymous), NA (Narcotics Anonymous), SLAA (Sex and Love Addicts Anonymous), and OA (Overeaters Anonymous) for the support and guidance they provide.

For more information on addictions, visit:

The 12-step recovery programs:

- AA (Alcoholics Anonymous): **www.alcoholics-anonymous.org**

- NA (Narcotics Anonymous): **www.na.org**

- SLAA (Sex and Love Addiction Anonymous): **www.slaafws.org**

- OA (Overeaters Anonymous): **www.oa.org**

- GA (Gamblers Anonymous): **www.gamblersanonymous.org**

- DA (Debtors Anonymous): **www.debtorsanonymous.org**

- Al-Anon/Alateen: **www.al-anon.alateen.org**

Additional resources:

- National Council on Alcoholism and Drug Dependence: **www.ncadd.org**

- National Institute on Alcohol Abuse and Alcoholism: **www.niaaa.nih.gov**

In Step 1, you've explored the lessons within your story and have considered the possibility that you may have diagnoses requiring attention. As you now know, the ultimate determinant of whether you meet criteria for a disorder is whether your symptoms match those in the *DSM* (*DSM-IV-R*, as of this printing). While I could not possibly reprint the whole manual, you can find it in your local library or bookstore and compare your symptoms with those of any disorder that you sense could fit.

If your story matches completely, you know you meet the criteria; if it doesn't, you don't. You can figure out a lot for yourself. In fact, I often share the criteria with my patients to be sure that we're on the same diagnostic page. The information isn't that tough to understand. It's easily accessible and the gold standard when it comes to making a psychiatric diagnosis.

Before moving on, I need to make a plug for a particular type of medical assessment. I want you to be open to the possibility that you could need an evaluation of your general health, because it turns out that there are quite a few general medical conditions that can look like psychiatric problems even though they're not.

For example, if you have an underactive thyroid, you may feel like a person with major depression. By contrast, if you have an overactive thyroid, you might feel as though you have an anxiety disorder. Minor and easily treated medical problems like vitamin-B$_{12}$ deficiency and thyroid abnormalities can also masquerade as mental illnesses. Occasionally, serious but very rare problems such as brain tumors and autoimmune diseases can appear to be psychiatric problems as well. Finally, many hormonal shifts, such as those that occur during perimenopause and menopause, can wreck havoc on the emotional brain.

So if your symptoms don't completely fit *DSM* criteria, or if you don't respond to the usual treatment interventions, something else could be going on. In that case, I recommend a general-health assessment with your internist, family practitioner, or gynecologist.

Before closing this chapter, I want to review a point we visited earlier on: *You don't choose your vulnerabilities or diagnoses. You only decide whether you identify and address them.* As we finish Step 1, please answer the following questions:

1. What have I identified (diagnoses, etc.)?
2. How do I want to address what I've found up to this point?
3. What are the lessons of my story?

As you move on to Step 2 in the next chapter, you'll begin to explore your need for medication. If you have clinical depression, an anxiety disorder, or ADD, medication *may* be part of your answer—and then again, it *may* not. There's no "one-size-fits-all" answer in the Take-Charge program. Your story and needs are unique, and your personal path is waiting for you. With enough information and support, your inner wisdom will guide you to your own best solutions. You can take charge, and you *can* heal!

STEP 2

Explore Your Need for Medication

Welcome to Step 2 of the program! In Step 1 you examined your story and looked for its lessons, exploring the question *Do I have a medical condition or clinical diagnosis?* In reviewing the checklists, you may have identified one or more disorders that could explain part of your struggle; or you may have discovered that a diagnosis you've been given doesn't fit your story.

In Step 2, you'll explore your need for medication, which is a mixed bag. Many lives have been transformed for good with this type of intervention—in fact, lots of people say, "Medication saved my life." But there are other voices out there, too, and some individuals blame drugs for actual deaths. The FDA has issued warnings about the possibility of increased suicide risk with the use of some prescriptions. We're entering an area of controversy and confusion as we begin Step 2 together.

But you don't need to get confused or overwhelmed by this issue, because I'll help you find your way through the labyrinth. You'll discover how to learn your own personal answer to the question *What's the place of medication in my journey?* There are four specific principles to consider in evaluating this, but first I need to give you some background.

Shakespeare wrote: "There is nothing either good or bad but thinking makes it so." Those who tell you that medication is all positive or completely negative are misguided in their thinking. Unfortunately, you're regularly exposed to extreme messages from both camps: champions and critics of this treatment option.

In reality, a particular prescription might be great for you, or it might be terrible; a drug may save your life or disrupt it. You might benefit for a brief period or need ongoing assistance. You may be tipped into your first manic episode by an antidepressant or experience unbearable side effects. Sometimes medicine is good and sometimes it isn't—it all depends on the situation. Your need is related to your vulnerability, your challenges, and your unique tale.

As you know, we're all born with different degrees of susceptibility to illnesses and disorders, which continue to be affected by our developmental and life experiences. Given our family histories, genetics, and particular challenges, some of us are much more prone to becoming clinically depressed, anxious, or addicted than others. With enough stress and loss, most of us will become depressed, worried, or overwhelmed, but our individual tolerance points are very different.

For example, I come from a family with strong genetic loading for clinical depression. Both my maternal grandfather and my mother took antidepressant medication for years to control insomnia, hopelessness, fearfulness, and negativity. Neither was particularly interested in, or inclined to do, much else that might have lifted their moods. But even had they chosen to do more, it might not have made a difference. On my dad's side of the family, I have some genetic loading for alcoholism. That wasn't in a first-degree relative, so it may not be as strong.

In any case, I've never yet experienced a full-blown clinical depression that required medication. But I surely could, and I'd take pills if I needed them to heal. And although I've never suffered from this condition, I can get down or blue if I stop my regular self-care regimen. I do a lot of things that are felt to be protective; several have even been shown to be natural antidepressants *for some people*. I exercise aerobically for at least 30 minutes five days a week. I sing, pray, attend religious services weekly, maintain ongoing social connections, see patients, teach, and give back in many other ways. I spend time outdoors under the Tucson, Arizona, sun daily (except when traveling);

write books and articles to foster personal empowerment and health; nurture the growth of my four children; and make time for fun with my kids, friends, and soul-mate husband.

As you can tell, I'm a super-busy lady who's juggling and balancing a lot, and as a result, I regularly do a bunch of things that decrease my vulnerability to illness. You'll learn more about those interventions in subsequent chapters. Because of my good fortune, genetic endowment, attitude, and life choices, I'm usually upbeat and hopeful. However, when I get thrown too many curveballs, my system can get overwhelmed, and I sometimes feel pretty anxious.

On rare occasions, I become so unsettled that I can't calm down enough to sleep at night. When that happens, I take a tiny dose of Valium; one milligram is usually enough to turn my system around. I may need to take a pill as often as once every three months. Whenever I do this, it interrupts my anxiety, and by the next day, I head for the gym first thing in the morning and am lucky enough to be back to feeling like myself again before breakfast. That's my story. I happen to be very resilient, and my dad was the same way. But you have your own history, endowment, and vulnerabilities. You may be like me, or you may be more like my mom and grandpa. You might not even be like any of us, because ultimately, you're just *you* . . . and it's *your* story that counts.

Pamela's story and Christina's tale are two more examples that illustrate how individual differences dictate the need for medication in the Take-Charge program. You might see the former as one side of the coin and the latter as the other, but it isn't so black and white. See what you think. . . .

Help along the Path: Pamela's Story

Pamela, a bubbly woman in her 50s, was referred to me by several close friends who were worried about her. Her husband of many years was dying of cancer, and she was quite overwhelmed and anxious—just not herself. She told me how grateful she was for the referral as she settled into a seat in my office for the first time.

Pamela hadn't been in therapy before and had never been evaluated by a psychiatrist. As she told me her story, I determined that she was suffering from what *DSM* calls an "adjustment disorder with anxious mood." That basically means that she was struggling with unsettlement caused by significant life stress. She didn't meet diagnostic criteria for an anxiety disorder, depressive illness, or anything additional. She needed supportive psychotherapy and practical guidance, yet her internist had started her on an antidepressant several weeks before.

I questioned her about his rationale. "Why did he put you on this medicine?" I asked.

"Well," she said, "I'm not sure. I told him that I wasn't sleeping and needed something for it. Was that a poor choice?"

Together we explored her story and determined that the antidepressant might not have been the best idea. However, since her husband was dying, she was at a higher risk than normal for developing an anxiety or depressive disorder. Because she was already feeling somewhat overwhelmed and wasn't having any problem with the drug, we decided not to stop it right away. Although I probably wouldn't have started it initially, I was concerned about ceasing the medication at such a challenging time in her life—after all, perhaps it was helping her somewhat. What if she were to become worse off without it? It made sense to continue her prescription for the time being.

Pamela and I met for several months as I helped her through the death of her husband and the grieving and rebuilding process that followed. She did extremely well through the whole ordeal. She then chose to taper off the medication after a total of six months from the original start date. This felt completely appropriate to me, and she did quite well thereafter.

An Ongoing Experience: Christina's Story

Christina, a 32-year-old graduate student, wasn't feeling very well: She was "down in the dumps" again. During her first appointment, she told me that at the suggestion of several health practitioners, she'd cut down her antidepressant dose during the prior week. Concerned about this decision and its aftermath, I asked Christina to tell me her story. Why was she on the drug in the first place, and how had it helped her?

It turned out that she'd been suffering from depressive illness since childhood. She'd been in and out of therapy over the years and had been repeatedly suicidal. Although she'd come quite close several times, she'd never made a suicide attempt. Medication had always managed to lift her depression. She'd been on it for a long time, yet she'd periodically find herself thinking that she ought to be okay without it, and that taking the pills was some sort of weakness. She'd then start cutting down on them. Invariably, she'd get depressed, and sometimes even suicidal, before resuming a therapeutic dose of the drug.

Christina had a very strong family history of mental illness as well. She told me that many of her relatives over several generations were known to have suffered from clinical depression. In fact, several close family members had committed suicide. There was a lot of psychosis, addiction, depression, and anxiety in her siblings, parents, cousins, aunts, and uncles.

My patient shared all of this information in a very matter-of-fact way; she seemed totally detached from its significance. She told me that no matter what her family history was, she ought to be able to handle her moods without medication. She was unrelenting in her self-criticism, and unrealistic in what she expected of herself.

In dealing with this situation, I needed to take a completely different position than I did in helping Pamela. I explained to Christina that she had a life-threatening, recurring illness that was beyond her control. For her, as for so many other people, depression was a chronic condition that could worsen over time. The vulnerability to this runs in families, and her genetic loading was very strong.

For individuals like herself who've suffered from at least two depressive episodes, the likelihood of an additional one is above 90 percent. She was at high risk for recurrence and suicide, so she needed to increase her antidepressant dose right away. I explained that taking medication might be an ongoing part of her life, and that acceptance of *what is* was going to be a big piece of her therapeutic work.

Although she was disappointed, Christina did as I suggested. She resumed her usual drug regimen and reported feeling more hopeful and energized by the next time we got together. Thankfully, she responded quickly to the dosage increase.

Before you read on, take a moment to reflect on these stories. Do you relate to my experience, Pamela's or Christina's story, or bits of each? Do you recognize that these three situations cover a spectrum of vulnerability and need? Perhaps you realize that so far, medication is *mostly unnecessary* for me, might have been *briefly necessary* for Pamela, and is *absolutely crucial* for Christina in an ongoing way.

Remember the enduring lesson from Step 1: The answer to the question *What's wrong with the patient and what must be done to promote healing?* is in the presenting complaint and the initial clinical history. Your need for medication depends on your background, unique vulnerability, and personal story.

THE FOUR PRINCIPLES

Earlier in this chapter, I said that there are four specific principles you could use to figure out whether you need to take medication as part of your Take-Charge program. In this section, I'll teach them to you and show you how to use them to evaluate yourself. As I explain the principles, I'll share some clinical examples and give you guidance on how to work with each one. Then in Step 3, we'll explore *how* to use pharmaceuticals in treating depression, anxiety, ADD, and nonspecific problems that fall outside of the diagnostic categories. By the end of the next chapter, you'll have a good idea of whether this treatment is an option, possibility, or necessity for you, and also how to use it.

Medication only makes sense and may be necessary when:

1. You've identified a specific problem or diagnosis.

2. You've established target symptoms.

3. A specific medication has been shown to relieve the identified target symptoms of your specific problem.

4. The risks of you taking that medication outweigh the risks of avoiding it.

These four principles are crucial to your success in the Take-Charge program. If you get them down pat and live by them, you'll transform your life. If you neglect them, you may very well find yourself overwhelmed and spinning out of control for a long time.

Principle 1: Medication Only Makes Sense and May Be Necessary When You've Identified a Specific Problem or Diagnosis

This is a basic concept: We doctors should not treat a set of symptoms without determining the actual cause behind them. And you, as the sufferer, shouldn't take prescription medication if you don't know or understand why it's being given to you.

Why is it important to identify your diagnosis or problem? Remember what you learned in Step 1: In giving a set of symptoms a name, or diagnostic label, we can begin to figure out what treatment interventions work. Our medications have only been studied and shown to be effective for specific disorders. If you take a drug but don't have any symptoms that have been shown to respond to that substance, there's a good chance that you won't be helped by it. You might even get derailed or suffer unnecessarily.

We need to know what we're treating; we have to figure out *what is*. When we use medication indiscriminately, we can make actual conditions worse. We can end up on the wrong path or even create brand new problems. All drugs have side effects. The last thing you need to experience when you're already distressed is a series of unpleasant or troubling symptoms from a medication you don't even need, so let's look at some examples of problematic and effective medicine use.

Do you remember Jake's story? When he came to me, he was being treated for back pain with a bunch of powerful medications. His suffering had been getting worse and worse over the course of three years, and the prescriptions were doing little to make his life work, as he was spending more and more time in bed. But his discomfort was the result of an undiagnosed, and of course, untreated, generalized anxiety disorder. Once we made the proper assessment together, Jake began appropriate medication (a long-acting antianxiety agent) and psychotherapy. He improved and was thus able to move on with his life.

What's the lesson? A faulty diagnosis led to the wrong medication and progressive deterioration; the right knowledge and correct drug opened the door to healing.

Recall the details of Pamela's situation: Her internist started her on an antidepressant when she was complaining of insomnia. Luckily, she tolerated the substance well and didn't suffer from side effects. But because it wasn't clear whether the substance was needed in the first place, we were reluctant to stop it for a while. Had she clearly met the criteria for depression or anxiety in the internist's office, and had she understood the diagnosis and need for treatment, she and I would have known that it was important to continue her prescription for six months to a year. What's the lesson? The confusion about the reason for starting the medication made it difficult to know whether it could be stopped; clarity would have determined the right path.

There's another crucial lesson to be learned from Pamela's story. Today, antidepressants are among the most commonly consumed medications in the world. Most prescriptions for these drugs are written by internists and primary-care physicians. Unfortunately, many doctors don't focus on making a diagnosis before prescribing these pills. Therefore, lots of people who are taking them don't know why. Some probably don't need them and shouldn't be on them!

Please don't begin taking prescription medications before you understand why you may need them, and don't stop taking a drug until you know it makes sense to do so. Ask your physician to explain her rationale for the treatment recommendation, and make sure you agree. Don't assume that a doctor knows best and you have nothing to contribute to the discussion. You *can* take charge of your emotional health, so expect to partner with your care provider. Speak up! Your inner wisdom is brilliant and may recognize a bad fit between the official assessment and your story. You know yourself a whole lot better than anyone else does, so you're uniquely suited to identify mismatches and proper fits.

Another aspect of the first principle is that *medication only makes sense, and may be <u>necessary,</u> when you have identified a specific problem*. Think about Christina's story in light of this principle, and focus on the word *necessary*. Remember, Christina met diagnostic criteria for recurrent major depression. Her diagnosis, scary family history of suicides, and ongoing experiences of suicidal thoughts made medication a necessity in her Take-Charge program. Nothing else had ever worked to transform her hopelessness and devastation, and with untreated depression, she was at high risk for suicide. The diagnosis dictated the medication choice, while the family history and personal story demonstrated the necessity of treatment.

Now that you have clarity about the importance of making a diagnosis before beginning drug therapy, let's move on to the next principle.

PRINCIPLE 2: MEDICATION ONLY MAKES SENSE AND MAY BE NECESSARY WHEN YOU'VE IDENTIFIED TARGET SYMPTOMS

You're probably wondering what these symptoms are. *Target* is a strange word to use when talking about healing, since it seems sort of aggressive. But if you conjure up the image of a target in your mind and begin to visualize yourself shooting arrows or darts in the hopes of hitting a bull's-eye, you'll make the connection. You see, the target represents the set of symptoms you're trying to treat with your "arrows" or therapeutic interventions.

Just as it is dangerous and pointless to shoot arrows into thin air, it's wasteful and potentially harmful to take medication if we haven't identified specific symptoms that we hope to improve or make better with the drug. Furthermore, without identifying and examining these target symptoms over time, we have no way to evaluate whether a drug or medication is working.

Let's look at an example to clarify this concept. Think back to Rhonda's story and what happened after her house was burglarized. She said:

- I can't get my work done.
- I can't concentrate.
- I don't care about what used to matter to me.
- Food doesn't interest me.
- I cry all the time.
- I wish I could go to sleep and not wake up.
- Life feels pointless.
- I don't feel like myself.

39

This list of problems helped me ascertain that Rhonda was suffering from a clinical depression. However, they also had another use. I made these statements the target symptoms, the specific issues, that I hoped to see improve once Rhonda began taking antidepressant medication.

Week by week, the two of us would look at shifts in these troubles. How would we evaluate change? We set up a rating system. The scale went from 1 to 10, where 1 was *not at all or never,* and 10 was *almost always.* I asked Rhonda to rate each statement before we started medication; each symptom was rated a 10 or almost always. Week by week, she categorized her symptoms. As time went on, the numbers got lower, indicating that the drug was working.

You might question why a rating scale and list of target symptoms is necessary. Perhaps you're saying to yourself, *I'd know if I were getting better. It would be obvious.* Although that idea may make sense to you, the reality is that it doesn't work that way. Quite often, the last target symptom to improve is the depressed, anxious, or hopeless mood. Your sleep, concentration, and energy level may change dramatically before you *feel* better. Without some way to document that the other symptoms are improving, people who are getting better may insist that nothing is changing. This tool can help you maintain perspective and stay with the program.

The list can also enable you to realize when treatment *isn't* working. If your list of troubles is unchanged in spite of intervention, you'll realize your need to switch to another medication or change course in some other way.

I don't know how I'd judge the success of any therapeutic intervention without using target symptoms. Remember, Principle 1 involves identifying the diagnosis or problem clearly before intervening; this is a crucial first step. But how do we get involved and ensure success? We need to identify our goals and use a rating scale. Without a specific list of day-to-day, nuts-and-bolts troubles to follow, we have no way of evaluating the benefit of any treatment.

As part of your Take-Charge program, you'll need to create a list of the target symptoms you hope to improve. This exercise is crucial, whether you pursue medication intervention or any other step we'll be covering. Not only will you need to know *what is* (the problem and the diagnosis) in order to take charge, you'll also have to track *how it is* (day-to-day struggles), too.

How do you create your list of target symptoms? Well, you can start by using the checklists in Step 1. If you related to any of the disorders there, you can use the statements you checked off. I suggest that you take some time to note your target symptoms before moving on to the third principle. Feel free to write your day-to-day difficulties on the lines provided here or on a separate piece of paper.

My List of Target Symptoms

The day-to-day difficulties I want to heal:

1. _____
2. _____
3. _____
4. _____
5. _____
6. _____
7. _____
8. _____
9. _____
10. _____

I've also provided a rating scale so that you can assess your progress. I suggest making additional copies of it so that you can keep using it over time. It can help you evaluate your improvement with medication, as well as with many of the other self-care and treatment interventions that we'll be discussing in later steps or chapters.

Please don't chart your progress more often than once per week. No change happens faster than that, and many improvements are much longer in coming.

MY PROGRESS: RATING SCALE

Use a scale from 1 to 10, where **1 = Almost Never,** and **10 = Always.**

SYMPTOMS	Date: / /	Date: / /	Date: / /	Date: / /	Date: / /
	Rating	**Rating**	**Rating**	**Rating**	**Rating**
1.					
2.					
3.					
4.					
5.					

PRINCIPLE 3: MEDICATION ONLY MAKES SENSE AND MAY BE NECESSARY WHEN THAT SPECIFIC DRUG HAS BEEN SHOWN (OR PROVEN IN CLINICAL STUDIES) TO RELIEVE THE IDENTIFIED TARGET SYMPTOMS OF THE SPECIFIC PROBLEM

Once you make a diagnosis and create a specific target-symptom list, the medication that you choose should be known to make your diagnosis and set of day-to-day troubles better. If you use a drug to treat a problem that it isn't known to improve, it probably won't help—and it may even make matters worse.

Let me give you an example of what I mean here. Daniel came to me with panic attacks, a type of anxiety disorder. Although he had attacks about once or twice a week, which would come on abruptly and last about 15 minutes, he'd been prescribed an anti-anxiety medication that takes more than 30 minutes to begin to work and lasts for eight to ten hours. Since the drug wasn't acting quickly enough, he was getting worse over time. And since he was taking something that lasted longer than he needed, he felt drowsy and depressed for hours after swallowing each pill.

This medication *has* been found to be useful in GAD. In fact, it's what I prescribed for Jake (the anxious man with headaches). It worked well for him because he was anxious all the time. However, it was a very poor choice for Daniel, who needed medication that was quick to take effect and short term. He should have something that he could use whenever he began to feel a panic attack coming on. When I switched him to one of those fast, short-acting drugs—one that's been shown to be effective in treating the target symptoms of panic disorder—he improved immediately.

As you take charge of your emotional health, I want you to find out how any medication you're taking or considering is used to treat your diagnosis and target symptoms. Ask your treatment provider, "Has this been shown to help my type of problem?" Be sure you understand what you should expect from the prescription and that you know how to use it, because if you don't take it in the way it's been shown to be helpful, it won't work.

For example, Daniel needed to use the short-acting anti-anxiety drug I prescribed as soon as he began to feel anxious or sense that a panic attack could be coming on. This technique is what works to stop escalating worry. If the anxiety continued to increase for more than 20 minutes, he was to take a second pill. This step-by-step approach has been shown to interrupt the cycle.

Jake, on the other hand, was to take his long-acting medication every morning, afternoon, and evening. He needed to adjust the dose according to his level of anxiety at the time. This method works for GAD.

As you take charge of your emotional life, be sure you identify your diagnoses (if any), target symptoms, and the role medication can play in addressing your particular problem and day-to-day difficulties. Before we move on to the fourth principle, I encourage you to reflect on how the third one applies to your story.

If you're on medication or considering a particular drug, is it a suitable fit? Has it been shown to help your problem and its symptoms? Do you know how to take the drug in the proper way? Are you able to work with your treatment provider to answer these questions? If the answer to the last question is no, I urge you to find a suitable partner before going much further. In the Take-Charge program, you must always choose professional relationships that are good fits for you. You deserve to have what works, and you can find it!

PRINCIPLE 4: MEDICATION ONLY MAKES SENSE AND MAY BE NECESSARY WHEN THE RISKS OF AVOIDING IT OUTWEIGH THE RISKS OF TAKING IT

We can think about this principle as the risk-benefit consideration. Each drug has potential risks or side effects, as well as possible benefits or healing results. Think about Daniel with panic attacks and Jake with generalized anxiety disorder for a moment. The same long-acting anti-anxiety prescription had more risk than benefit for the former patient, but vice versa for the latter—in other words, Daniel got worse on it, while Jake got better.

Each illness, disorder, problem, and diagnosed condition poses a certain degree of risk to your life and well-being when untreated, and offers benefits if treated. For example, Christina's recurring episodes of major depression and ongoing suicidal thoughts meant that she was at high risk for death without treatment. Although she was reluctant to take an antidepressant, she tolerated it with few problems and experienced dramatic improvement.

Every medication that's available has been studied, and shown to offer some value in addressing some sort of problem, and every single drug has hundreds of possible side effects. Some people are extremely responsive to the benefits and experience few side effects, while others are quite sensitive and have more difficulty finding drugs that work without causing undue distress. No person is equally responsive to the ups and downs of all medicines, since every agent acts and is metabolized differently in the body. There's no way to predict your reaction, so finding the right drug to treat your anxiety, depression, or ADD will always involve some trial and error.

A particular medication may help you somewhat, but not enough. It may cause you to be less anxious or depressed—for example, taking your target symptoms from a level 10 to a level 5. This suboptimal response may be the result of an inadequate dose. If so, increasing the amount you're consuming will also up your benefit. Or it could be that you're experiencing a partial response to the maximum suggested dose, which isn't unusual.

We often need to switch drugs or include additional ones. Furthermore, most medications are only one piece of the treatment puzzle.

We routinely need to add other interventions to our Take-Charge programs, and we'll visit these complementary steps in subsequent chapters. In the meantime, let's summarize and take stock of where we are so far.

REVIEW YOUR STORY AND THE POSSIBILITY OF MEDICATION

By now, you know that taking medication is a mixed bag: It can help and harm. Your life can be transformed with pharmacological intervention, and this step might even be the door to your future! Adding a proper chemical adjustment to your system may be the first and most crucial action you'll take in this program, but how can you know what you ought to do? What are the risk-benefit issues related to medicine in your story?

I want you to begin to think about your problems, your diagnoses, and your level of distress. You, and only you, are inside your body, living your life day after day. You're the only one who really knows how much you struggle, what amount of pain you experience, and how hard it is for you to keep going. You know what your problems have cost you emotionally, physically, psychologically, financially, interpersonally, and spiritually. If you had to rate the severity of pain, difficulty, or loss you've experienced on a scale of 1 to 10, where 1 is minimal and 10 is too much to bear (or "I'd rather be dead"), how would you score your experience? By and large, the higher the number, the more likely it is that you need some chemical intervention, at least for a while.

Lots of us are reluctant to take psychotropic medications. We tell ourselves, as Christina did, that we ought to be able to manage without drugs. We see our need as a weakness, flaw, or laziness. But I know for sure, in the deepest recesses of my being, that no one wants to suffer or do a bad job. If you're overwhelmed with distress or pain, are unable to accomplish your goals, or have trouble participating in what usually matters to you, something is going on that you can't control. You may need medication. Perhaps it's time to work on acceptance of your need and openness to pharmacological management.

You might be concerned about the risks of serious side effects with drug treatment. While you may realize that intervention is necessary, you could also be scared or confused about how to evaluate the dangers. I want to teach you something that I do to minimize risk: I *never* use a *newer* medication to treat a problem when there are *older* available drugs that work *just as well.* Newer is not necessarily better—in fact, it's often worse. The longer a substance has been around, the more people will have taken it. Time gives us the opportunity to identify problems that might not have shown up in the smaller clinical trials or drug tests that are required to get the pill on the market. So if a drug is a necessary piece of your Take-Charge program, choose one that's been around for a while.

I want you to do something else that I do to minimize serious risk with medication: Monitor side effects regularly and frequently with all new prescriptions. Even the reports you may have heard about anti-depressants causing increased suicidal thoughts found that the side effect came on early and escalated in severity over time. In the clinical trials, where there was careful and frequent monitoring of the patients, no one who developed this problem took his or her life. As soon as the thoughts came, the medicine was stopped. The side effect resolved once the medication was discontinued.

In Step 3, you'll find a table that you can use to rate your degree of benefit and the severity of side effects with medication. I urge you to use this monitoring tool as you take charge of your emotional life. Risks can be scary, but you can do a lot to minimize them, and you may need medication. While you need to be cautious, I don't want you to hesitate to treat your difficulties. You deserve to heal!

The assessments you've just completed will help you avoid losing time to illness the way that a woman I recently spoke with did. Last night, Michelle called in to my weekly radio show. She'd just decided to begin medication treatment for bipolar disorder (or manic-depressive illness). She shared that she'd been given the diagnosis a long time beforehand, but hadn't wanted to take drugs. She had "done every-thing else": She left a job she didn't like, trained for a new career, and pursued lots of self-healing and care.

In spite of it all, she found herself so depressed that she was unable to work or attend exciting job interviews. She realized that she needed to start medication because she "had no choice." I congratulated her on her willingness to take this step. Drugs can do a lot to make manic-depressive illness better.

This disorder is associated with extreme episodes of depression and a high risk of suicide. While Michelle couldn't control her vulnerability to the problem, she was able do a lot to help herself live a full life! I was grateful for her call. She needed the support that I could give, and her story was helpful to many other listeners struggling with a similar dilemma.

Before we move on to look at how you can use medication to treat depression, anxiety, ADD, and nonspecific problems that fall outside of a diagnostic category, I'd like you to pause and recap what you've learned so far in Steps 1 and 2. Complete these sentences and the chart:

1. I've considered my story and its lessons. I've learned:

_____

_____

2. I've identified my problems or possible diagnoses. They are:

_____

_____

3. I've created my list of target symptoms. It includes:

_____

_____

4. I've taken time to rate the severity of my symptoms on a scale of 1 to 10. I'll fill in the chart on the next page to document my experience.

SYMPTOM	TODAY'S SCORE	WORST IT'S EVER BEEN	BEST IT'S EVER BEEN

5. When I begin to evaluate my need for medication and look at the severity of my *overall distress* on a scale of 1 to 10, where 1 is minimal and 10 is unbearable, I score a _____. This means that I may need to be open to my need for medication. **True** or **False** (circle the correct answer)

In the next step, I'll be teaching you how to use medication in your Take-Charge program, since you're probably wondering how it works, how you should take it, and when you should stop it. Let's take a look at that now.

STEP 3

Follow Treatment Guidelines When Medication Is Necessary

In Step 2 of your Take-Charge program, you considered your need for medication. Perhaps you decided that it's a crucial piece of your healing plan, or you think that it might help. In this step, you'll learn some guidelines to follow when taking medicine. They're found in the answers to the following questions:

1. *How do* medicines work for anxiety, depression, and ADD?

2. *How well* do drugs work for these problems?

3. *How much* is enough?

4. What about *side effects?*

5. How do I pick the *right one(s)?*

6. *How long* should I take a medicine?

7. What is involved in *starting and stopping?*

8. Could I need medication even if *I don't have a diagnosis?*

Let's take a look at the answers to these questions. For each one, I've included important guidelines for you to follow if a prescription is part of your Take-Charge program.

HOW DO MEDICATIONS WORK FOR ANXIETY, DEPRESSION, AND ADD?

The simple answer, and the most truthful one, is that we don't know. We have some pretty good ideas about how different drugs affect brain chemistry and neurotransmitter levels, and we think that some of these actions on nerve cells and chemicals in the brain lead to the benefits or improvement in symptoms that we see. But the human body is extremely complex, and we aren't very sophisticated in deciphering its many secrets.

That said, we do know some important things about how different pharmaceuticals work, and you need to learn some of that information to be your own best advocate! Here's a fundamental fact: *Different classes of medications work differently.* Some have a direct effect on the brain, while others are indirect. This concept explains how quickly a drug can begin to work, and how you'll need to use it.

A medication that has a direct effect binds or attaches itself to a receptor on a nerve cell and causes an immediate change by being there. Substances that work in this way cause a rapid (within minutes to hours) change in symptoms. To understand what I mean, think about alcohol for a moment. Like some other drugs, it has a direct effect on the nerve cells in the brain. So within 30 minutes of drinking some wine or beer, you might feel calmer, giddier, or more relaxed.

Another property of this type of drugs is that once they're metabolized, and thus removed from their receptor spots on the nerves, their benefit disappears and symptoms return. Think about wine or beer again: When you have a couple of drinks, you may feel calm or giddy for a while. But within an hour or two (the length of time depends on your rate of metabolism), you'll be back to your baseline or usual self. To feel different again, you'll need to have another drink or two.

What about drugs that have an indirect effect? These substances work by causing a series of things to happen. They, too, bind to receptors on the nerve cell. But unlike direct-effect medications, their presence begins a cascade of changes that ultimately shifts the neurochemical balance. Think of a superlong row of dominos, falling in *very slow* motion as each piece hits the one next to it. Eventually they all fall down, and the landscape shifts.

Indirect-effect drugs cause all sorts of cellular changes before their ultimate result is seen. They often alter the levels of chemical messengers that are being produced and released into the space between the nerve cells in the brain. These shifts in chemical balance are probably responsible for the improvement in symptoms, but it can take weeks to see this result.

So how does this lesson about direct- and indirect-effect drugs relate to the treatment of depression, anxiety, and ADD? Well, many of the medications used to treat anxiety problems, and almost all of the medications used to treat ADD, are direct-effect drugs. That means they work quickly but don't last long. To achieve a consistent benefit, you have to keep taking them.

By contrast, all the medications used to treat depression—some of which are also used to treat anxiety problems—are indirect drugs. That means they can take days or weeks to bring about a noticeable change, but the benefit isn't short-lived.

This difference in the mechanism of action in various drugs is very important. It explains why the antidepressant you were prescribed last week may not have changed your symptoms yet, whereas the Ativan or Valium you were prescribed to take the edge off your anxiety is working like a dream. This is also the reason why the Ritalin or Adderall prescribed for your ADD, which you take with breakfast each day, works well to improve your focus, concentration, and memory throughout the morning but does nothing for you at the dinner table if you forget your afternoon dose.

So the take-home message in answer to the first question, *How do medicines work?* is that some of them act directly and quickly but don't last that long. Others function indirectly by creating an ongoing shift in neurochemistry and take a while to improve symptoms. Their effect is more lasting.

Important guidelines: Once you've identified the diagnosis or reason that you need medication and have a prescription to address it, be sure you know the answers to these questions:

1. How quickly is the drug meant to work?

2. How often do I need to take it?

3. Do the time frame and mechanism of action fit with my need for relief?

If the answer to the third question is no, please request a different or additional prescription! You may need to take both a direct- and an indirect-effect drug together until the latter starts to work, or even indefinitely to cover a mix of symptoms. Your need depends on your story. Use your knowledge of yourself as you partner with your care provider to create your optimal and unique Take-Charge medication plan.

HOW WELL DO DRUGS WORK FOR ANXIETY, DEPRESSION, AND ADD?

This is a crucial question. Medications can be lifesavers for lots of people, but they aren't magic bullets. Even the best antidepressants, for example, don't work for everyone. Studies comparing them to placebos in individuals with clinical depression show that the real thing works only modestly better than a fake. Not everyone responds to medication, and some individuals respond to sugar pills when they think they're getting a drug!

Furthermore, even when patients respond, all of their symptoms may not go away completely. Often people get *somewhat* better. That said, 18 or 19 million Americans suffer from depression each year. If just 60 percent of them take medication and partially respond to it, that's more than 10 million who have changed for the better. And depression is one of the greatest causes of morbidity and mortality in the world, so a lot of lives would be transformed or saved. In fact, a huge study of 65,000 individuals that was published in *The American Journal of Psychiatry* in January 2006 found that treatment with antidepressant drugs did reduce the risk of suicide in depressed teenagers and adults. Just remember that this treatment option *can* be a lifesaver, but it's not a miracle cure. It's simply a piece of the puzzle.

The same goes for anxiety disorders: Medication is a godsend for many folks and somewhat helpful for others. Most sufferers get some benefit from short-acting medicines, but these are bad choices if your condition is ongoing and long lasting. You'll get rebound anxiety, or an increase in those feelings, when the drug wears off.

Many anxious people do well on what we call antidepressants. These are good choices for chronic, ongoing anxiety. In fact, there's really no good reason for the drugs to be linked only to depression. Although most were first created to treat mood problems, studies have shown them to help a lot of other troubles, too. For example, they're beneficial for obsessive-compulsive disorder (an anxiety condition), panic disorder, and social phobia.

What about medication for ADD? Well, again, popping a pill isn't the whole answer. The vast majority (over 90 percent) of sufferers will get *some* benefit from stimulants such as Ritalin and Dexedrine; occasionally other types of medication are helpful, too. While drugs don't eliminate all the symptoms, most patients can focus better and control their impulsivity more easily when they take something.

How does medication do in treating manic-depressive illness? Although bipolar disorder involves periods of depression, it's different from what we call unipolar depression. Because it's cyclical in nature, we often need to use several substances together and adjust them over time to treat this illness. While drugs don't prevent depression or mania, they surely decrease the severity and frequency of symptoms. Remember, this illness has a high risk for suicide. Many people suffering from it need to take a mood stabilizer such as lithium in addition to their antidepressant. While medicine isn't the whole story, it's usually critical.

So the take-home message in the answer to the second question: *How well do drugs work?* is "Pretty well." Medication can make a huge difference in the symptomatic relief of the mood and anxiety disorders and ADD. It can also decrease the frequency of episodes of mania and depression, although it isn't a panacea. Using this treatment option may make a huge or moderate difference in your life.

Important guidelines: Once you've identified your target symptoms, evaluate each drug and dose you try with the rating scale entitled "My Progress Including Drug, Dose, and Side Effects" that you'll find later in this chapter. If you don't see adequate improvement *on your rating scale* with the proper dose of medication over the appropriate period of time, you may need to try something else or to add another treatment to your plan. Talk to your care provider about your observations and experiences as you use your rating scale to take charge of your emotional life.

HOW MUCH MEDICATION IS ENOUGH?

This may seem like a silly answer, but the right dose is however much you need to feel better. By and large, your level of response will be dose dependent. In other words, the more you take, the greater the benefit you'll experience. But since all medicines have side effects and these are dose dependent, too, you don't want to overshoot your need. If you take more than necessary and feel too ill from side effects, you may not be able to continue using that medication. So you want to "start low and go slow." You'll progressively move the amount up until you see enough improvement without too much fallout.

Although there are recommended starting levels for all medications, these are only useful to a point. Each person has a unique sensitivity to each drug's benefits and set of side effects. Your profile is based on your genetics, biology, and metabolic processes, and there's a great deal of difference from one person to the next. There's no way to predict your response in advance, so finding your right dose will involve trial and error.

Years ago I was treating two tiny, depressed 95-pound women (who didn't know each other) at the same time. Both were taking Prozac when it was only available in a 20-mg capsule. One woman needed four pills or 80 mg a day to treat her depression, and she had no side effects. The other patient had dramatic side effects on a 20-mg dose, but actually needed only 2 mg a day to treat her illness. How could she get such a tiny amount? She'd open the capsule and dump out the granules. Then she'd lick her finger, dip it into the grains, and lick her finger again. She tolerated that amount well and felt she was back to being herself after several weeks.

So how much medication is enough? It all depends on your story. Think of my two tiny ladies: They were the same size, had the same diagnosis, and were taking the same medicine. But one needed 40 times as much Prozac as the other did for healing. It's all about your unique story and body chemistry.

Important guidelines: Once you've begun a medication trial, keep track of your dosage level as you evaluate your improvement in target symptoms. Use the expanded rating scale following the next question to evaluate your improvement and your level of side effects. As you work the Take-Charge program, share your rating scale with your treatment provider. This will help you and your doctor find your best drug and dose.

WHAT ABOUT SIDE EFFECTS?

Every single drug has side effects, but what does that really mean? Remember that each medication is designed to hit a target or decrease certain "target symptoms." But we haven't gotten sophisticated enough in our drug development to create agents that only affect the cells and symptoms we want to change. Therefore, whenever you take a pill—even an aspirin or Tylenol—it will travel throughout your body and touch billions of cells and many metabolic processes. It can cause many upsets as a result of its actions all over the body, and these unintended disturbances are what we call side effects.

If you look at any print advertisement for a drug or open the *Physicians' Desk Reference (PDR)* and look up any medicine, you'll see hundreds of possible side effects, risks, and cautions listed. In current times, this downside is inevitable, because we haven't gotten sophisticated enough to avoid it.

All medications have a bunch of common side effects and a myriad of not-so-common ones. Before you start taking anything, ask your doctor to review the former. Be sure you're comfortable with what you hear before starting the pill, and then keep track of your responses, both positive and negative. You may develop a common side effect, a rare one, or one that's never even been reported. Most of these tend to decrease in severity over time, so if you can tolerate them early on, try to hang in there with your plan. The problems will probably become less prominent.

So the answer to the question: *What about side effects?* is that they're unavoidable and sometimes problematic.

Important guidelines: Use the following rating scale to evaluate your symptom response and side-effect profile with various medication doses. Make as many copies of the chart as you need to document your ongoing experience. Use it to partner with your treatment provider in finding your best course of action as you take charge of your emotional life.

My Progress: Including Drug, Dose, and Side-Effects Rating Scale

Use a scale from 1 to 10, where **1 = Almost Never** and **10 = Always,** for target symptoms. List the side effects you experience in each week, and rate them on a scale of 1 to 10, where **1 = Very Mild** and **10 = Intolerable.**

	Date: / /	Date: / /	Date: / /	Date: / /	Date: / /
	Drug & dose	Drug & dose	Drug & dose	Drug & dose	Drug & dos
TARGET SYMPTOMS	Rating	Rating	Rating	Rating	Rating
1.					
2.					
3.					
4.					
5.					
SIDE EFFECTS	Rating	Rating	Rating	Rating	Rating
1.					
2.					
3.					
4.					
5.					

HOW DO I PICK THE RIGHT MEDICINE(S)?

Unfortunately, the answer to this question is similar to the others. Although we doctors have some idea of what to try, we aren't very advanced in this area.

Of course, whatever medication we choose must be one that's effective for your diagnosis. But there will probably be several drugs like that, so what guidelines do we use? Well, first and foremost is your past history. If you formerly responded well to something, there's a good chance that you'll respond to that agent again. By contrast, if you didn't respond positively to a particular medicine before, it's unlikely that you will now.

If your personal past doesn't help, family history sometimes does. You may do well on a drug that's helped a biological relative with similar problems, or do poorly on one that someone you're related to couldn't tolerate.

Many researchers and clinicians are trying to find ways to match symptoms to the best treatment option. Some of their techniques may ultimately be highly effective. But for now, the answer to the question: *How do I pick the right medicine?* is largely diagnosis, history, and hunch.

Important guidelines: Get as much historical data as you can to partner effectively with your doctor, and then vigorously evaluate your progress and problems with every intervention. You can take charge of finding your best fit here, and it's crucial that you do so.

HOW LONG SHOULD I TAKE A MEDICINE?

The duration of a prescription depends on the type, length, and severity of the problem you're being treated for. If you have a chronic or recurrent problem, it may make sense for you to remain on medication indefinitely. This is often the case for people with anxiety disorders, depression, bipolar disorder, and ADD. On the other hand, if you're experiencing a first-time episode of crippling anxiety and depression, then a six-month to one-year course may be appropriate for you.

In another scenario, if you've been prescribed medicine for a brief increase in some ongoing symptoms that are usually tolerable, it might make sense for you to take the drug for an even shorter time. That said, antidepressant medications are rarely meant to be used for less than six months. Remember that they're indirect-effect drugs. They take a while to work, and therefore they only make sense for challenges that are somewhat ongoing.

So the answer to the question: *How long should I take a medicine?* depends on the diagnosis, length, and severity of your problem.

Important guidelines: Be sure that your story and experience of trouble jibes with your treatment provider's recommendations. Your history dictates the type and length of interventions in your Take-Charge program.

WHAT'S INVOLVED IN STARTING AND STOPPING A MEDICATION?

Well, we've covered beginning treatment (start low, go slow) but not the stopping part. This is when you need to know about withdrawal syndromes and reemergence of symptoms.

Medicines that you take episodically (or as needed) for anxiety or sleep can usually be stopped without tapering off. This applies to pills that you don't take every few hours or every day. Similarly, stimulants for ADD can almost always be cut off at any point.

Most drugs that are regular and ongoing, however, shouldn't be stopped abruptly. You might have a withdrawal syndrome or a return of your symptoms if you don't go off slowly. *If it's time for you to try stopping a medication, work with your prescribing doctor to do so at an appropriate rate.* You may discover that you need the drug more than you realized, or that you have to cut your dose much more slowly than you had anticipated.

So the answer to the question, *What's involved in starting and stopping a medicine?* is that it depends on what drug you're taking, and what problem you're trying to treat. There's no one-size-fits-all solution to this process, but there is a perfectly right answer for you.

Important guideline: Include your doctor, and make sure your plan to stop medication fits your story and experience with the drug.

COULD I NEED MEDICATION EVEN IF I DON'T HAVE A DIAGNOSIS?

The answer is a qualified yes. Remember my story: I occasionally take a tiny dose of Valium when my system is too revved up to settle down and sleep. I don't meet diagnostic criteria for an anxiety disorder or anything else, but I do benefit from a pinch of periodic intervention. That could be the case for you, too. However, the answer to this question is a *qualified* yes, because before treating your symptom, you need to rule out a medical or psychiatric condition as its cause. Don't assume that you don't have one. Even when no diagnosis fits, you'll need to identify a specific set of target symptoms to guide your medication use. And of course, you must always evaluate your risk, benefit, and response.

Important guidelines: Make sure you know what symptoms you're treating with the drug. Monitor your need and response just as you would in treating a formal disorder. Just keep in mind that even if you lack a diagnosis, medication might still be a crucial piece of your Take-Charge program.

Congratulations! You've just completed Steps 1, 2, and 3, an intensive course in evaluating your need for medication and learning guidelines for its use. Although you aren't ready to be your own treatment provider, you're highly qualified to partner with your doctor in taking charge of your emotional life.

You've learned how to use four principles to assess your medication requirement. You now know how to include diagnoses, target symptoms, and risk-benefit concerns in finding the right path. You even understand a lot about how medicines work, how much is enough, how to start and stop drugs, and when it makes sense to include pharmacological interventions even if you don't have a diagnosis.

Before moving on to Step 4, please take a moment to respond to the statements on the next page either on the lines provided or on a separate piece of paper.

1. When I evaluated my need for medication with the four principles, I realized that:

    _____

    _____

    _____

2. When I review the eight questions and answers in Step 3, my take-home lessons and guidelines are:

    _____

    _____

    _____

You've just taken stock of where you are with diagnostic and pharmacological issues. Without further ado, let's move into Step 4 and see what you can add to your Take-Charge plan!

STEP 4

Include Complementary- and Alternative-Medicine Interventions

Welcome to Step 4 of your Take-Charge program, where you'll learn all about complementary and alternative medicine (CAM). Before I teach you what CAM is, why it matters, and how to use it, I need to give you some background. I want you to understand how these options came to be separated from mainstream medicine in the United States.

You see, our current health-care system, with its focus on disease, illness, and chemical intervention, is relatively new. Until the 19th century, natural, folk, and home remedies played a significant role in achieving and maintaining wellness. Herbs, plants, dietary restrictions, spiritual practices, and intuitive interventions were intrinsic to this model. Over the years, through trial and error, what worked became accepted practice. Lessons were passed from generation to generation, and healers carried that acquired wisdom forward. The care provider was felt to support the individual's innate capacity to recover. As far back as 400 B.C., Hippocrates said that the "natural forces within us are the true healers of disease." Hippocrates, Aristotle, and Galen (a classical Greek physician and writer) were all holistic. They saw the body, mind, and spirit as interrelated—or maybe even as one!

In the mid-1600s, the philosopher René Descartes began a movement to separate the soul-mind (which became the responsibility of the church or religion) and the body (which became the concern of science) from one another. He espoused an approach that viewed human bodies as resembling clocks. When a clock broke, you were to take out the broken piece and replace it. Then voilà—it was fixed! When a person became ill, you were to excise, replace, or treat the sick *piece,* and the patient would be healed. This reductionist view took hold fast.

As science began to advance, medical and surgical interventions became the cornerstones of Western medicine; natural, holistic, and folk practices began to take a backseat. Since many of those approaches had evolved by trial and error over countless generations, as opposed to being created by technological design, they were often discounted by scientists and the medical establishment. Their value hadn't been rigorously proven, so they couldn't possibly be of merit.

In spite of this devaluation, many native healers and practitioners of CAM persisted in their work, and a variety of new CAM providers began to emerge. But most schools of Western medicine ignored this growing movement. The lessons of these other approaches were left out of the routine training of doctors. As a result, mainstream physicians didn't learn how to deal with these other disciplines.

The growing divide between enduring, ancient wisdom and modern-day allopathic medicine gave birth to the confusion and discontent that many of us feel today. Eventually, this split led to the CAM movement. Lots of folks within the medical community and outside of it who saw value in the disregarded interventions began to demand attention, consideration, and study. As a result, the National Institutes of Health established the National Center for Complementary and Alternative Medicine (NCCAM). This center was created to explore complementary and alternative healing practices in the context of rigorous science, train CAM researchers, and disseminate authoritative information to the public and professionals.

The NCCAM has defined CAM and organized it into five major modalities. The following information comes from one of the center's publications, titled: "Get the Facts: What is Complementary and Alternative Medicine?" You can find the full text at **www.NCCAM.nih. gov/health/whatiscam**. I've added the *italicized* information to the text; you'll find definitions of many of the terms in the Glossary at the end of this book.

WHAT IS COMPLEMENTARY AND ALTERNATIVE MEDICINE?

Complementary and alternative medicine, as defined by NCCAM, is a group of diverse medical and health-care systems, practices, and products that aren't presently considered to be part of conventional medicine. While some scientific evidence exists regarding some CAM therapies, for most there are key questions that are yet to be answered through well-designed scientific studies—questions such as whether these therapies are safe and whether they work for the diseases or medical conditions for which they're used.

The list of what's considered to be CAM changes continually, as those therapies that are proven to be safe and effective are adopted into conventional health care and as new approaches emerge.

IS COMPLEMENTARY MEDICINE DIFFERENT FROM ALTERNATIVE MEDICINE?

Yes, the two are different.

- **Complementary** medicine is used **together with** conventional medicine. An example of complementary therapy is using aromatherapy to help lessen a patient's discomfort following surgery. *Other examples include using yoga with an antidepressant to treat depressive illness, adding regular singing to medication interventions for panic disorder, and cutting down on sweets while taking medication to decrease the symptoms of ADD.*

- **Alternative** medicine is used **in place of** conventional medicine. An example of alternative therapy is using a special diet to treat cancer instead of undergoing surgery, radiation, or chemotherapy that has been recommended by a conventional doctor. *Other examples include using SAM-e (a dietary supplement) to treat ADD and exercise to treat moderate depression.*

WHAT IS INTEGRATIVE MEDICINE?

Integrative medicine, as defined by NCCAM, combines mainstream medical therapies and CAM therapies for which there's some high-quality scientific evidence of safety and effectiveness. *This is what I do in my clinical practice, and what you're doing as you use the ten-step approach to create your personal Take-Charge program.*

WHAT ARE THE MAJOR TYPES OF COMPLEMENTARY AND ALTERNATIVE MEDICINE?

NCCAM classifies CAM therapies into five categories, or domains:

1. Alternative medical systems. These are built upon complete systems of theory and practice. Often, these systems have evolved apart from and earlier than the conventional-medical approach used in the United States. Examples of alternative medical systems that have developed in Western cultures include homeopathic and naturopathic medicine. Examples of systems that have developed in non-Western cultures include traditional Chinese medicine and Ayurveda.

2. Mind-body interventions. Mind-body medicine uses a variety of techniques designed to enhance the mind's capacity to affect bodily function and symptoms. Some techniques that were considered CAM in the past have become mainstream (for example, patient-support groups and cognitive-behavioral therapy). Other mind-body techniques are still considered CAM, including meditation; prayer; mental healing; and therapies that use creative outlets such as art, music, or dance.

3. Biologically based therapies. These use substances found in nature, such as herbs, foods, and vitamins. Some examples include dietary supplements, herbal products, and the use of other so-called natural but as yet scientifically unproven therapies (for example, using shark cartilage to treat cancer). *Other examples include using SAM-e, vitamin B$_{12}$, folate, and omega-3 fatty acids in the treatment of depression; using Chinese herbs to regulate hormonal imbalances that affect mood; and decreasing carbohydrate consumption while increasing protein intake to regulate both mood and attentional symptoms.*

4. Manipulative and body-based methods. These are based on physical manipulation and/or movement of one or more parts of the body. Some examples include chiropractic or osteopathic manipulation and massage.

5. Energy therapies. These involve the use of energy fields. They're of two types:

— **Biofield therapies** are intended to affect energy fields that purportedly surround and penetrate the human body. The existence of such fields hasn't yet been scientifically proven. Some forms of energy therapy manipulate biofields by applying pressure and/or moving the body by placing the hands in, or through, these fields. Examples include qi gong, Reiki, and therapeutic touch.

— **Bioelectromagnetic-based therapies** involve the unconventional use of electromagnetic fields, such as pulsed fields, magnetic fields, or alternating-current or direct-current fields.

SOURCES OF NCCAM INFORMATION

NCCAM Clearinghouse
Toll-free in the U.S.: 1-888-644-6226
International: 301-519-3153

TTY (for hearing-impaired callers): 1-866-464-3615
E-mail: **info@nccam.nih.gov**
Website: **nccam.nih.gov**
Address: NCCAM Clearinghouse, P.O. Box 7923, Gaithersburg, MD,
  20898-7923
Fax: 1-866-464-3616
Fax-on-Demand service: 1-888-644-6226

The clearinghouse provides information on CAM and on NCCAM. Services include fact sheets, other publications, and the ability to search federal databases of scientific and medical literature. It doesn't provide medical advice, treatment recommendations, or referrals to practitioners.

Congratulations! You now know more about CAM than most people. Before moving on, use the following space (or a separate piece of paper) to record your CAM experiences, listing all the interventions you've used to date. Which ones have worked or caused you problems? Do any still serve you well?

_____

_____

_____

_____

_____

Now think about how CAM came to be split off from current-day Western medical practice. Does this division between modalities disturb you as much as it does me? When I was a medical student at the University of Pennsylvania, I was so troubled by the limitations of the model I was learning that I took outside courses in massage therapy and Chinese medicine. I needed to balance the Western approach with one that focused on the whole person; the intrinsic capacity to heal; the wonder of wellness; and the power of faith, energy, and touch to make a difference. I always try to combine the lessons of ancient wisdom with the science of modern medicine, because I believe all disciplines contain offerings that can enhance our lives and our work. Do you agree?

Before examining the specific modalities that will be the focus of Step 4, let's look at the frequency of CAM use in the United States. As you consider the statistics, you may be struck by the number of people who actively include these options in their lives. Many of us are looking for more integration! The most used intervention is prayer, and since spirituality and prayer are so crucial to healing, I've devoted a whole chapter to them. This will be your focus in Step 10.

The information on the next page comes from a report titled "The Use of Complementary and Alternative Medicine in the United States" (reviewed July 2004, updated September 2004). The survey was completed by 31,044 adults in the U.S. The full text can be found at **www. nccam.nih.gov**. (I added the italicized comments.)

Respondents answered questions on various types of CAM therapies commonly used in the United States. These included provider-based therapies, such as acupuncture and chiropractic, and other therapies that don't require a provider, such as natural products, special diets, and megavitamin therapy. The number of interventions included was quite significant. How many of them are familiar to you?

CAM THERAPIES INCLUDED IN THE 2002 NATIONAL HEALTH INTERVIEW SURVEY (NHIS) *AN ASTERISK (*) INDICATES A PRACTITIONER-BASED THERAPY.*	
Acupuncture*	Massage*
Ayurveda*	Meditation
Biofeedback*	Megavitamin therapy
Chelation therapy*	Natural products
Chiropractic care*	(nonvitamin and nonmineral, such
Deep-breathing exercises	as herbs and other products from
Diet-based therapies	plants, enzymes, etc.)
Vegetarian diet	Naturopathy*
Macrobiotic diet	Prayer for health reasons
Atkins diet	Prayed for own health
Pritikin diet	Others ever prayed for your health
Ornish diet	Participate in prayer group
Zone diet	Healing ritual for self
Energy healing therapy*	Progressive relaxation
Folk medicine*	Qi gong
Guided imagery	Reiki*
Homeopathic treatment	Tai chi
Hypnosis*	Yoga

— **How many people use CAM.** In the United States, 36% of adults are using some form of CAM. When megavitamin therapy and prayer specifically for health reasons are included, that number rises to 62%.

While the NHIS did not include questions on spending, a 1997 survey found that the American public spent $36 billion to $47 billion on CAM, and these numbers have continued to rise. Of this amount, between $12 billion and $20 billion was paid out of pocket for the services of professional CAM health-care providers. This is more money than people paid from their own funds for all hospitalizations in 1997, and about half the amount of all noncovered physician services. Five billion dollars of out-of-pocket spending was on herbal products.

— **CAM domains used the most.** When prayer is included in the definition of CAM, the domain of mind-body medicine is the most commonly used (53%). Excluding prayer, biologically based therapies (22%) are more popular than mind-body medicine (17%).

— **CAM therapies used the most.** Prayer specifically for health reasons was the most common. The majority of people who use these therapies do so to treat themselves, as only about 12% of the survey respondents sought care from a licensed CAM practitioner. The ten most common choices were:

1.   Prayer for oneself: 43.0%
2.   Prayer for oneself by others: 24.4%
3.   Natural products: 18.9%
4.   Deep-breathing exercises: 11.6%
5.   Prayer in groups for oneself : 9.6%
6.   Meditation: 7.6%
7.   Chiropractic care: 7.5%
8.   Yoga: 5.1%
9.   Massage: 5%
10. Diet-based therapies: 3.5%

— **Health conditions prompting CAM use.** In the U.S., people are most likely to use these methods for back, neck, head, or joint aches, or other painful conditions; colds; anxiety or depression; gastrointestinal disorders; or sleeping problems.

— **Reasons for using CAM.** When people were asked to select from five reasons to describe why they used CAM, results were as follows (respondents could select more than one reason):

- 55 percent felt that it would improve health when used in combination with conventional medical treatments.

- 50 percent said it would be interesting to try.

The survey found that most people use CAM along with conventional medicine rather than in place of it.

INTEGRATING CAM INTO YOUR TAKE-CHARGE PROGRAM

Now that you know what CAM is and how widely it's used, you're ready to dive into examining its place in your Take-Charge program. Like most people, you probably believe that combining CAM with conventional medicine can help you—I sure do. So how should you include these interventions in your life?

The reach and depth of CAM is huge. We can't possibly cover all the domains and specific modalities in just one chapter. Since there are many entire texts devoted to alternative medical systems such as Chinese medicine (for example, *Between Heaven and Earth,* by Harriet Beinfield and Efrem Korngold) and Ayurveda (as in Deepak Chopra's work), we won't focus on that domain except to look at yoga. Keep in mind that alternative medical systems have a great deal to offer. You might find through your own research that one of these approaches speaks to you and offers interventions that work. I encourage you to explore what calls out to you.

Similarly, we won't be studying the energy therapies, but for a different reason. These approaches are among the most controversial of CAM practices because we haven't yet been able to demonstrate the presence or effect of energy fields. Remember, however, that this lack of "proof" doesn't tell us anything about the value of the domain. Energy healing has been a part of almost all societies and religions for thousands of years. For example, Chinese medicine is organized around the life-force energy it calls *chi* (pronounced "chee"). Asian Indians focus on *prana,* and the Judeo-Christian traditions value the energy described as halos around powerful people.

In spite of the controversy, these methods are growing in popularity and are actively being studied in medical centers around the country. The 2002 survey found that 4.6 percent of participants had used some form of healing ritual, 1 percent had used Reiki, and 0.5 percent had used qi gong. In the integrative medicine program at the University of Arizona School of Medicine where I teach, my Chinese medicine colleagues often recommend qi gong to our clinic patients. So if one of the energy interventions appeals to you, I encourage you to explore it; perhaps you'll find some healing there.

In the rest of this chapter you'll consider the role that some specific CAM interventions could play in your Take-Charge program. The modalities you'll examine are:

- Music

- Yoga

- Biologically based therapies: Saint-John's-wort, SAM-e, vitamins, omega-3 fatty acids, and nutritional interventions

- Exercise

- Guided imagery, meditation, and other relaxation techniques

- Massage

- Light therapy

I've chosen these representative CAM interventions because they're reasonably well understood and easy to implement. The list isn't meant to be exhaustive, but rather to expose you to some options, so don't allow yourself to be confined by the limits of this particular selection. Consider each intervention, but as you do so, keep thinking about how to create the best and broadest Take-Charge plan for your needs. (As I mentioned earlier, you'll examine prayer and spiritual practices in Step 10.)

MUSIC

Music plays a crucial role in every culture and in most spiritual traditions. It's deeply healing. In fact, chanting and drumming have been among the major tools of practitioners such as shamans for thousands of years. Recent studies have shown that music affects immune function, pain thresholds, cognitive function, blood pressure, and levels of anxiety and depression. In *Molecules of Emotion,* Candace Pert describes how music and meditation bring about their healing benefits. These practices actually activate the natural feel-good chemicals in the brain, called "endorphins"!

There are many ways for you to include this modality in your Take-Charge plan. You can turn on your CD player or radio and listen to calming pieces to help you settle your nervous system. Choose energetic and lively ones when you're feeling down or blue and need a boost, and turn on background music for better focus. This last technique helps many ADD sufferers concentrate better.

You can also create the sounds yourself by playing an instrument or singing. While all forms of music can be healing, playing a wind instrument or using your voice is especially helpful if you're hoping to calm an agitated state. These activities force you to breathe slowly and deeply and to relax your chest muscles. This process settles your nervous system in the same way that breathing into a paper bag interrupts a panic attack.

You can even whistle! In the musical *The King and I,* the heroine, Anna, whistles a happy tune whenever she feels afraid. In trying to fool those around her by presenting a calm and in-control demeanor, she settles her nervous system so much that her fear actually disappears.

When I do workshops, I often have the group sing with me. In this way, we step out of the thinking mode and into the doing-being mode together. As a beautiful melody fills the room, participants often rediscover how crucial music has been to their wellness. The exercise teaches them to include this art form in their Take-Charge plans.

I sing in a choir. No matter how lousy I feel when I head to practice, I always feel better on the way home. This recurring experience has taught me how much I need to sing for my mental well-being.

There's actually a whole field of music therapy. Practice guidelines have been established by the American Music Therapy Association (AMTA). You can find more information here:

- American Music Therapy Association: **www.musictherapy.org**

- The International Arts-Medicine Association: **www.members.aol.com/iamaorg**

- The Society for the Arts in Healthcare: **www.thesah.org**

Each of us is unique, so we each heal differently. Consider how music might fit into *your* Take-Charge plan. Think about what kind of tunes you like and how you feel when you hear, play, or sing them. What about the sound gives you pleasure? Write your reflections below.

_____

_____

_____

_____

Perhaps you realize that music should be included in your plan, and you may have committed to a regular practice. If so, bravo! If not, don't worry; it may not be your thing.

Let's move on to consider the role of yoga in healing.

YOGA

Yoga practice is on the upswing in the Western world today. Teachers, practices, and options abound for including it in your life. You can find classes in studios, retreat centers, online, and at your local gym; aspects of this discipline have even been combined with aerobic exercise in some popular courses.

But what *is* yoga, and how might you want to use it in your Take-Charge plan? Well, it was developed and has been practiced in India for thousands of years. The name means "union with the divine," and it's based on the philosophy that we create our experiences by the decisions we make in life. It sees the self as a "seed," or piece of the divine with infinite potential, and encourages personal development as the path to peace and self-actualization. The philosophy focuses on acceptance, self-observation without judgment, compassion, connecting with oneness, and deep centering.

This ancient system uses breathing exercises, posture, stretches, and meditation to balance the body's energy centers. There are many forms of practice, and you may find that a particular one appeals to you. Yoga has been used in combination with other treatments for depression, anxiety, and stress for years.

Sudarshan Kriya

A particular type of yogic breathing called Sudarshan Kriya (SKY) has been studied and shown to relieve depression, anxiety, stress, and post-traumatic stress disorder (PTSD). While it's a very powerful healing technique, it can also exacerbate mania. Please don't use it if you are a rapid cycler or have bipolar disorder. It can also lead to a drop in blood levels of lithium, so if you're taking this medication, you shouldn't use it either. If you're bipolar but stable on medications other than lithium, yogic breathing might be an option for you, but please check with your doctor to be sure it's safe for you to experiment before attempting to use this tool.

So what is yogic breathing anyway? SKY consists of a specific sequence and order of breathing patterns designed to calm the nervous system, promote attention, and increase the sensation of pleasure. I first learned about SKY at a course I attended at the annual meeting of the American Psychiatric Association in May 2004. Richard Brown, M.D., and Patricia Gerbarg, M.D., who have written extensively about SKY, taught the course. (See "Complementary and Alternative Treatments in Psychiatry" that Brown, Gerbarg, and Muskin wrote for the book *Psychiatry*, 2nd edition.)

If you're interested, you can learn how to practice SKY through the Art of Living Foundation. This nonprofit organization is affiliated with the United Nations and teaches SKY techniques in over 100 countries. In fact, volunteers offered free courses to hundreds of traumatized and grieving New Yorkers after the terrorist attacks of September 11, 2001. For course information, visit **www.artofliving.org**. You may even discover a yoga instructor in your community who can teach you this technique.

Evaluating Yoga

You'll find many books, CDs, and other resources to help you decide whether to include yoga of some kind in your Take-Charge plan. But, before you buy a lot of materials, I suggest that you check out a few classes. See if the practice appeals to you. It may, or it may not. For example, while I deeply resonate with music, I don't with yoga. I've tried a number of classes over the years, and although I enjoyed them,

I haven't felt drawn in enough to begin a regular practice. But my story may not be yours, so check it out and see. Lots of people love it!

At this point, pause and consider whether to include yoga in *your* Take-Charge plan. Think about your experiences, if any, with the practice. Do you enjoy it? Do you wish to learn more about its potential benefits? Might you want to find a class, teacher, or retreat? Use the space below (or a separate piece of paper) to record your thoughts.

_____

_____

_____

_____

Perhaps you realize that yoga belongs in your Take-Charge plan, or maybe you want to learn more about it. If so, terrific! If not, that's fine too; it may not be your thing.

Let's move on to consider the role of nutritional and biologically based therapies, including SAM-e, Saint-John's-wort, vitamins, and omega-3 fatty acids.

NUTRITIONAL ADJUSTMENTS

We're obsessed with food, diets, and the ideal way to eat for optimal health and weight loss. There are countless books on this subject, and the diet industry thrives in our culture.

While we can't possibly cover all that's known about nutrition and mental well-being, let's review a couple of crucial points. First, anxiety and ADD are made worse by excessive caffeine consumption, and depression is often exacerbated by alcohol intake. Please examine your use of these substances in relation to your struggles.

Second, ADD, mood, and anxiety symptoms are exacerbated when our diets are loaded with carbohydrates and deficient in protein. For detailed guidance on how to adjust your diet for optimal health, I recommend Christiane Northrup's book *The Wisdom of Menopause,* and Daniel Amen's books *Healing ADD* and *Healing Anxiety and Depression* (with Lisa Routh). Dr. Northrup, for example, recommends a diet composed of 40% protein, 35% low-glycemic-index carbs, and 25% fat for optimal mood balance in women during the perimenopausal and menopausal years. I've had great results following this regimen.

I recommend that you begin to keep track of the relationship between your food choices and your symptoms. Some minor adjustments in your meal and snack choices can make a major difference to your well-being.

BIOLOGICALLY BASED THERAPIES

I've chosen to include some biologically based therapies in your Step 4 exploration because there's growing interest in using nutritional and dietary supplements for wellness. In fact, U.S. sales of these products in 2002 were $18.7 billion, with herbal/botanical supplements accounting for $4.3 billion. We're anxious to take substances that we think of as natural, healing, and less dangerous than prescription medications. But we need to be aware of what we assume will work, and the risks we may tend to minimize. That said, several nutritional adjustments and supplements have been shown to make a difference in mental well-being.

SAINT-JOHN'S-WORT

This herb (*Hypericum performatum* in Latin) has been used for centuries for medicinal purposes, including the treatment of depression. (See the NCCAM for the fact sheet on Saint-John's-wort that's excerpted here.)

Here are some key points about it:

- The composition of Saint-John's-wort and how it might work aren't well understood.

- There is some scientific evidence that the herb is useful for treating mild to moderate depression. However, recent studies suggest that it's of no benefit in treating major depression of moderate severity. More research is required to help us know whether it has value in treating other forms of depression.

- Saint-John's-wort interacts with certain drugs, and these interactions can be dangerous.

- It's important to inform all your health-care providers about any therapy that you're currently using or considering, including any dietary supplements. This is to help ensure a safe and coordinated course of care.

If you'd like to try Saint-John's-wort, please be sure to discuss it with your doctor. This herb can interfere with some heart and cancer medications, decrease the effectiveness of birth-control pills, and be occasionally toxic when used together with some prescription anti-depressants. That said, it's been used successfully in Europe for many years and could be a good choice for you.

SAM-e

SAM-e was discovered in 1952 and has been widely used in Europe for the treatment of depression, arthritis, and liver disease. It's an essential molecule in all living cells in the human body. We get about one-third of the amount our bodies need from our diets, and our livers produce a lot as well. But some people may be deficient in SAM-e and need supplementation; you could be one of them. This substance was approved by the FDA as a nutraceutical in 1998. You can purchase it over the counter without a prescription.

SAM-e has been shown to be an effective antidepressant by itself. In fact, some people respond to it who haven't done well with prescription medication. It's also been found to be useful in increasing some patients' responses to prescription antidepressants when taken in combination with them. I occasionally add SAM-e to such a drug when I've gotten a partial response and can't go up on the medication dose.

This supplement should always be taken with B_{12} and folate, since these vitamins are necessary for it to be effective. These can also be bought over the counter.

SAM-e is less dangerous than Saint-John's-wort in terms of drug interactions, but it shouldn't be used by bipolar individuals because it can cause mania. For more information, visit:

- NCCAM Clearinghouse: **www.nccam.nih.gov**
- CAM on PubMed: **www.nlm.nih.gov/nccam/camon pubmed.html**
- Office of Dietary Supplements (ODS), National Institutes of Health (NIH): **www.ods.od.nih.gov**

B_{12} AND FOLATE

You may be taking these vitamins already, but it's worth knowing that they can help your mood substantially. Folate brightens your outlook when used alone, can improve antidepressant response, and may increase your response to SAM-e. The usual dose is 800 mcg to 5 mg a day.

Vitamin B_{12} can improve mood and enhance energy when used alone. It may also increase the antidepressant response of SAM-e.

If you're struggling with mood issues, you might want to try adding these two supplements to your Take-Charge program. They're well tolerated and can make a big difference.

OMEGA-3 FATTY ACIDS

We're hearing a lot of talk about the health benefits of omega-3 fatty acids or fish oil found in cold-water fish such as salmon and tuna. Supplementation is effective in treating depression in people whose diets are deficient in this oil, but we don't know whether taking a pill is enough by itself. Antidepressants may also be necessary.

I sometimes encourage people on antidepressants to add fish oil to their Take-Charge programs to get a further boost in mood. A 1,000 mg capsule containing the two fatty acids eicosapentaenoic acid (EPA) and docosahexaenoic acid (DHA) is a good dose. Be careful not to take more than 2,000 mg a day from supplements in order to avoid problems with excess bleeding.

For a free software download that contains information about the omega-3 fatty acid content of foods visit: **http://efaeducation.nih. gov/sig/kim.html**.

Having looked at a smattering of biologically based therapies, I'd like you to pause and consider what role these agents might play in *your* Take-Charge plan. Write your thoughts below, or on a separate piece of paper.

_____

_____

_____

_____

Perhaps you've decided to include or abandon the use of an herb or supplement, or maybe you have no interest in including biological interventions at all. Whatever feels right for you is fine.

EXERCISE

We all know that exercise is good for our general health. It helps with weight control, blood-pressure reduction, and keeping our hearts healthy. You may also recognize that regular movement improves your mood, reduces your stress level, and helps you focus. The importance of physical activity for a sound body, mind, and spirit has been recognized for countless generations, and was a cornerstone of ancient Greek culture. Their wisdom has been passed forward and continues to be manifest in the universal appeal of the Olympic Games.

I've been personally aided at times of great stress and depression by intense aerobic exercise of 30 minutes' duration, five days a week. My patients have routinely and consistently had similar experiences. Additionally, ADD sufferers I've treated experience improvement in their ability to focus and control their impulses on their regular workout days.

Recently, a series of studies has even shown that exercise has an "antidepressant" effect. In other words, regular intensive aerobic activity has been found to reduce the symptoms of *moderate* depression, *just as well as antidepressant medication,* in some people. Of course, many depressed individuals can't motivate themselves enough to exercise regularly, and some who can may still need to employ additional tools and interventions. But the take-home message is that whether you use medicine or not, routine physical activity can make a huge difference to your mental well-being.

What role might exercise play in your Take-Charge program? Think about your experiences getting your body moving. Have you played sports, walked, run, or taken exercise classes? What else have you done? How have you felt after aerobic activity? Make a note of your reflections below or on a separate piece of paper.

_____

_____

_____

_____

Unlike the other CAM interventions, which may or may not be for you, I urge you to include exercise in your Take-Charge plan. If it isn't yet part of your routine, start something. If it is, do you need to make it more regular or increase the intensity of your workouts? Check with your doctor to be sure that you can include this option, and then go easy at first, but don't avoid activity! Exercise is a powerful tool for taking charge of your emotional life.

RELAXATION TECHNIQUES AND GUIDED IMAGERY

Relaxation techniques and guided-imagery exercises are phenomenally effective in stopping anxiety because they sidestep the logical and analytic centers of the brain. In other words, these tools avoid the area that's involved in spiraling your worries out of control. Instead, they affect the sensory, emotion-based channels and bring about a direct and powerful calming response. These techniques also improve mood and decrease the amount of medication some people need to control their ADD symptoms.

You might want to pick up my *Stop Anxiety Now Kit* (available June 2007 from Hay House), which includes a guidebook and CD that teaches you how to use three of these self-soothing techniques:

1. Meditative relaxation
2. Progressive muscle relaxation
3. Guided imagery

Whether you use the kit or some other tool, I suggest you try all of these approaches. You may discover that one of them is especially appealing to you. Regularly use the one that suits you best.

MEDITATIVE RELAXATION RESPONSE

You've probably heard of Transcendental Meditation (TM) and may even have experience using it. It's one of the many techniques that brings forth the relaxation response; and it uses a specific, secret mantra. However, Herbert Benson, M.D., of The Mind/Body Medical Institute, has found a similar benefit when any sound, phrase, prayer, or mantra is paired with a quiet environment, a mental device, a passive attitude, and a comfortable position. When you meditate, you'll achieve calmness and relaxation by suspending the stream of thoughts that usually fill your mind. The process reduces stress and elevates your mood. While this is a wonderful option, please explore any meditative practices that appeal to you.

PROGRESSIVE MUSCLE RELAXATION

This technique involves a focused relaxation of all the muscle groups of your body. I usually start with the left hand, moving up the arm, across the shoulders to the head and neck, down the right arm, through the trunk, into the left thigh, down to the left toes, then on to the right thigh, and down to the right toes. I personally find progressive contraction and then relaxation of each muscle group to be the most effective way to promote tension release. I also find that it's best to work each muscle group two times.

There are many ways to relax your muscles in a progressive fashion. You can talk yourself through this exercise, or you can find a series of CDs that appeal to you. Once you discover something you like, use it regularly for a while and see what happens.

GUIDED IMAGERY

Guided imagery is a deliberate, focused sort of daydreaming: It uses words, music, and phrases to engage the imagination in creating a state of deep receptivity, calm, and inner peace. This technique is particularly beneficial for settling the nervous system and calming anxiety. Like meditative practices, it focuses attention and calms the mind, but it also works on the emotional part of the brain and skips over a lot of the talking and thinking areas.

Most people find guided imagery easier than meditation because it requires less focus and discipline. And because of the multisensory nature of the tool, they find it less difficult to hold their attention and absorb the images. While there's a lot of guidance available in tools, there's also plenty of space for finding yourself in the experience; it's a phenomenal balance.

Guided imagery has been found to increase levels of serotonin in the bloodstream—in other words, it works like an antianxiety or antidepressant medication, affecting the same chemical messengers that medicines such as Prozac, Paxil, and Luvox do. Guided imagery can be beneficial by itself, or it can be added to medication management for an increased effect.

While my *Stop Anxiety Now Kit* (available June 2007 from Hay House) contains a guided-imagery CD, there are many others on the market, and you'd do well to experiment with them. (I especially like the ones created by Belleruth Naparstek.) I suggest that you use such a tool daily for *at least* several months. You'll find that your ability to enter the experience increases exponentially over time, and the calming effect lasts for many hours after each use. Many people love this technique because it's an extremely effective tool to stop anxiety and improve mood.

For additional resources, visit:

- Academy for Guided Imagery: **www.academyforguided imagery.com**
- Health Journeys: **www.healthjourneys.com**
- The Healing Mind: **www.thehealingmind.org**

Please pause now to reflect on the role relaxation techniques and guided imagery might play in your Take-Charge program. What has your experience been with this realm of healing? What have you tried, and what has helped? Is this all new to you? What about it do you find appealing? Make notes of your reactions below or on a separate piece of paper.

_____

_____

_____

_____

You may have decided to explore or include a relaxation technique in your plan, or perhaps you're turned off by this realm right now—no matter. Whatever works for you is best for you.

MASSAGE

Massage has a long history. It was first written about in 2000 B.C. and is mentioned in ancient Egyptian, Persian, and Japanese texts. Hippocrates described its medical benefits, and the earliest Olympic athletes were treated with massage techniques prior to competitions.

According to the Centers for Disease Control's Advance Data publication number 343, May 2004, massage therapy involves pressing, rubbing and otherwise manipulating muscles and other soft tissues of the body. This causes them to relax, lengthen, and allow increased blood flow to the area. Using their hands, elbows, and feet, massage therapists may employ over 75 different methods—such as Swedish, deep-tissue, and neuromuscular massage and manual lymph drainage—to promote relief and healing.

This intervention has been used for symptomatic relief of anxiety, stress, depression, and ADD. *Massage Therapy Journal* did a wonderful piece titled "Massage Strategies for Depressed Patients" in the Fall 2003 issue. Dean Ornish also provides lots of examples of the healing power of massage in his book *Love & Survival.*

While I've never considered massage to be the whole answer to a psychiatric challenge, I do find that it routinely benefits my patients. Beyond diminishing anxiety and depressive symptoms, it provides a safe place to experience challenging emotions. You may recall that I mentioned studying massage therapy while in medical school. I love what it adds to the healing equation, and I'm driven to bridge the gap between Western medicine and these techniques. Today, I even write a regular column for *Massage Therapy Journal!*

Without knowing much about its benefits, many of us still feel drawn to this intervention. We might even say: "Wow, I really need a massage!" The soothing nature of the experience calms and heals our revved up systems. In fact, it's the most requested service in day spas!

For more information, visit:

- American Massage Therapy Association (AMTA): **www.amtamassage.org**

- Massage Magazine: **www.massagemag.com**

- National Certification Board for Therapeutic Massage and Bodywork (NCBTMB): **www.ncbtmb.com**

- Touch Research Institutes (TRI): **www.miami. edu/touch-research**

Take a few moments to reflect on the role massage might play in your Take-Charge program. What's your experience with it to date? Would you like to experiment with this ancient practice? Use the space on the next page (or a separate piece of paper) to record your thoughts.

_____

_____

_____

_____

You may have decided to get your first massage, add regular treatments to your schedule, or avoid this option all together. Whatever speaks to you is what you're meant to do.

LIGHT THERAPY

Do you feel better on a bright sunny morning or a cloudy, rainy one? Does the length of the day affect your mood? Are you more chipper in the summer than in the winter? Sunlight affects most people in powerful ways.

Many individuals who suffer from depression and bipolar disorder experience a seasonal variation in the severity of their problems. Perhaps you've heard of something called seasonal affective (*affect* means "mood") disorder or SAD. People with this condition usually experience either the onset of their depressions (or a worsening in the severity of their ongoing problem), in the fall and winter months, when the hours of daylight decrease and the strength of the sun's rays diminishes. Many of these folks get better if they sit in front of a bright light box every day; this is called "light therapy."

Recently, a study done in Denmark (*Acta Psychiatrica Scandinavica,* Aug. 2005, Klaus Martiny, M.D., Ph.D.) found that people with depressions *not of a seasonal variety* who were on antidepressant medication improved within one week when daily exposure to bright-white light of 10,000 lux was added to their treatment plan. The control group, who were on medication without bright light, didn't improve at the same rate. In addition, the benefit of light exposure wasn't confined to the winter months. Although the study was small and leaves a lot of questions unanswered, it highlights the importance of light in wellness.

Think back to your childhood. Do you remember your parents or teachers saying, "Go outside and play! It's a beautiful day. You shouldn't be indoors." That folk wisdom—that being in nature is healing—has been passed from generation to generation.

While you may not need a light box in your life, you probably do need more time outdoors and more sun exposure (with sunscreen) than you currently get. Our spirits lift when we spend time in Mother Nature's playground.

I've always noticed that my moods are impacted by the weather. Having lived in the Northeast for most of my life, I was routinely more down in the dark times and up in lighter ones. My experience of mood and weather is common.

Just listen to the word choices of our language: We describe depressed periods as being dark, blue, or black and upbeat ones as bright spots. I now live in Tucson, Arizona, where it's bright and sunny almost all the time. Whenever I feel down, spending a half hour in the sun lifts my spirits. In order to prevent the down times from coming on at all, I try to enjoy time outdoors every day.

Take some time to think about your sunlight or light-box exposure. Do you get enough? What role might this option play in your Take-Charge program? Record your thoughts below or on a separate piece of paper.

For more information on light therapy, visit:

- The Cleveland Clinic Health Information Center: **http://www.clevelandclinic.org/health/health-info/docs/1400/1484.asp?index=6412**

- Columbia University: **http://www.columbia.edu/~mt12/blt.htm**

- The Mayo Clinic: **http://www.mayoclinic.com/health/seasonal-affective-disorder/MH00023**

Congratulations! You've now completed Step 4 of your Take-Charge course. As you create your own program from the steps we're covering, think synergistically. For example, might you want to meditate, exercise, or even sing outdoors in the sunlight? Would you do well to have a medical assessment, increase your medication dose, and begin a yoga practice?

Moving on, do you need to examine your life choices to see if some of your problems are the result of a poor fit between your nature and what you are trying to accomplish? In Step 5, you'll look at that "round-peg-in-a-square-hole" question and learn how healing is about honoring your gifts and respecting your limitations. Let's move into that area now!

STEP 5

Make Life Choices
That Fit Your Nature

Welcome to Step 5! I hope you're as excited as I am to be beginning this step. Here's where we get to start having fun together. From now on you'll be working in ways that are designed to access and nurture your core self. What could be more joyful than discovering and developing the wonder of you?

In Steps 1 through 4, you addressed the diagnostic and intervention issues necessary for building a healthy foundation for your Take-Charge structure. If you'd skipped or brushed past those chapters, the subsequent lessons of Steps 5 through 10 wouldn't work. You see, trying to access your inner wisdom, intrinsic capacity to heal, and ability to connect when you have an undiagnosed or untreated disorder is like constructing a building without a foundation. You can't really get anywhere, no matter how much you try. So even though slogging through diagnostic and intervention issues isn't the most fun, it's crucial and deeply liberating. Doing so opens the door to real pleasure because it allows you to step boldly into what makes you tick and sing.

So what's the lesson of Step 5? You have unique gifts and talents that you're meant to access, develop, and share with others. We all need what you have to offer. Similarly, you have your own distinct personality and way of being in the world, just as everyone does. Certain kinds of experiences, relation-ships, and environments will nurture you, while others will unsettle you. Whenever you operate from a connection to your essence and purpose, you'll feel at peace. But, being human, you have areas of limitation and challenge. If you ignore, disregard, or refuse to accept your nature and problems, and push yourself into places you don't belong, you'll experience discomfort and failure of some sort.

No one wants to do a bad job, be unsuccessful, or feel miser-able, but we all do sometimes. Whenever something's not working in your life, there's a reason for it; you are, in some way, disconnected from your essence and life path. But you can fix that. Perhaps you're unknowingly trying to fit a round peg into a square hole. You could be doing that in your choice of friends, lovers, or even career path.

In order to take charge of your emotional life, you need to identify and respect your nature, gifts, and challenges. In this chapter, you'll visit your passions and problems. You'll begin to consider your life choices in light of your growing wisdom, identifying what you can do to nurture what works for you and transform what doesn't. But before you begin, I'd like to share some stories that illustrate the lessons of this step.

THE IMPORTANCE OF SELF-KNOWLEDGE

In *There's Always Help; There's Always Hope,* I tell the story of two brilliant graduate students (who didn't know one another) who came to me with severe, major depression and a complete inability to function. One was in dental school, and the other was in a program in elementary education designed to create teachers. Both young women, who'd always done well academically, had begun failing their graduate-school course work. Then, seeing no way to succeed, each had become ill and unable to go forward.

You can read the details of their amazing journeys in my earlier book, but I want to share a key lesson of their stories with you now. Each of them had been unable to succeed because *she was pursuing something she wasn't meant to do.* And each of them was able to tri-umph upon finding and pursuing her proper path.

What do I mean by this? Well, as it turns out, the dental student had an unrecognized spatial learning disability. Her mind couldn't translate the flat images of teeth on x-rays into the three dimensions of the actual mouth. So, for example, she could never figure out which side of a tooth had the cavity. As a result of her limitation, a learning issue that couldn't be altered, she kept failing her lab courses. There was no way she could become a dentist.

When she'd originally decided to go to dental school, she didn't know how ill suited she was to that career. Once she got there and found herself unable to do the work, she became overwhelmed and depressed. By the time I met her, she was sick and devastated; she felt like a failure. Once the two of us identified her disability, she chose to switch to a more appropriate career path. She's now an accountant, and very successful in her work.

The elementary-education graduate student turned out to have undiagnosed ADD. Her brain chemistry made it impossible for her to balance the demands of maintaining order in a rowdy class and sticking with her lesson plan, so she kept failing her student-teaching course. Although she loved working with young kids, she couldn't handle them in a busy classroom, so she, too, became depressed. By the time I met her, she was ill and hopeless.

Once she and I identified her ADD and the mismatch of her career choice and her inborn limitations, she was able to forgive herself for failing. She decided to switch gears and work with children in a capacity that would fit her gifts and nature. She's now a pediatric nurse. She cares for one child at a time and loves her work!

So both women were unable to succeed and became sick when they tried to pursue careers ill suited to their gifts and limitations. Both were able to thrive upon discovering and pursuing paths more appropriate to their unique passions, talents, and challenges.

Pursuing Our Passions: My Story

We all have strengths, passions, and gifts; and we all have limitations, challenges, and hang-ups. Given our unique natures, we each feel comfortable in some situations and miserable in others. But we don't tend to honor our personalities or cut ourselves much slack. We often focus on our flaws and devalue our gifts, beating ourselves up when we don't like someone or feel that we don't fit in. We view those around us as better, more talented, or even perfect! We compare ourselves to others and neglect to see the whole picture. My patients often enact this dynamic with me. In their eyes, I'm flawless and they're failures.

The reason I look gifted is because I'm pursuing my passion and doing what I do well. I'm a healer, doctor, writer, connector, mom, wife, friend, speaker, and teacher. I've always been drawn to psychic pain and seen ways to help heal it; this comes naturally to me. I love hearing people's stories and stepping into their lives. I thrive on sharing myself with others and being in relationships. That's who I am and what makes *me* tick.

But I'm horrible when it comes to technology; and I also hate tension, conflict, and passivity. I'm the solve it, can-do peacemaker. I'm all there with anyone who wants to connect and work out issues, but I get unsettled by those who refuse to own their stuff and grow themselves. Furthermore, I recoil from computers. I know I have to use them, but they make me cuckoo! If I tried to be a programmer or engineer, I'd fail miserably. In fact, my aversion to technology could be a real hardship in today's world, but I don't let my limitation stop me.

I write my books, articles, and kits by pen, and then my beloved husband keyboards them for me! And if he couldn't do it, I'd find someone else who would. When I write, I need to feel the words flow from my brain and being, through my body, and into the tips of my fingers. I need to grasp my pen and hold it to the page. I have to physically *write* as I manifest my gift. I can't imagine being able to create with a keyboard, because it's just not me. It never has been and probably never will be either. Unbelievable, huh? But it's absolutely true: I'm deeply flawed and wildly successful!

I don't even like to use e-mail, because I want to see and hear you. I need to feel connected. I can't do what I do without human contact, and technology gets in my way. If I have the right setup, I can succeed. But if you were to put me in a cubicle with nothing but a computer, I'd probably become extremely depressed and unproductive. I need to be in relation and creation in order to be well.

I'm successful now because I've found my path, but I got fired from one of my first jobs, working in a furniture store, when I was 17 years old. When I hadn't learned what my trainer thought I should have mastered after three weeks, she showed me the door. To this day, I don't even know what I did wrong! But I learned something powerful from that experience: A paperwork- and sales-oriented desk job wasn't for me, and there was no way I was ever going to take another one. Neither the work nor the environment was right. I was meant to do something else—something that respected my nature, gifts, and significant limitations. I made it my business to figure out what that was.

Today, my work, family, social, and spiritual lives largely reflect who I am and what matters to me. But living authentically is an ongoing project; the work is never done. Life is about change, so I'm constantly tweaking, altering, and fine-tuning the mix. I expect to be doing that forever, but my building blocks are in place.

FINDING YOUR PATH

You, too, can become adept at identifying your nature, essence, gifts, passions, limitations, and areas of challenge. Using the right building blocks, you can create a big-picture plan that works for you. As you take charge of your emotional life, you'll learn to make choices that fit your unique and wondrous nature. Your inner wisdom is brilliant; you can access it and use it to make your life work.

So let's start to look at your story and the lessons of your journey. I've said that there's a path you're meant to travel that's uniquely yours, but what am I talking about? And how might you have gotten removed from living your own story? Let's go back to the beginning and see what we can discover together.

You were born with everything you need. You came with special gifts, intuitive wisdom, burning passion, and a particular purpose for entering this wondrous planetary sea of beings. You exited the womb ready to manifest your own special greatness, and those of us already here were waiting for you to arrive. This is a spiritual law of the universe.

But you were just a helpless baby, so you couldn't yet manifest all you were meant to become. You needed to be cared for, nurtured, and raised by grown-ups. You needed someone to hold, feed, and rock you—and to teach you the ways of the world. You needed this home, hearth, and help in order to survive, thrive, and prosper.

As a child, you were very much in touch with your essence, vibrancy, and passions. You were powerfully drawn to foods, people, and activities that resonated for you. You were equally put off by that which disinterested or unsettled you. But, like all children, you were driven by the need for approval, because when people thought well of you, they gave you the attention you needed in order to survive.

But in seeking that approval and taking on the beliefs and biases of those around you, some parts of yourself got squashed, shushed, pushed down, and ignored. Over time, as you continued to grow up, some of those key bits of your essence may have even become so secret that you stopped knowing they were there at all!

Like all of us, you learned to do some of what was expected of you, rather than all of what you might have been meant to do. Our parents and teachers unknowingly convey both growth-promoting and limiting lessons. Remember that song from the musical *South Pacific,* "You've Got to Be Carefully Taught"? As its lyrics remind us, we even learn whom to hate and fear from those who raise us. Given what we go through to get "growed up," many of us find it hard to know who we are or to believe that there's any value in being true to ourselves. But I'm here to tell you that there is, and to help you reconnect with who you are and what you're meant to do with your life.

As you work this step of your Take-Charge process, you'll find a series of exercises designed to help you connect with your essence, identify your limitations and life choices, and change the pieces of your plan that don't work for you anymore. Unlike Steps 1 through 4, Step 5 is much more action oriented. You'll be thinking, writing, reflecting, and examining your inner world as you seek your truth. If you draw, paint, sculpt, sing, or engage in any other art form, feel free to respond to the exercises below in your chosen medium.

So, let's start by identifying your gifts, passions, and other precious pieces. In your mind, go back in time to your early childhood and growing-up years. Without thinking too much, start filling in the blanks of the exercise below (or write your answers on a separate piece of paper).

REDISCOVERING ME

1. When I was a kid, I most wanted to give the world _____

   _____

2. My favorite things were (write down any associations that come to you; include the what and why):

   a. Songs _____

   b. Books _____

   c. TV shows _____

   d. Foods _____

   e. Heroes _____

   f. Friends _____

   g. Relatives _____

   h. Teachers _____

   i. Subjects _____

   j. Radio stations or programs _____

   k. Colors _____

   l. Games _____

   m. Toys _____

   n. Outfits _____

   o. Seasons _____

   p. Holidays _____

   q. Hobbies _____

   r. Movies _____

3. The best gift I ever got was _____

4. I could lose myself and all sense of time when I _____

    _____

5. I loved learning about _____

6. I was most joyful when I _____

7. My happiest memory is _____

8. I never minded _____

9. I could _____ for hours and not get bored.

10. I was really good at _____

11. My favorite folk or fairy tales as a child were _____

    _____ I especially liked the

    part when _____ because

    _____

12. The sayings that spoke (or still speak) to me include _____

    _____

    _____

13. Scenes that touched (or touch) me are _____

    _____

    _____

14. Art that moves me includes _____

    _____

15. Happiness is _____

16. Joy is _____

17. My secret dream is _____

18. I fantasize about _____

19. I know for sure _____

20. I love being _____

21. I am _____

22. If I were to make a treasure box and fill it up with what's most important to me (which could contain symbols of what matters), it would include _____

_____

23. If I had one day left to live, I'd want to _____

_____

24. When I was a kid, I wanted to be _____ when I grew up.

25. As a child, I imagined that as a grown-up, I _____

_____

26. The story I most like to tell about myself is _____

_____

27. I know that I am meant _____

28. My life wouldn't be complete if _____

_____

29. I am most grateful for _____

_____

30. My most moving life experiences to date include _____

_____

31. Even though I'm scared or doubtful, I know _____

_____

32. I'm living my passion when _____

33. I wish I could _____

34. Maybe I can _____

35. I'd love to be able to _____

36. If I were financially comfortable enough to do anything at all, I would _____

37. My private prayer is _____

38. I need to trust that I _____

Hopefully, you've now completed the "Rediscovering Me" exercise. If not, I urge you to give yourself the gift of doing it. Finding your personal right path requires you to fully step into the process, and the exercises in this chapter are designed to help you do that.

The premise behind the "Rediscovering Me" exercise is that somewhere in the back of your mind or deep within your soul, you know who you are, where you belong or fit, and what you're meant to be doing with your life. Given enough unencumbered space, you can begin to access your deep wisdom.

Reflect on your responses. What have you learned about what makes you tick and sing?

_____

_____

_____

_____

Now reflect on your life. How much does your life reflect what matters to you?

_____

_____

_____

_____

One way to get clarity about the fit between your essence and your life choices is to make two lists. In the first one, write down all the people, places, things, activities, and values that you hold dear. Rank them in order of importance to you, with number one being the most important, and so on.

Then make a list of all the ways you invest your energy and time. Think of a typical day, week, or month. How much time in a given week do you spend on each activity? List your involvements in order of energy spent, with number one being the most demanding, and so on.

In the ideal world, you'd be devoting the bulk of your energy or time to what's most important to you, and the numbers would line up between the two lists. If you find that your number one priority consumes the bulk of your time, and your next concern the second greatest amount of time, and so on, you're amazing and well on your way to wholeness!

Most people, however, find the comparison of their two lists to be far from ideal. But take heart, because you can only start from where you are. And by discovering the mismatch in your lists, you've identified your problems. This recognition and acceptance are the first steps in transforming your life.

Remember, Step 1 was about discovering and honoring the lessons of your story. If you think back to the questions you answered in that chapter, you probably recall considering these: *When in your life have you felt the best? The worst? What or who heals you? Unsettles you?* and so on. These queries were designed to get at the "right-fit" issue, and we're now looking at that topic from another vantage point.

Begin thinking about the mismatches between your two lists, or about the disconnects you've noted between your essence and life choices. You can actually fix some of the problems by simply identifying them and making a conscious choice to allocate your time differently. For instance, you may value your marriage more than your social life, but realize that you're spending more time hanging out with your work buddies than with your spouse. Simply cut down on activities with co-workers and plan more couple time into your week.

But what about the more complicated mismatches, or the confusion that lingers about who you really are? You may be concerned about the roadblocks you've encountered as you've tried to make your life reflect what matters to you the most. Are you worrying about your "stuckness"?

I'd like to tell you a story in order to show you how your answers to the questions in this step can help you find your own personal right path. While the road to authentic living may be long and tortuous, the actions you need to initiate in the Take-Charge process are straightforward and accessible. Read about Stan's journey to see what I mean.

Discovering the Lost Self: Stan's Story

Many years ago, Stan, a 52-year-old technician in the casino industry, came to me for help. He was down on himself, addicted to stimulant drugs, and living with undiagnosed ADD. He'd always felt "less than," and actually believed that he was worthless. Although he could do his job well, he was working in a terrible setting for an addict looking to heal, and he didn't find his work especially fulfilling either.

I was troubled by Stan's self-assessment and worldview. Believing that all people have gifts, passions, challenges, and right fits and that his troubles had to be due to some mismatch, I urged him to tell me about his childhood and adult life. I wanted to know when he felt joyful, successful, empowered, and decisive, because his salvation depended on him accessing the essential pieces of himself and growing them. Without making a connection to his core being, Stan would have difficulty maintaining the hope and commitment necessary for doing the hard work of addiction recovery.

As my patient began to share his story, I learned that he was a gifted photographer, and he'd even previously had some professional success in pursuing his passion. But he'd come up against a brick wall when his career trajectory required him to be both organized and successful at self-promotion. Neither skill set came easily to him. On top of that, his undiagnosed ADD and addictive issues fed his problems. Without a better foundation (addressed in Steps 1 through 3) and major adjustments in the structure of his work, he couldn't succeed—but he didn't know that.

Seeing himself as a failure in business, Stan gave up on his love of taking pictures and entered the casino industry. By the time I met him, he'd been there for so many years that his other life was a distant memory.

I knew that this man was suffering because he was so disconnected from his core self. That split needed to be mended. I had to help him rekindle his inner flame, so I asked him to start bringing me samples of his photographic work.

Eventually, he did so, and they were great! I offered support and encouragement. I pushed him to clean out his darkroom, which had become a storage area, and to start using it again. After some time, he did that, too. As he immersed himself in the world of photography, be began to feel competent and joyful. The empowering energy that Stan generated by pursuing his gift enabled him to stay with the arduous process of therapy to take charge of his emotional life.

Stan and I worked together for a long time. We devoted the bulk of our effort to transforming his self-concept and worldview, combatting his addiction, and addressing his ADD. By the time he graduated from my care, he was much more self-confident. Although he was still working in the casino industry, he'd made photography a big part of his life. He ended his treatment feeling reborn.

Some years went by, and Stan and I lost touch with one another. Then my first book, *There's Always Hope; There's Always Help,* came out. While on a book and seminar tour, I reconnected with this patient when he came to one of my workshops. He was doing phenomenally well! He was clean and sober, having maintained his sobriety for nearly ten years. He'd recently saved up enough money to purchase a whole new set of photography equipment so that he could invest more fully in his passion. Empowered and clear about how to make his life work, he was elated and grateful. He'd come to thank me for helping him get back to knowing, trusting, and becoming who he was really meant to be.

Examine Your Past

You, too, can find and live your gifts; your answers are in your story. Think about Stan's journey, and then think about *your* adult life. Begin to identify your experiences of success, joy, fulfillment, or flow, as well as your episodes of challenge, disappointment, frustration, or personal failure. When have you felt most creative, empowered, and decisive in your life? What were you doing? Who was supporting you? In contrast, when have you felt the most demoralized, bored, confused, overwhelmed, and hopeless? What were you doing? Was anyone making it harder for you? Write your answers on the next page or on a separate piece of paper.

_____

_____

_____

What tasks, skills, demands, and structures were part of each experience? Think about the details. What are your gifts or talents? What do you need to do to reclaim these pieces of yourself? How can you begin? What might you need to do to make sure your life choices fit your nature? (You may write your answers here or on a separate piece of paper.)

_____

_____

_____

Now, think about stuckness. What's difficult for you? What do you need to do to address your difficulties? What sort of help might you need? What are you ready to take on? Commit to a plan and outline it in writing.

_____

_____

_____

It might help you to hear more of Stan's story. You already know that he had to be willing to look to his history for answers about what he was meant to do. He had to commit to a long process of many tiny steps in order to transform his life. *But Stan also required medication, 12-step recovery-program tools, marital counseling, and psychotherapy in order to take charge of his emotional life.*

Would you do well to adopt some of those same techniques? Where are you, and why might you be stuck on your path to take charge of your emotional life? What should you do to get moving again?

You can't make life choices that fit your nature if you're trapped in one place, so let's examine some common reasons for this state. If you've hit a roadblock, there must be an explanation. Here are some possibilities. Which ones speak to you?

1. You have an undiagnosed or untreated condition that keeps you from being able to take charge of your emotional life.

2. You're trying to fit a round peg into a square hole.

3. You don't know what you ought to be doing.

4. You're afraid to trust what you know.

5. You don't feel entitled to live your story.

6. You're overwhelmed by the size of the project.

7. You're afraid of failure.

8. You devalue your gifts or magnify your limitations.

9. Your assumptions are faulty.

10. You're living a common definition of insanity: doing the same thing over and over again but expecting different results.

11. You haven't made yourself enough of a priority.

12. You're making progress but don't realize it.

13. You're impatient with yourself or the process.

14. You're a perfectionist.

15. You're actually there, but don't take the time to acknowledge the blessing of where you are!

As we explore each of these possibilities, look for yourself in the descriptions. Use the tips to overcome each of the roadblocks that you experience. Feel free to add in your own strategies as well.

1. You have an undiagnosed or untreated condition that keeps you from being able to take charge of your emotional life. As you know, this is a common reason for stuckness. Think of Stan's story or the tales we reviewed in Step 1. For example, depression makes it hard to get out of bed and concentrate; anxiety makes it difficult to think straight; ADD affects memory, concentration, focus, and level of interest; and mania makes it tough to sit still or remain on an even keel.

Tip: Whenever you're having trouble in your life, ask yourself whether you could be suffering from an illness, disorder, or hormonal issue that's compromising your capacity to be "in flow." Don't hesitate to seek help. Even if you're already being treated for something, the interventions may need to be changed, or you may have a second, unrecognized issue. Get help to get well!

2. You're trying to fit a round peg into a square hole. You probably recall that I experienced this mismatch when I tried to succeed in a paperwork/sales desk job. I was ill suited to the setting and work demands. Whenever we push ourselves to do something we aren't wired for, we'll become unsettled.

Tip: When you feel overwhelmed or frustrated, ask yourself: *Am I striving to do something that's wrong for me? Could I be trying to do the equivalent of running a marathon with a broken leg or singing in a chorus when I'm tone-deaf? Am I telling myself that I ought to be happy in this job, relationship, or outfit even though it's not really my thing?*

Be honest with yourself. If it feels wrong, there's a good chance that it is. Let yourself move on to something better suited to your nature and gifts.

3. You don't know what you ought to be doing. My experience is that most people say this when they're making the "meaning-of-life" question too big in their own minds. Every single person I've ever worked with can identify something that gives them pleasure and something that causes them pain.

Tip: Even if you need to start from the tiniest ember of light—such as knowing that you like to sing, dance, read, write, teach, do puzzles, or build things—you can begin to find your way. You need to fan the ember, create a big flame, and ignite the passion. You can do this by making time to pursue what appeals to you.

Start with a tiny effort and grow your investment until there's no question in your mind that you're in flow. Don't hesitate to experiment with various sparks until you find the ones that really glow for you; stay with the process. Your inner wisdom will guide you to the place where your light is meant to shine.

4. You're afraid to trust what you know. Many of us live in fear of stepping into our wholeness. The unknown is scary, and the devil we know seems somehow less troubling to us than the one we don't. But Franklin D. Roosevelt said it well: "The only thing we have to fear is fear itself." The worries we manufacture in our own heads are our biggest problem. We must take calculated risks if we're to take charge of our emotional lives.

Tip: Whenever you feel afraid, remind yourself of your power to prevail. Affirm: *I am meant to trust in my inner wisdom. My intuition is my guide. I owe it to myself to take on the challenges and rewards due me. I can prevail, and I intend to do so.*

5. You don't feel entitled to live your story. This is a common mantra, but it has no basis in the spiritual laws of the universe. You were put here for some reason that's unique to you, and the world needs your contribution.

Tip: When you start doubting your right to be you, talk back to your inner critic. Don't engage in a dialogue; just repeat a new belief over and over, creating a statement that works for you. I like this one: *I need to do what I am meant to do.* Or, *I exist to share my passion with the world.* Write your own mission statement, and say it whether you believe it or not. Doing so will empower you to live your own story.

6. You're overwhelmed by the size of the project. Most of us find that whenever we focus on the magnitude of a goal, we get overwhelmed. This is why, for example, 12-step recovery programs urge people not to think about giving up their addictive use forever. Their mottos "One day at a time" and "Keep coming back" speak to the need to start small and build from there.

Tip: Think in terms of the big picture and little steps. In other words, identify your goal, but focus on what you need to do *today* in order to get there. Remember the tortoise and the hare: Slow but steady won the race.

7. You're afraid of failure. One of my favorite lines about this subject is: "There are no failures, just slow successes." The most accomplished and fulfilled people on the planet have lived stories of setbacks, dead ends, mistakes, and adversities overcome. The only route to fulfillment is *through* the dread. Eleanor Roosevelt expressed this idea eloquently: "I believe that anyone can conquer fear by doing the things he fears to do."

Tip: Whenever you find yourself expressing fear, talk back to it. Say: *There are no failures; only slow successes. The way to conquer my fear is to take action—then my fear will melt away. I can and need to do this.*

8. You devalue your gifts or magnify your limitations. Many of us continue to believe that the grass is always greener on the other side of the fence. We agree with Groucho Marx and say, "I don't care to belong to any club that will have me as a member." But your talents are wondrous, and your challenges really do pale in comparison to them. It's not your essence that's the problem; it's what you're telling yourself about who you are that's tripping you up.

Tip: Focus on what you do well, figure out what's working in your life, and remind yourself of the good choices you've made to get to where you are. Or think of a challenge you've overcome, reminding yourself of your accomplishment. You can also come up with a way to nurture yourself in spite of your negative self-talk. How about a bath, a massage, or just a visit with a dear friend? You can begin to love yourself to wellness!

9. Your assumptions are faulty. Last week, a brave woman called me for advice during my weekly radio show. She shared her loss of joy and growing sense of helplessness, and she wondered what was wrong with her. Some years ago, in order to have more control of her time, she'd left her job to grow her own business. Now she was experiencing great success, but she was working 12 hours a day with no breaks! She'd made her life more unbalanced rather than easier, and she was feeling like a failure.

As we explored her situation, she said, "I made a lot of faulty assumptions when I decided to go this route."

I reassured her that we all do that sometimes, and we talked about the fact that her journey into entrepreneurship was meant to teach her something. She needed to discover the lesson and move on. She was overwhelmed, joyless, and depressed because it was time to change her course.

I said, "There's a reason you've gone this route. Your job is to figure out the lesson and take it with you into the next thing you do."

"Thank you," she responded. "I was feeling the same way. I guess I needed to hear it from someone else in order to acknowledge it."

Tip: If you're stuck, question your assumptions. Do you need to adjust your expectations of yourself or others? Should you cut your losses, learn your lessons, and move on? Perhaps you need to alter your beliefs about what will happen in order to be able to step into what comes next and beckons you. Assumptions can really hang you up, so challenge them!

10. You're living a common definition of insanity: doing the same thing over and over again but expecting different results. We all do this; it's a function of the way our minds work. Certain patterns become so ingrained in our neural circuitry that we replay them over and over. In other words, our brains become almost hardwired; they behave the way computers do. But of course, anytime we replay our situation, we get back the same old result. So, for example, if you keep going from one waitress job to another, and you get fired by your manager each time, then you're apt to get fired again—so maybe waitressing isn't your thing.

Tip: Look at your patterns. Do you see yourself reenacting the same problem over and over again, or even the same dialogue? If so, change at least one tiny piece of your behavior at a time and see what happens. Even small shifts can move mountains.

11. You haven't made yourself enough of a priority. Many of us neglect to put ourselves high enough up on the care list. But you can't succeed, thrive, grow, and give back if you're strung out and depleted. Taking charge of your emotional life requires time, energy, and other resources. Are you too busy taking care of everyone around you? Are you drained or depleted at the end of the day? How much of your schedule, energy, and money do you devote to your self-care, as compared to what you lavish on others?

Tip: Begin to examine your place on the priority list. Commit to treating yourself at least as well as you treat your friends, spouse, children, colleagues, pets, and even plants. Give yourself the best you have to offer. Only then will you accomplish what you're meant to achieve!

12. You're making progress but don't recognize it. This is one of the most common problems I see in my practice. We all focus so much on our limitations and what doesn't work in our lives that we neglect to see our gifts, growth, and progress. I spend a great deal of my clinical-care time reminding my patients of their own histories and accomplishments. It's striking to me that they invariably agree with my account and feel better after hearing it. I think about how much healthier we'd all be if we took the time to acknowledge and celebrate our own achievements.

Tip: Make it a point each day or week to reflect on your goals and small successes. Write them down in a journal and reread them periodically. You'll probably be amazed to discover how much you *are* changing.

13. You're impatient with yourself or the process. We live in a fast-paced, drive-through, shrinking world that's only getting more demanding, pressured, and frenetic. Gone are the days when you could get away and be truly inaccessible. We're expected to be consistently present, productive, and perhaps even superhuman. It's no wonder that we have unreasonable expectations of ourselves and tend to lose patience quickly. We expect a quick fix and feel like failures when our growth and transformation process follows its slow but steady course. But significant progress takes tons of time. We must hang in there if we're to achieve our goals.

Tip: Remind yourself that nothing worth striving for comes easy. In fact, if your journey doesn't feel slow, arduous, and frustrating, you're probably cutting necessary corners. Tell yourself that you're not in a race to the finish; you're meant to savor your travels and relish the pauses. You need breaks and downtime!

14. You're a perfectionist. So many of us are! If you're expecting yourself to be perfect, it will be hard for you to effect change, because it's difficult to build on your accomplishments when none of them are good enough for you. And it's tough to take risks and step into the unknown when you're expecting yourself to do a perfect job. That goal is too big for any human being. No one is perfect; to err is to be human. We're all a little broken, limited, flawed, and challenged. In fact, our vulnerabilities are often what's most appealing about us!

Tip: Tell yourself, *My best is good enough. Perfection isn't the goal. To err is to be human.*

15. You're actually there, but don't take the time to acknowledge where you are! We seem to believe that we haven't taken charge of our emotional lives if we still have work to do. But being alive involves facing and negotiating challenges every day. If you have your building blocks in place, you're in charge! You may regularly need to reorganize the pieces, but as you make life choices that fit your nature, you'll be "there" in an ongoing way.

Tip: Regularly ask yourself, *Am I making life choices that fit my nature?* If the answer is yes, celebrate. If no, then make the changes necessary to get to yes. You can live the life you were meant to lead—you might even be doing so already!

As you conclude your Step 5 work, let's review what you've learned. You now know that you're genetically and spiritually endowed with gifts and challenges, and you're meant to identify and honor both in your efforts to take charge of your emotional life. You've called forth some of your essential pieces—those embers, sparks, or even the internal flames that give your life meaning. You've explored mismatches between your true self and your life choices and chosen to implement some steps and strategies to better align your being with your doing. You may even have decided to explore medical or psychological assessment, counseling, coaching, or therapy.

I urge you to invite in all the supports you need in order to work your Take-Charge program. Guides and mentors are crucial in healing. We often benefit from the voice and insight of others.

That said, we also have an amazing capacity to self-heal. We carry around a lot of beliefs that imprison us. Given enough guidance in identification and transformation of our self-destructive brain circuits, we can actually learn how to reprogram some of our negative self-talk loops on our own. And even if we can't do it *all* alone, we can (and need to) do a lot of self-talk to take charge.

In Step 6, you'll discover how to identify the learned beliefs that imprison you. You'll master some cognitive-behavior techniques that you can use to transform your stuck-in-a-rut thinking and take charge of your emotional life.

STEP 6

Identify the Beliefs
That Imprison You, and
Reprogram the Brain Circuits Involved

Welcome to Step 6! The premise behind this chapter is that what you believe—what you tell yourself both consciously and unconsciously—affects what happens in your life. We might even say that you actively *create* your own world. Although you may not recognize your power, you do wield it. And with enough persistence, you can identify the beliefs that imprison you. You can then develop powerful mind-body tools to reprogram those negative mental circuits. Using those strategies, you'll literally change your brain to change your life.

How can you possibly have so much power? You probably doubt that you do, and you may be thinking, *If I had that, I would be using it to make my life better, easier, and more fulfilling. What person in their right mind would choose the pain and suffering I experience? You can't possibly be right.*

Well, you wouldn't consciously create distress for yourself, but you do so without knowing it. You see, we all carry around internalized messages, ideas about ourselves and others. Some of them are healing, and others harm us. We're aware of some of those beliefs because of the chatter we hear in our heads, but are unaware of many others, in spite of their power.

You learned most of those lessons early in your development and stored them away without realizing it. But your internalized messages affect the course of your life. The healing ones are encouraging, gentle, loving, optimistic, honest, and fair; the harmful ones are critical, discouraging, pessimistic, and harsh. Your ideas determine your behavior and what the universe gives you back in response. But how do you acquire these beliefs? How is it that they affect you as they do, and how can you change them?

THE ORIGINS OF SELF-CONCEPT

Well, the lessons we learn about ourselves in childhood determine our self-concepts as adults. The models you were exposed to or taught during your formative years dramatically affect your mind-set. For most of us, our primary learning laboratory is our family of origin. We learn how to think about ourselves and others from what our parents teach us by word and example.

Although our teachers, classmates, and religious leaders may exert powerful developmental influences on us as well, we experience the messages contained in our "home base" as the most powerful. Obviously, if you were raised in an environment other than a traditional family with two parents, then you were exposed to messages and models of a different nature. The home environment has the greatest power to affect the mind-set of a developing child, whatever form it takes.

As children, we learn and store away information with the degree of cognitive development that we have at the time of the event. For example, if we're young and still very concrete or literal in our thinking, we may simply store away a lesson such as "I am a bad boy" or "I am a naughty girl." Since our capacity to understand what might make a person good or bad hasn't yet been developed, we store the information as a simple fact.

Without being consciously aware of these stored self-concepts, we're influenced by them throughout our adult lives. Since these old messages can cause dysfunction and intense pain, we may find ourselves questioning our ideas and choices enough to identify some of our negative core beliefs over time. Having figured out what they are, we can use our adult ideas to talk back to our childlike ones. By recognizing and subsequently challenging our internalized beliefs, we can change and replace them with more constructive and positive notions. This healing process involves using a cognitive-behavior technique, a form of self-talk called "affirmations," to reprogram destructive thoughts. You'll learn more about that later in this chapter.

But before discovering how to change the mind-set, we need to ask: *How do those negative lessons actually affect us? What do we do with them? What does it really mean to be influenced by our past?*

MARKING TIME

Strange as the idea may seem, we all reexperience our pasts in the present as we tell ourselves what we learned. Having been called stupid or lazy in childhood, we may tell ourselves the same things now. We also hear our self-concepts and worldviews reflected back in the words of others, even when those people aren't actually saying those words. So we may "hear" our friends or bosses calling us dumb or unmotivated, when they're simply following up with us to determine where we are with a project.

Additionally, we re-create familiar family dynamics in our adult relationships, even if the original situations were (and often still are) painful to us. We may pick critical friends, bosses, lovers, and life partners. What's familiar somehow feels right, hence the popular notion that "women marry their fathers" and "men marry their mothers."

In spite of our adult desires to experience joy, fulfillment, and pleasure in our relationships and pursuits, we often unknowingly re-create the pain, sadness, and loss of our childhoods. We do it minute to minute by what we tell ourselves, and year after year as a result of the choices we make. Our biggest challenge can be trying to figure out how to live the life we're meant to have, as opposed to the one someone else might have taught us.

You've probably heard the expression "You're your own worst enemy." I believe this statement to be true. We are, in many ways, what we believe. Both my personal life and clinical work with patients have shown me how frequently our troubles are the result of self-sabotage. We often impose limits on ourselves that trap us into what doesn't work. Until and unless we challenge our beliefs, we remain stuck in unproductive, even self-destructive, positions.

Breaking Free from Our Misconceptions

I'm going to give you a silly, simple example of what I mean by staying trapped by an idea. A long time ago when my now-teenage son was three years old, he and I had a battle of wills about vegetables! I'd made dinner, and we were sitting down to eat. Gabe announced that he didn't like broccoli (having never eaten it before) and refused to sample it.

I insisted that he try one bite, and if he disliked it, he could have a substitute. He refused to do so. He was given multiple chances to challenge his belief and cooperate. But even knowing that his rigidity would land him in bed without any further dinner, treats, or bedtime story, he refused to try the broccoli. He was eventually carried off to his room, kicking and screaming.

Gabriel was a stubborn little boy, but I was even more determined than he was when it came to health issues. So when we sat down to green beans the next evening and he pulled the same routine, he was carried off to bed as he had been the night before. This went on for four days, with Gabe insisting each night that he didn't like the vegetable on his plate, no matter what it was. It didn't make a difference if he'd never tasted it before, or if he'd eaten it with gusto in the past.

Finally, on the fifth night, we sat down to broccoli again. The familiar routine began to play itself out until just before the trip to bed. Then, wonder of wonders, Gabe lifted the tiniest spear of broccoli to his mouth and put it in. And guess what? His reluctant face broke into a smile. He finished that first piece, and as he was stabbing the second one with his fork, he said "I like broccoli! Can I have some more?"

"Of course, Gabe," I answered. "But wouldn't you have saved yourself a lot of upset if you had just tried the broccoli the first time?" He nodded.

"There's a lesson here," I said. "Don't insist you know something when you don't know for sure that it's true. Your stubbornness will only cause you grief. Other people might even get angry with you, and do or say things that upset you. It's best to be open-minded and willing to try new things. Do you agree?"

By now Gabe was on his third helping of broccoli. He nodded again and said, "I don't know why I wouldn't try it, Mom. But I learned my lesson."

I believe that he did learn to challenge his stuck thinking. In fact, we never had an argument like that again—not about anything! What a relief that was to all of us in the family.

Now this may seem like a silly story about a three-year-old child and vegetables. But is it really so irrelevant? Have you ever enacted this kind of dysfunction in your adult life? For instance, have you ever insisted that someone didn't like you, that you couldn't accomplish a goal, or that your input wasn't valued when you didn't know for sure that you were correct? I doubt that you can truthfully answer no to this question.

We all fall into "stinking thinking" sometimes. And when you get stuck in one of those ruts, what happens? You act on the basis of your assumption. You treat the person whom you believe doesn't like you in a way that may actually lead them to feel that way. You shy away from pursuing goals that you believe you can't achieve, so you never meet them. Or you keep your mouth shut, thinking that no one values your input, and thus lose the opportunity to have any say in what happens to you. Your beliefs can get you into a lot of trouble. In fact, what you think can alter the course of your life.

UNEARTHING DESTRUCTIVE ASSUMPTIONS

Some of your counterproductive thoughts are easy to identify, while others are deeply buried. The ideas that are readily accessible are the ones that you hear in your head. For instance, your internal voice might say, *That was a stupid thing to do* or *You're such a loser.* You can discover these perceptible beliefs by attending to the dialogue in your mind. But identifying your more deeply buried assumptions requires more digging. It involves examining your destructive life patterns and tracking their origin. What did you learn that you're unconsciously playing out? You need to do some detective work to discover the underlying beliefs that you haven't as yet given voice to. Let's look at some examples of each scenario—accessible beliefs and buried ones—so that you get a handle on what I mean.

Reworking Accessible Beliefs

If you think back to Stan's story, you'll recognize the thought that imprisoned him. Remember when he hit a wall in his photography business? He told himself that he couldn't succeed in that line of work. The idea *I can't do photography for a living* led him to give up on his passion and take a job in the casino industry.

With a lot of time and help, Stan was able to challenge his belief and rediscover his inner flame. In this case, his counterproductive thought was relatively easy to identify. But since so many of his life choices had followed from it, the reprogramming effort involved a lot of work.

What about a more simple example of a destructive belief—one that's easily identified, challenged, and reprogrammed? Well, my patient Sam was a particularly anxious fellow who tended to expect the worst possible outcomes to problems. One day he came in over-wrought because his boss hadn't responded to voice-mail or e-mail communications about a pressing work matter. Sam was convinced that he'd made some fatal error, that his boss was avoiding him as a result, and that his job was in jeopardy. He was afraid to go back to work. "I'm about to be fired," he insisted tearfully.

But Sam actually excelled at his work. His performance reviews were routinely exceptional. In fact, he'd just been given a glowing evaluation! I reminded him of his workplace history and challenged him to consider alternative reasons for his boss's lack of response. As he began using his rational brain to challenge his dysfunctional belief, he was able to settle down.

Armed with a list of possible causes for the situation, Sam chose to change the belief that told him, *I'm in serious danger whenever someone is slow to respond to my questions.* Instead, he decided to say, "Not everyone responds as quickly as I do when queried. I need to tell myself: *Calm down. No news is good news. If I'm at risk, I will surely be told about it.*"

Sam committed to making these few sentences a new mantra, and he repeated them in his head all the way back to work. When he got there, he discovered the reason for the silence—his boss had the flu!

I continued to work with Sam for several months. Occasionally, he'd start to express that old, crippling belief. But before he even finished the sentence, he'd stop himself and state: "I don't know why I'm saying that, because I know it's old thinking. No news is good news. If I'm at risk, I'll surely be told about it."

By changing his mind and reprogramming that dysfunctional pattern, Sam's anxiety progressively diminished. Empowered to take charge of his emotional life in a new way, he was able to graduate from my care.

Reworking Hidden Beliefs

Now let's look at an example of someone with a deeply buried but disabling belief. I'd like to tell you about Melissa, who came to me hoping to heal her romantic life. Her marriage had ended some years before when her husband shared his infidelity and desire to repartner with his lover.

Melissa was devastated. "Perhaps I haven't fully recovered," she said, "because I shy away from romantic relationships. And whenever I do get involved with someone, I hold myself way back. Eventually he always leaves. It becomes a replay of my marriage experience."

The two of us got down to work, trying to sort out the lessons of Melissa's history. What did she believe, and why was she replaying an abandonment dynamic over and over again? As it turned out, she came from a family with a disabled sibling. She was a good student and a quiet child, and her parents didn't recognize the attention she needed in order to thrive. She was often expected to take care of her brother, having to put aside her schoolwork and whatever else she wanted to do. As a result, Melissa learned the lesson: *My needs aren't important; I have to help those less fortunate, no matter what the cost to me.* Although she was somewhat aware of this conviction, she didn't recognize its influence.

When it came to relationship issues in her adult life, that internalized idea exerted its silent power. During Melissa's courtship, she often played the role of silent caretaker, putting up with and even accommodating her then-fiancé's troubling behavior. When he proposed, her inner-wisdom voice said *Don't do it!* but her dysfunctional belief countered with *You can't hurt his feelings. He's a nice enough guy. He needs you. You have to say yes.* Without recognizing that the childhood message *My needs aren't important; I have to help those less fortunate* was at play, she said yes.

Upon entering the marriage, Melissa buried her inner wisdom along with her turmoil and misgivings. She tried to make things work, but out of sight and mind is not out of life. In spite of her efforts to build a loving partnership, she couldn't alter what she'd known to be true: Her husband wasn't ready and wouldn't fully commit to the union.

When he left, Melissa was devastated. She didn't remember that she'd had her own misgivings from the very beginning. She personalized his decision that she wasn't good enough for him, and then carried this sense of low self-worth into subsequent relationships, dating unavailable men who'd never commit enough to hurt her so deeply again.

It took Melissa and me months to identify the crippling belief that had been behind her acceptance of the marriage proposal. By looking at her childhood, we finally figured out where the idea had come from. Armed with this knowledge, we began to reprogram the self-destructive brain circuit.

As an adult, Melissa understood the importance of caring for herself and her own needs in life. She came to recognize that she'd abandoned herself in choosing to enter a marriage that wasn't meant to be. The demise of the union was inevitable. *She* was good enough, but she'd made the wrong choice. *It* wasn't right! She'd set herself up to suffer when she ignored her inner wisdom and enacted the learned belief. She'd put her own needs aside to avoid "hurting his feelings." As a result, she unknowingly hurt herself.

Her internal script needed to be rewritten. It became: *My inner wisdom is my guide. I need to honor my feelings, give them a voice, and act on them. I am meant to silence the voices telling me that I don't count. Those aren't really mine. I am good enough, and I deserve to experience joy.*

Melissa and I worked together for some time. She needed to develop skill in identifying and heeding the wisdom of her inner voice, ferreting out and challenging the old belief and living more authentically. Throughout her work, she repeated the new script she'd created. This exercise enabled her to reprogram the old tape as she strove to believe what she now knew to be true. She graduated from my care several years ago, feeling empowered and transformed.

The universe acts in synergistic and strange ways sometimes. When I wrote down Melissa's story, I hadn't heard from her in quite a while. We'd connected perhaps two or three times since her graduation. Yet, as I was writing *about* her, she was writing *to* me. Within days of completing this passage, I received a New Year's greeting card from her. She'd just read my first book and loved it. She was writing to tell me that, and to let me know how well she was doing. She was engaged to a wonderful man, and she'd truly reprogrammed her mind and changed her life. She was grateful and delighted to have me share this story of her transformation in order to help you.

THE POWER OF YOUR MIND

We've now covered three examples that demonstrate the power of beliefs to affect life paths, and I'm sure you resonated with some elements of each story. What struck you? To whom do you relate the most—Gabe, Sam, or Melissa? Have you ever engaged in an effort to reprogram your destructive beliefs? How well did you do?

Perhaps you have some experience with affirmations or other cognitive-behavior techniques. These methods are extremely powerful in altering problematic brain circuits, because they work by creating new neural pathways. You see, when you tell yourself something over and over, the same pattern of neurons fires repeatedly. Eventually, that circuit takes on a life of its own. So when you encounter the familiar situation, your brain begins to tell you what it already knows (almost without thinking). After feeding yourself something negative for years, such as *My needs aren't important,* your mind has that thought pretty well fixed in place.

But you can change this! The way to do so is by telling yourself something different over and over again until *it* becomes ingrained. You don't have to think the new message is true for it to take; you just have to keep saying it. After a while, it will become fixed enough that you'll believe it instead.

There's something else I need to teach you about the strength of your thoughts to affect your life. It concerns the minute-to-minute power of your mind-body connection. Whenever you give yourself encouraging or positive messages, internal chemicals are released that calm the deep limbic system of your brain. This makes you feel happy and relaxed.

By contrast, when you focus on sad, angry, worrisome, or critical thoughts, your brain releases chemicals that activate your deep limbic system and make you feel tense, anxious, and unsettled. So even before you reprogram your problematic circuits, you can harm or heal yourself by what you allow your mind to say.

LOOKING INWARD

In the remaining pages of Step 6, you'll identify the beliefs that imprison and harm you. You'll then develop strategies to bring about both immediate relief and long-term change. The first part of this process involves figuring out what thoughts you need to alter . . . and perhaps you know some of them already. If so, write them on the lines below or on a separate piece of paper:

_____

_____

_____

Most imprisoning thoughts are the result of fear, self-devaluation, guilt, pessimism, overgeneralizing, and "catastrophizing" (or expecting the worst). Let's look at each of these categories a bit to help you find your inner demons.

— **Fear** is a big issue—in fact, it can cripple the most mighty! As I mentioned earlier, according to Franklin D. Roosevelt, the only thing we have to fear is fear itself. That's how prominent this force is in our lives. In fact, it's the greatest cognitive distorter. We can't think straight when we're anxious. We may worry about our health, our financial security, the strength to endure challenges, or the ability to perform at an acceptable level. We might be afraid of flying in an airplane, losing our keys, or driving our car in snowy conditions. We may dread abandonment, abuse, annihilation, or failure. These are just a few examples.

What are you afraid of? Is this an area of stuck thinking for you? What do you say to yourself?

— **Self-devaluation** is very common in negative thinking. You might enact this by labeling or calling yourself names, for example: *I'm a failure and a jerk.* Or perhaps you devalue yourself by comparing yourself unfavorably to others: *I'm not as smart as Sally, or as funny as Jon.* You might even put yourself down by overgeneralizing (which you can also do with fear, guilt, and the like): *I'll never be promoted, I'm always left out;* or *No one will be interested in my ideas.* I often hear the ultimate self-devaluation from my patients. It sounds like this: *I'm not enough, I don't matter; The world would be better off without me;* or *I'm a burden to those around me.*

How do you devalue, criticize, label, or belittle yourself? What do you say?

— Let's move on to **guilt.** We feel this emotion when we neglect to say or do something that we believe we *should* do, or when we do or say something that we think we *shouldn't.* Whenever the word *should* comes into your mind, you're holding yourself to someone else's standard. Often, you're articulating a rule of behavior that you learned while growing up. Think back to Melissa's story. She learned to put herself second, and that felt right. So she said to herself, *I should accept this marriage proposal. My feelings aren't important. I can't hurt him.*

Guilty thoughts can also surface when people survive disasters that take or destroy the lives of others around them. This is called survivor guilt, and may sound like this: *It should have been me.* You might also feel guilty for outperforming your siblings or parents: *I shouldn't have embarrassed them or shown them up;* or for failing to meet the expectations of others: *I should have stayed in that marriage. My parents loved my ex-spouse.*

Finally, you may even feel guilty when someone else criticizes or hurts you. You could be enacting an old dynamic and assuming that you're responsible for the other's behavior. The thinking is: *I shouldn't have said or done what I did. I regret my behavior.*

What's the role of guilt in your internal dialogue? How often do you find fault with yourself for what you should have done but didn't, or what you shouldn't have done but did? What do you say to yourself?

———————————————————————————————

———————————————————————————————

———————————————————————————————

— **Pessimistic thinking,** seeing the cup as half empty instead of half full, is a powerful warden. It can imprison you and forever keep you from taking charge of your life. Studies looking at how well children learn when teachers are told that their students are bright versus intellectually limited demonstrate that the way the instructors *view* the pupils—whether it's accurate or not!—determines classroom performance. Smart kids who are treated as if they're limited do poorly; average children approached with high expectations perform extremely well.

Think about the implications of this: If you expect yourself to fail, you most likely will. Additionally, if you expect others to treat you poorly, or if you think that unpleasant things are going to happen, you'll search for and find the negative outcome. Each time you do so, you'll reinforce your belief that the world is a big, bad, or scary place. You'll withdraw more and more, and take less and less charge of your life.

But we're imperfect beings who live in a flawed world. Perfection can't be the goal. Every single moment is full of opportunities and problems, blessings and curses. You can choose to focus on the negative and *feel* bad or on the positive and *feel* good. For example, during a wonderful celebratory meal, you can let a chipped plate destroy your pleasure in the company and wonderful food. Or at the theater, you can permit the occasional distraction of someone coughing in the audience to diminish your enjoyment of the play. When your co-worker calls in sick and your workload increases for the day, you can tell yourself, *I bet she won't be in for weeks and I'll be overwhelmed* or *Thank heaven I'm well and can manage the extra work for today.* Which thought do you believe will make for a better day?

Are you pessimistic at times? When do you expect the worst for yourself or others? What do you say in your head?

_____

_____

_____

— We all **overgeneralize** at times, and whenever we do, we set ourselves up. When we use words such as *always* and *never,* we're falling into this trap. Telling ourselves *I'll never get promoted, I'll always be abandoned,* or *No one could possibly love me* is a recipe for staying stuck.

Similarly, saying *I can't change my life, You never listen to me,* or *Everyone is out to get me* keeps us stuck. Nothing in life is absolute. When we make global statements, we leave no space for growth, options, or creativity. Taking charge of your emotional life requires you to follow a unique path specific to your challenges and gifts. You can only find your way if you are open-minded and flexible in your thinking.

In what ways do you overgeneralize? Is it mostly when thinking about yourself, others, or both? What do you actually say?

123

——————————————————————————

——————————————————————————

——————————————————————————

— Perhaps the most crippling series of thoughts emerges when we **catastrophize.** In this behavior, both fear and pessimism come together, and we assume the absolute worst. For example:

- Our spouse is late, so we say, *He must be dead.*

- When our friend needs to talk, we decide, *He's chosen to end the relationship.*

- Upon receiving a letter from the IRS, we believe, *I'm going to be imprisoned.*

The excessive fear that accompanies catastrophizing unsettles our nervous systems in dramatic ways, and we feel absolutely awful. At this point, we're often unable to take action of any kind.

When do you catastrophize? What's the fear behind your thoughts? What do you tell yourself?

——————————————————————————

——————————————————————————

——————————————————————————

BEGINNING TO CHANGE YOUR MIND

Now that you've done some thinking about the beliefs that imprison you, it's time to get into the real work of Step 6: identifying and reprogramming your dysfunctional thoughts. You've already written down some of your problematic beliefs as you read through the examples, descriptions, and questions in this chapter. What other ones might you be carrying?

You'll be cataloguing all your counterproductive beliefs later in the chapter by completing "My Negative-Thought List." In preparation, think about your areas of success and challenge. What ideas may have contributed to your difficulties? Write them down on your list. You may have 3 statements, or you may have 22. Remember to include your experiences of fear, self-criticism, guilt, pessimism, overgeneralizing, and catastrophizing.

To help you identify more negative thoughts, do the following "Sentence-Completion Exercise." As you go through it, write down whatever comes into your mind without thinking about it. Just let what's in there pop up. You may be surprised by what's revealed to you when you create this opportunity.

Sentence-Completion Exercise

I am _____

I can't _____

Men _____

Aging _____

Women _____

Children _____

Other people _____

Death _____

God _____

Money _____

No one _____

Sickness _____

Everyone _____

Sex _____

Love _____

Anger _____

Sadness _____

Loss _____

Forgiveness _____

Life _____

Hope _____

Now read your completed sentences, putting a mark next to those that you recognize as imprisoning beliefs. Include them in your Negative-Thought List.

My Negative-Thought List

1. _____
2. _____
3. _____
4. _____
5. _____
6. _____
7. _____
8. _____
9. _____
10. _____

Visualization for Healing

Before I teach you how to reprogram your imprisoning beliefs, I'd like you to pause and do a visualization exercise with me.

Imagine an all-powerful, all-knowing, loving, compassionate, and caring being beside you. Allow yourself to see, hear, smell, feel, and fully sense the presence of this wise entity, and get comfortable. Breathe deeply into the moment. Perhaps you'd like to hold hands with this visitor or get close in some other way. Your guest is your helper, protector, assistant, and co-healer. It may be someone you already know, or someone who's coming to you for the first time.

In the presence of this wise being, read your negative thought list aloud. Allow your co-healer to feel concern for you. Let yourself recognize the pain your wise friend experiences as you voice your harmful beliefs. Invoke compassion for yourself as you sit with this pain for some moments.

Then open your heart and mind as widely as you possibly can. Repeat the following affirmations out loud three times:

- *I am at one, at peace, and at ease.*
- *I have all that I need.*
- *I am safe, abundant, blessed, and wondrous.*
- *I carry the mystery and beauty of the infinite within me.*
- *I am lovable and loved.*
- *I am more than enough.*
- *I am meant to be.*

These words come from your wisdom healer. As you repeat them, recognize the peace that descends upon you and your guide simultaneously. Feel the soothing chemicals suffuse your brain and body, and allow yourself to relax fully into this healing. You're at one, at peace, and at ease. You want for nothing.

Sit with the blessings of these affirmations for as long as you wish, repeating the words that touch you. Feel them cushioning you, comforting you, and forming a protective energy field around you. Let your body and spirit relax deeply into this safe space. Stay there as long as you wish, and know that you can return to this place anytime that you want. It's always there for you.

TRANSFORMING NEGATIVE SELF-TALK

Now that you're calm, it's time to start developing positive, affirming thoughts to speak back to your internal critic. This exercise involves taking each negative idea on your list and fashioning an uplifting antidote in response.

How do you decide what sort of statements to create? Well, following are some guidelines:

1. All affirmations need to be in the present tense. So let's say that the negative statement on your list is *I'm a failure.* Rather than saying *I will be successful,* you might try *I am successful* or *My best is good enough.*

2. Write statements that are positive rather than negative. For example, if your imprisoning thought is *No one will ever love me,* your antidote might be something such as *I am lovable and loved,* as opposed to *I am <u>not</u> going to be abandoned.*

3. Your validating statement doesn't need to be believable to you at this moment. In fact, it probably won't be or you wouldn't have to create and say it. The affirmation is something you choose to say now in order to bring about changes in your belief system and in what comes to you in the future as a result.

Let's practice this exercise. Take your list of negative thoughts and start writing positive antidotes for each one. Here are some examples:

*   "I'm fat and ugly" **becomes** *My body serves me well,* or *I appreciate the miracle of my body.*

*   "I can't take care of myself" **becomes** *There's always help; there's always hope.*

*   "People are scary" or "The world is unsafe" **becomes** *I am at one, at peace, and at ease. The universe provides for me.*

*   "I won't be happy until I have financial security" **becomes** *I am comfortable and safe. Abundance is mine for the asking.*

*   "I'm a nobody" **becomes** *I am a blessed child of the universe.*

*   "I'm weak" **becomes** *I am vibrant, energetic, and empowered.*

- "I'm alone" **becomes** *I am held in the warm embrace of the infinite.*

- "I should be more outgoing or friendly" **becomes** *I am wonderful just as I am.*

- "I'm scared" **becomes** *My Lord is with me. I do not fear.*

- "My anxiety will escalate out of control" **becomes** *I have tools to use to interrupt my anxiety.*

- "I am destined to fail" **becomes** *I create my own destiny, and I choose to succeed.*

Sometimes finding the proper affirmation or antidote to a self-imprisoning thought takes a while. Don't get discouraged. Instead, sleep on it, get help, and experiment. The right answer will be revealed.

Once you've created affirmations for each of your negative ideas, write these positive statements on index cards. These will become your reprogramming tools. But how are you to use them? Each morning and evening, you are to take three deep belly breaths, thank the universe for giving you the power to heal, and then read the statements on your cards. Say each one out loud three times before going on to the next, letting the words sink into your being. When you're finished, thank the universe again for supporting you, and then go on with your day.

It's crucial that you read your affirmations regularly. Remember, you're up against entrenched ideas. Each time you affirm yourself, you'll feel the immediate, self-soothing benefits. Over time, you'll alter your mind-set loops and dramatically change your life.

A Powerful Transformation: Carol's Story

You may doubt my words. Perhaps you're thinking: *I can't really change my life by choosing to say stuff I don't even believe. Affirmations can't do that much to make a difference. That's magical thinking!* I'd like to share one of the most dramatic tales I know in order to demonstrate the power of your mind, the effect of affirmations and visualizations, to change your body and your life's course.

Some years ago I attended a Women in Leadership conference in San Francisco that was sponsored by Leadership, Inc. One of the speakers was a runner who described how she used her mind to qualify for the Olympics when a serious year-long injury prevented her from training for the team tryouts.

Since I unfortunately can't remember the name of the speaker, I'll call her Carol. She was a schoolteacher who ran track, a fast and gifted athlete whose dream had always been to qualify for and compete in the Olympic Games. So one year before the tryouts (which come up every four years), she chose to take 12 months off from her job, rent a home adjacent to a track, and devote her time to training for the qualifying races.

Soon after she moved into her new home, she injured her leg very seriously. As I recall, she tore some ligaments. She was unable to even walk, and was told that the recovery process would take a year. Perhaps she'd be able to run by the end of that time, but she surely couldn't train for the Olympics. It was unlikely that she'd be able to run by the tryout date!

Carol was devastated. As she hobbled around on her new crutches, she felt the hopelessness wash over her. *What will I do now?* she wondered. *The next qualifying opportunity won't arrive for four more years. I'll be too old to compete then, and I can't take another year off. I'm doomed.*

But then her inner wisdom spoke up. *Don't give up,* she heard from deep inside. *Train anyway.* Confused, but hopeful, she began to puzzle about the message. *How can I work toward my goal if I can't stand, walk or run? What might I do?*

And then she hatched a plan: She'd use her mind to change her body; she'd train her brain to change her life. She'd tell herself: *I am qualifying for the team* and work to see herself do it. She'd imagine herself in her Olympic outfit and at the games—and she *would* be there!

Carol set to work. She procured tapes of all the prior Olympic races in her category. She watched the winning athletes over and over, slowing the tapes down to analyze their movements frame by frame. Each time she watched a tape, she imagined herself running in the place of that competitor, only faster. She spent hours a day doing this, and she also affirmed herself constantly: *I am outrunning everyone in my category. I am at the Olympics.*

When she was able to stand comfortably on crutches, she stood at the starting line on the track and visualized herself running the course—*fast!* She told herself, *I am winning.* Eventually, she could stand without crutches, and she kept doing the same thing. After some months, she could walk a bit of the track, then a little more, and eventually the whole course. She continued to excel *in her mind,* even though she couldn't really run a single step.

When the qualifying day arrived, Carol had trained daily—in her mind—for a full year, but she hadn't actually run at all. She put on her running clothes, wrapped her ankle and foot in all sorts of protective bandages, and stood at the starting line. The bell rang and she was off, doing what she'd told herself she'd do, enacting what she'd visualized, and living her belief.

And she qualified! She ran her best time ever, and she was going to the Olympics as a member of the U.S. team. She'd talked herself to triumph. Her mind—the things she'd chosen to tell herself over and over, the images she'd called up, and the persistence she'd exhibited—had literally changed her physical being and her destiny.

Can what *you* tell yourself change your mind, body, and life? Of course. You simply have to choose to step into the challenge and do the work persistently and consistently, without fail. Can you visualize and talk yourself to wellness? You certainly can.

What you choose to tell yourself will change your path. Use the daily affirmations you've created, and you *will* take charge of your emotional life.

STEP 7

Learn the Language of Your Body and Make Friends with Your Inner Healer

Welcome to Step 7. So far in your Take-Charge program, you've looked at the possibility that you have a medical condition or clinical disorder, explored your need for medication, learned how to use drugs and complementary and alternative medicine (CAM) for healing, examined the relationship between your nature and life choices, identified the beliefs that imprison you, and begun working at reprogramming your self-destructive brain circuits. You ended Step 6 by reading Carol's story, where you discovered the power of the mind to literally change the body.

In this chapter, you'll examine the ways that your body talks to you—how you physically express your emotional state. You'll learn to use your mind to heed the language of your inner healer, and to register its lessons and make the changes necessary to take charge of your emotional life. You'll do so by traveling back in time to explore your story from another angle, discovering your "body-language fingerprint." You'll then develop affirmations and guidelines to use in accessing and honoring your "body-speak." Finally, you'll learn how to use guided imagery to facilitate your Step 7 work.

EXAMINING PHYSICAL MESSAGES

Often, our body's symptoms are manifestations of our unrecognized psychic pain—of stress, depression, anxiety, grief, and fear. When we're out of touch with our emotional challenges and needs, our bodies feel and express the problem. We may suffer from sleep difficulties, muscle tension, or shortness of breath. We may become irritable, sweaty, short-tempered, tearful, hypertensive, or "wiped out." We can even develop problems such as headaches, colitis, back pain, cardiac disease, asthma, and esophagitis. Sometimes when we're carrying traumas that we don't even realize exist, our bodies struggle to let us know what's going on by making us sick.

Every moment, our physical selves are registering experiences and communicating with us about what's happening. When someone smiles at us, our bodies register joy, our blood pressure and heart rate diminish, and calming chemicals suffuse our systems. We feel good. Yet when another person cuts us off in traffic and gives us the finger, our bodies register upset. Our blood pressure and heart rate rise; we may get sweaty and jumpy. We feel bad.

Scientist and author Candace Pert talks about the molecules of emotion that affect every cell in the body. Hundreds of chemical messengers (informational substances) are registering and communicating emotional experiences throughout our bodies all the time. Whether we recognize it or not, we're physically *feeling* things.

Sometimes our minds can't, don't, or won't register the emotions that impact us. When this disconnect gets large enough, we may feel sick. Our "illness" may take us to the emergency room or to our family doctor. After a thorough assessment and a bunch of tests, we might even be told that there's nothing wrong—in other words, nothing can be found on an exam, x-ray, or blood panel to explain our distress.

But something *is* wrong: We're ill. We feel bad because something is going on, and our bodies are trying to let us know what it is. It's our job to learn the language of our physical selves, to determine what's amiss, and to allow our symptoms to guide us in finding our unique path to wellness. We can all do this, and I'm going to show you how.

Let me give you some examples of what I'm talking about. I'll start by telling you something about how my body talks to me, and how I've learned to heed its lessons.

Developing Awareness: My Story

Many years ago while I was in a residency training program to become a psychiatrist, a psychologist was teaching our class about psychological testing, which is a system of structured questions and exercises designed to be administered and scored to provide help in understanding brain function and diagnoses in patients. He told us that a new computer-based tool had just come out, one that would spit out a psychological profile of anyone who completed a several-page questionnaire. He offered us residents the opportunity to be evaluated in this way so that we could see what we thought of the tool. My whole class chose to do it, and we got our results back the following week.

My profile said that I was a stable, well-adjusted person with an optimistic outlook and a clear sense of self and my goals in life. But it also reported that I had a propensity for somatization—that is, at times I'd feel my distress through physical symptoms such as headaches or stomach pains. *How odd,* I remember thinking. *I have no awareness whatsoever of doing this.* But I hadn't yet learned the language of my body.

The teaching stayed with me, and I began to pay attention to what my body might be telling me that I was missing. I started to appreciate the wisdom in my physical responses to life occurrences. I found that I'd get headaches or stomachaches when I was operating from a place of guilt, or when I was trying to do what I thought I *should,* instead of what I wanted to do.

Each time this occurred, I challenged myself to change my behavior and thus eliminate the symptom. I learned to do it so well that eventually the need for the physical sign went away, and I rarely do anything from a place of "should" or guilt today. On the infrequent occasions that I begin to be drawn in that direction, I start to feel ill or unsettled. At that point, it's my job to stop, look at the situation, listen to myself, and then shift gears.

My body has talked to me in other ways over the years. It has, for example, taught me a lot about how to take charge of my needs in my family life. I've been in a stable, happy marriage with the same man for almost 25 years, but my husband, Rick, and I have been through some challenging times, just as most couples have who stay together long enough.

On several occasions when my husband wasn't dealing with his own issues adequately and his behavior was compromising my well-being and that of our family, I developed weird physical symptoms. There was a period when I had such severe pain in my feet that it hurt to walk or stand. A full medical workup found no abnormality, and I eventually realized that my body was saying, *I can't stand this anymore. I can't keep walking this road. Something has to change or I'll need to leave this relationship.*

On another occasion, I developed severe chest pain that was diagnosed as mild esophagitis. Although the abnormality did show up on an endoscopy, I knew that it was a result of my reaction to my husband's behavior. The pain would come and go, day by day, in response to how comfortable I felt with what Rick was doing to address his problems. My body was saying, *I can't stomach this. I can't take this in. Enough is enough.*

I learned to use these messages from my inner healer to guide me in self-care and marital communication. I spoke and lived my needs. Eventually, my marriage improved and the symptoms resolved.

Our bodies store and remember our histories. Every one of our cells is involved in this process. So, as I sit here writing about these challenging times in my own life, I am actually reexperiencing—in a much milder form—the foot and chest pains I just described. Although my marital problems are long gone, and my husband is on the other side of avoiding challenge, the experiences have become a piece of my personhood. They live in my heart, soul, brain, and body, and your system works the same way. Your body knows, remembers, and has a lot to teach you about how to take charge of your emotional life.

I want to share one more example from my life before I tell you about some patients. This one concerns the language of body memory. When I was in my residency training, I did a rotation under a particularly critical and nasty supervisor. Dr. Jones was the head of a department in the hospital and everyone had to put up with his treatment to get through a required rotation. I found my two months under him to be among the most traumatic of my training years. When they were over, I breathed a deep sigh of relief. Never again would I have to deal with Dr. Jones.

Some years passed, and I graduated and set up my own private practice. Then one day as I was seeing patients in my office, a phone call came in. Between appointments, I checked my voice mail. As soon as I heard Dr. Jones's voice on the recording, I felt anxious. Unsettled, I listened to his brief request that I give him a call. *What did I do wrong?* I found myself thinking. I then immediately reassured myself: *There's nothing he can do to hurt me now.* My body had stored the trauma of dealing with this man, and I had to use my mind to talk back to the fear. But the sensation was also there to warn me: *Stay away from that guy.*

I mustered the necessary courage to call Dr. Jones back. Imagine my surprise when I discovered that he was calling to offer me a job—and my pleasure in being able to politely (and self-protectively) decline the offer!

I want to share a few additional clinical vignettes—examples of different ways our bodies tell us our stories—from my practice. As you read each one, think about your own body's language. How do your cells and organs talk to you?

Worrying Herself Sick: Sandra's Story

I was having coffee with a colleague when she said, "I'm really worried about my friend Sandra. Something is really wrong with her. She has all these neurological symptoms—numbness, weakness, and pain. She had to take a leave of absence from work. She's been hospitalized and evaluated at several medical facilities, but no one can figure out what's wrong with her. Would you be willing to see her?"

Concerned and perplexed, I responded, "Of course."

As I sat with Sandra the next day, she described a significant disconnect between her spiritual life and her work. "I hate my job," she said, "but I don't know what I want to do instead. My spiritual practice is totally separate from everything else I do." As she told me her life story, I kept getting the sense that she wasn't really in the picture. She'd had many interesting experiences, but very few of them seemed to reflect her choices, passions, purpose, or even interests. They sounded more reactive to others than driven by self-knowledge or drive. She was anxious and very self-critical.

Sandra also described her neurological symptoms and the extent of her medical evaluation. She had numbness, weakness, pain, and sensitivity in her arms and legs that would come and go. It didn't follow the usual distribution of any neurological illness. She described the pain as mini-explosions all over her limbs. I thought, *Something is pushing to get out, screaming to be heard.*

As I sat with Sandra and immersed myself in listening to her story, dreams, symptoms, and pains, *my* inner voice began to scream, *There's nothing neurologically wrong with her!* Her workups had been exceptional; it was her *story* that was shouting to be heard. Her body had forced her to pause—to stop doing what she *had* been—so that she could examine and fix her life.

"There's nothing neurologically wrong with you, Sandra," I said, voicing my inner wisdom after sitting with her for two and a half hours. "You're not in your own story. Your body is telling you that you need to stop, take stock, and figure out how to take charge of your life. You need to bring what matters to you together with what you're doing, and I can help you do so. You're going to be fine."

Sandra began to cry with relief; her inner healer had been recognized. "I know you're right," she said. "I'm just so anxious and overwhelmed." Her physical complaints were masking her generalized anxiety. She was scared and confused, not neurologically ill.

"You need to stop focusing on the symptoms," I said. "The more you worry about them, the worse they'll get." I taught her a thought-stopping technique to use whenever she began to worry. You, too, can learn this tool from my *Stop Anxiety Now Kit* (available June 2007 from Hay House), or my first book, *There's Always Help; There's Always Hope.*

I explained that whenever she began to experience the symptoms, she needed to say, "There's nothing wrong with me. I'm just anxious. What is my body trying to tell me?" She could also use some anti-anxiety medicine briefly to take the edge off her worries if she couldn't easily get them to settle down, or if she had trouble pulling herself out of the negative thought loop. The physical manifestations would be quieted, but the real work—the process that would eliminate these signs all together—involved figuring out how to heed the language of her body. We had to determine what she needed to do to take charge of her emotional life.

Recognizing the truth in my explanation, Sandra began to quiet her body with the thought-stopping technique, anxiety management, and self-exploration. She was soon able to return to work and start examining the pieces of her current life that suited her and identify the ones that needed to be changed. Although Sandra isn't finished with her long-term work, she's on the way to wellness, and she's come to see her symptoms as messages from her inner healer. They're to be welcomed, not feared.

Recognizing External Stressors: Frank's Story

Frank, a 53-year-old police officer, was referred to me by a colleague. In his initial phone call, Frank said, "I was abused when I was a kid and treated for depression when I was a young man. I've even been hospitalized for being suicidal. I've been fine for 20 years without therapy or medication, but recently I began to feel that old stuff again. Right now I'm suicidal and overwhelmed. I wonder if you can help me. I just restarted an antidepressant, but I think I need to talk some stuff out." I agreed to see him for evaluation.

When Frank came to see me, he had a great deal of trouble sharing any more of his history. It was clear that he didn't want to talk about his past, or even that much about his current struggles. But he did tell me that a number of his buddies from work had recently been killed in the line of duty, his beat was getting more dangerous, and he was overwhelmed by the amount of trauma and violence that he was exposed to on a daily basis.

"I'm finding it harder and harder to keep my work separate from the rest of my life. I'm hanging on to my job because I have to put in three more years to retire with full benefits and a pension, but it's tough. In the last year, I've developed high blood pressure, depression, severe chest pains, and back troubles. My best friend, a cop who started with me, just had a heart attack. It could easily have been me. I'm in your office now, but I don't really want to talk about my past or my work at all."

"Frank," I said, "your desire not to talk about your history and current trauma is healthy. Your resistance is there for a reason, and we must honor it. You need all your energy to keep on going when you're so overwhelmed. I don't think you can add to your stress by sharing the details of your pain right now. You'd have to relive it in order to do so, and you can't afford to harm yourself that way.

"Your body is screaming to get out of the stress you're under as it is. To keep on working your beat feels so bad to you that you'd rather be dead! How about transferring to another position within the police force for your remaining years? I think your job is killing you. You don't need to do psychotherapy work, because the problem isn't internal. It's between you and what you're trying to force yourself to do. Change your work and I bet that your depression, blood pressure, and back and chest pain will improve. There's a lot of stress-related illness in police officers, firefighters, and other first responders, as well as veterans and other trauma survivors. It's finally catching up with you."

Frank replied, "I know you're right. I just didn't want to admit it to myself, because it's not macho . . . but I have to make a change, and I will. Being a cop takes a big toll on a person. I've put in my time."

He requested a change the next week and was given another job two weeks after that. He and I reconnected after he'd been in his new position for a couple of months. By then, all of his symptoms had resolved: no more high blood pressure, back or chest pain, or suicidal thoughts. He felt well and whole. Having learned to heed the language of his body, he'd healed himself.

Separating the Past from the Present: Lisa's Story

I'd like to share another vignette and affirmation response with you right now. It involves a call I received recently while doing my radio show, *Healing Your Body, Mind, and Spirit.*

Lisa called in and said, "I've been through a lot of trauma in my childhood. I was sexually abused, my house burned down, and I was raped three times. I've gotten a lot of help, but in recent years, I've been more fearful, such as when I'm driving. I often have numbness and tingling. My sleep is terrible and I'm really jumpy."

I told Lisa that she was describing symptoms of post-traumatic stress disorder, which often arise in response to life-threatening experiences (see Step 1). That made sense to her, but she was confused because she'd been better for some years. She wondered why she'd gotten worse since her attack of acute appendicitis and emergency surgery several years ago.

When Lisa developed appendicitis, she had to have an operation immediately in order to save her life. She had no time to think about her situation, and she lost all sense of control. She was told by "powerful doctors" that they'd be putting her to sleep to cut her open and remove her appendix before it burst.

Lisa's experience of helplessness and violation in the emergency room reactivated her physical memory of rape and abuse. As her body began to relive its past, all her associated symptoms came alive, too. Not realizing the trigger, she'd been unable to settle her system again.

While still on the air, I taught her to affirm herself to promote healing. "Lisa," I said, "your surgery led you to relive the trauma of your past. In the hospital, you felt the way you did when you were being abused, but you weren't really in danger. You need to talk to your body, and comfort yourself by saying, *I am in no danger now. The surgery saved my life. My body is remembering old trauma. I am safe now, and I need not fear.*

Relieved and grateful, Lisa thanked me for my time and the guidance. She hung up, empowered. She'd discovered the reason for the return of her symptoms and learned how to affirm her self and quell her worries.

LEARNING YOUR OWN LANGUAGE

Having read my own story, plus Sandra's, Frank's, and Lisa's, you've learned a great deal about how the body identifies emotion and does its job to communicate its wisdom. You've also discovered what it means to register and heed the lessons of an inner healer.

What do you know about the language of *your* body? How do your cells, organs, limbs, and other body parts talk to you? What do they say? How do you express fear, sadness, anxiety, and joy? What happens minute to minute versus long term? How might you register and respond to your body's language? What is it trying to tell you? To whom—me, Sandra, Frank, or Lisa—do you most relate? Do you see bits of your story in all the examples? Please record your thoughts below or on a separate piece of paper:

_____

_____

_____

Your patterns of body-speak are enduring and unique to you. They have early origins and are, in effect, your "body-language fingerprint." Just as your real fingerprint defines you and only you in an ongoing way, so does your physical way of registering, processing, and communicating your experiences.

TIME TRAVEL: WHAT IS MY BODY-LANGUAGE FINGERPRINT?

In an effort to get more in touch with the language of your body, I suggest that you begin thinking about your early years. Call up scenes from your past—moments of joy, challenge, and fear. Visit your earliest memories, perhaps the first day of school, meeting a best friend, birthday celebrations, or a bedtime routine. As you step into your past, pay attention to what your body, mind, and spirit register. Notice your heart beating, your sense of anxiety or peacefulness, and how you feel in general.

Recollect moments of physical discomfort, sickness, and physical strength, and focus on your body. What do you notice? What might you need to pay more attention to if you are to hear your inner voice more clearly?

Now travel forward in time. Visit scenes from your young-adult years and more recent occasions. See yourself at work, at play, and in relationships. Listen in on your conversations; and see and hear yourself speaking, singing, crying, and yelling. Notice your tone of voice, body position, and physical and emotional state. Watch yourself when you feel good and when you feel bad, when you feel safe and when you feel scared. What do you discover?

Think about times in your life when you knew something for sure. How did you feel? Remember times when you silenced your deep knowing. What happened in your body? How did it try to talk to you? How did you respond? What did you learn? Write some of your reflections below or on another piece of paper:

_____

_____

_____

_____

_____

To get more in touch with the language and lessons of your physical self, complete the statements in this exercise without thinking too much. Just focus on your body, and write whatever comes to mind.

My Body Talks

1. When I'm happy, my body _____

2. When I'm sad, my body _____

3. When I'm overwhelmed, I _____

4. When I'm scared, _____

5. I know I'm excited when _____

6. Feeling good _____

7. Stress _____

8. Sickness _____

9. When I feel safe, I _____

10. I make myself sick _____

11. My greatest fear about my health _____

_____

12. Muscle tension _____

13. My heart beats really fast _____

14. Love _____

15. Pain _____

16. My doctor _____

17. Medication _____

18. Body language means _____

19. My inner wisdom _____

20. My job _____

21. Prayer _____

22. Music _____

23. Friends _____

24. My spouse, lover, or best friend _____

25. Cancer _____

26. Heart disease _____

27. Depression _____

28. Anxiety _____

29. Meditation _____

30. Being in nature _____

31. Internal peace _____

32. I self-soothe when _____

33. I heal myself when _____

34. Others help me _____

35. My pet(s)_____

36. Plants _____

37. Balance for me means _____

38. I take charge of my emotional life when _____

_____

39. I listen to the language of my body when _____

_____

40. I honor the wisdom of my inner healer _____,_____

_____

41. I know for sure _____

42. My body always _____

43. I can heal _____

44. I know that out of mind isn't out of body because _____

_____

Now read the 44 statements you've just created. Do you see any patterns? Does anything jump out at you? Are there lessons that you might want to explore or even implement? Perhaps the following example will help clarify that question.

HEALING LESSONS FROM THE PAST: JOHN'S STORY

When John, a thin and fit 48-year-old gentleman with colitis did the "Time-Travel" and "My-Body-Talks" exercises, he recalled being fat as a child. He saw himself being teased by his peers, recoiling as they called him "Porker" and "Fatso." He then revisited scenes of himself being too sick to go to school, doubled over in pain because his stomach was killing him.

John had never realized that there might be a connection between his abdominal pain and his emotional distress. But as he stepped back into his history, he felt the deep sadness and shame of this period in his life. He discovered that his childhood affliction was a manifestation of

145

his deep psychic distress: It was easier to be sick than to go to school and face the hurt he felt there.

Could this be a pattern? John had come to see me because his bipolar wife, Wendy, was becoming increasingly critical and emotionally attacking of him during her manic episodes. Fearful of setting her off more, he'd been retreating from the relationship. As he did so, his colitis had flared up. He was in a lot of physical pain and couldn't do his daily routine. In his words, he was "a mess."

"I think my body is telling me how upset I am," John said. "The more I avoid confronting Wendy, the worse my stomach gets. I can't go on like this. It's killing me! I need to let her know what's going on. I think she needs to have her medication adjusted again."

Empowered in a new way to take charge of his emotional and physical life, John went on a psychiatric visit with his wife. While there, he described what was happening to him when she was in an altered state. Concerned and deeply distressed to discover what she was doing, Wendy worked productively with her psychiatrist to improve her medication. As her condition improved, John's abdominal pain disappeared.

BEGIN IDENTIFYING YOUR BODY-SPEAK

Your body is talking to you every single second, and you can become expert at identifying and making sense of its messages. Do you doubt that? Reflect on John's story. Visiting his history, looking for patterns, and acting on the lessons he learned enabled him to heal his marriage and himself. Think about me, and how I became aware of my physical language from a screening tool used in my residency. It taught me to look for my body's expressiveness. As I began to look inward, I discovered emotions that I'd been unaware of before. Paying attention to your body-speak is all it takes to become fluent. And you can learn the language of your system.

Have you ever gotten a cold or virus when you pushed yourself too hard, a headache when you were really anxious, or a stomachache while eating a meal with someone you didn't especially like? Have you ever ended up sick when you just needed a day off or hurt yourself when you couldn't say no in another way? Have you been so exhausted that you couldn't stay awake when you were actually depressed or overwhelmed? Perhaps you've been unable to fall asleep at bedtime because you were deeply troubled by something. Do you remember losing your wallet, locking yourself out of your car, or forgetting your own phone number because you were emotionally overwhelmed? How has your body rebelled when you've pushed yourself beyond what's comfortable for you?

Now think about a time when you felt at peace, calm, or optimistic. Where were you, and what was going on? How has your body rewarded you when you've taken good care of yourself? Write your responses on the lines below or on a separate piece of paper.

_____

_____

_____

By immersing yourself in the language of your body, you might benefit from thinking about your ideas regarding ailments and where they come from. I, for example, was taught by my mom's words and example that physical sickness was acceptable and unavoidable, but emotional distress and psychiatric illness was to be denied and hidden from both the self and others. I routinely heard: "Laugh and the world laughs with you. Cry and you cry alone." Although I now know that lesson is hogwash, it took me years to reprogram it. It's no wonder that I learned to express my distress somatically!

Look at your family history. What illnesses did your mom, dad, siblings, and other relatives have? What was said about these health challenges? What health problems do you have? How do you think and talk about them? Do you see any connection? What did you learn from your parents about sickness, emotional distress, depression, and anxiety? How are those ideas active in your life today? What might you need to do to reprogram your beliefs?

_____

_____

_____

Use the lessons and tools of Step 6 to reprogram the problematic ideas that you identify here by creating the necessary affirmations. For example, to combat the message my mom conveyed, I used something like this: *My healing is about listening, honoring, and sharing my distress. Connection is the route to recovery!*

To combat his fear of conflict, John learned to remind himself, *If my stomach hurts, it probably means that I have to ask for what I need.* And this statement will help combat the fear of somatic symptoms: *When my body talks to me, I listen, learn, and heal.* Write down some affirmations that will help you honor the language of your body:

1. _____

2. _____

3. _____

Write your statements on index cards and say them the way you learned to use affirmations in Step 6. Doing this exercise will help you be open to learning the language of your body and making friends with your inner healer.

You probably realize that Step 7—learning the language of your body and implementing its lessons—actually involves the two smaller steps of discovery and application. This process is similar to the one that you just worked with in the last chapter, where you identified the beliefs that imprison you and reprogrammed the brain circuits involved. Both Steps 6 and 7 require you to figure something out and then actively adjust your behavior as a result of your newfound understanding; this will be easier to do if you devote some thought to this idea.

As you work Step 7, you should wind up with a series of two-part sentences. Their structure should look something like this:

When my body _____ *, I* _____

Here are some examples of that process as expressed for me, Sandra, Frank, John, and Lisa.

- **Me:** *When* my feet hurt, my body is telling me that I can't go on like this, and *I* need to change the situation or get out. *When* I get anxious upon hearing someone's voice, *I* need to reassure myself of my safety and beware of stepping into an unsafe situation.

- **Sandra:** *When* I feel weird neurological symptoms, my body is telling me that I'm unhappy and anxious in what I'm doing. *I* must stop focusing on my symptoms, calm my anxiety, and change what doesn't work in my professional life.

- **Frank:** *When* I have chest or back pain, high blood pressure, or suicidal thoughts, my body is telling me that I'm trying to do something I can't handle. *I* need to stop right away.

- **John:** *When* my stomach hurts, my body is telling me that I feel criticized and ashamed. *I* need to set limits with the person who's hurting me.

- **Lisa:** *When* my PTSD symptoms arise, my body is revisiting past trauma. *I* need to ensure my current safety, and then reassure myself that I am not at risk.

Take some time to write your two-part statements here or on a separate piece of paper. Remember to use the structure:

When my body _____ *, I* _____

_____

_____

You might want to create additional affirmation statements from these Step 7 Take-Charge sentences. Use the familiar procedure from Step 6 to do so.

PSYCHOTHERAPY AND BODY-SPEAK

Let's talk a bit about the role that psychotherapy might play in helping you master Step 7 of your Take-Charge program. I'd like you to think about the stories I shared in this chapter (mine, Sandra's, Frank's, Lisa's, and John's). Perhaps you realize that therapeutic guidance and support was helpful in each Take-Charge journey.

Does that mean psychotherapy or counseling are always necessary? Absolutely not! But I want you to know that we can all get a little stuck in the mind-body disconnect of this step without someone to offer another perspective. As you work this step, I encourage you to be open to getting outside consultation. Don't hesitate to give voice to your struggles in the company of someone you trust. You may be amazed to discover how much you benefit from a wise advisor.

Remember Sandra, Frank, and John? All found great relief after just a few hours of consultation. They knew that their bodies were trying to tell them a specific truth. But they needed external validation and support to accept and act on what they already knew. Do you feel a resonance with this need? If so, pursue it!

I'd like to close this chapter with a guided-imagery exercise to support you in learning the language of your body and making friends with your inner healer. Our greatest healing happens from a place of peace, presence, self-respect, solitude, and deep personal connection. While in that state, we can access our pain and inner wisdom. We must go there to hear the still, small voice within and be guided toward healing . . . and I'll help you travel to that space.

Practice this technique when you have at least 20 minutes free, are in a comfortable and safe physical space, won't be interrupted, and can play soothing, gentle background music. Think about where you might do this. The more often you complete this exercise, the easier it will be to enter that calm, knowing place.

When you've chosen your space and have the time, dim the lights, get comfortable, turn off all phones and ringers, let others know not to interrupt you, and put on some quiet music if you wish. Make sure that you feel at ease in your space, position, and so on before beginning. When you're ready, read the exercise to yourself, have someone else read it to you, or record it as you read it and then play back your recording. Pause between each sentence and phrase; don't rush the words. Your body will respond to the pace and tone of the language, so be soothing, slow, gentle, and loving to yourself.

GUIDED IMAGERY FOR HONORING YOUR BODY'S LANGUAGE

Take some deep, slow, cleansing breaths. Feel each one as it goes in through your nostrils and out through your mouth; allow your belly to rise and fall. Imagine yourself relaxing into your body more and more each time you breathe.

Feel the floor beneath you—your grounding to Mother Earth. Hear, smell, and feel the wind of your breathing—that miraculous physical manifestation of your being. Notice your body and sense the air around you. You're safe, grounded, and protected by a cushion of healing energy. You're surrounded by warmth, light, love, and gentleness. You're connected to all that heals. Your inner wisdom is brilliant, and you're at peace.

Rest in the knowledge of your safety, the energy of your wholeness, and your place of deep peace. As you breathe into the experience, pay attention to your body's language. Gently notice your arms, legs, head, heart, back, neck, and gut. Allow your roving attention to see, hear, feel, and touch all parts of your being.

Notice, without judgment, what is there. You may feel pain, joy, sadness, heaviness, lightness, burning, or numbness . . . or you may feel other things. Let them all be. Simply observe what is, since all exists for a reason. You're curious, open, and willing to learn. Allow the lessons of your body to come to you.

You may visit all parts of yourself or feel powerfully drawn to certain places. Go where you're called, and explore. Look, listen, sense, feel, and hear . . . and let it be. Notice, observe, experience, and pay gentle attention. Stay in this peaceful attentiveness for as long as you wish, simply noticing what is, welcoming without judgment, being at one and at peace with your body and deep wisdom.

Whenever you're ready, begin to ask your body, your inner healer, yourself: What do you want to teach me? Do you have something to say? Let come what may. Perhaps a powerful lesson, a clue, or nothing will emerge just yet. Whatever happens is meant to be, so just sit in openness. Your inner guidance will emerge when it's time. Don't rush or push; simply be. You'll be given exactly what you need at precisely the right moment. Let your body talk to you, and allow your wisdom to emerge as it's ready. You'll be enlightened . . . you will heal.

Now think of a special destination you'd like to visit. Allow yourself to travel to that wonderful place. Imagine yourself there. Feel, see, hear, and touch your surroundings—perhaps the wind or sun on your cheeks, the grass between your toes, the smell of flowers, or the feel of a recent rain. Know that you can return to this place at any time. Relax gently into this spot and remain there as long as you wish.

When you're ready, emerge slowly from your journey. Savor the peacefulness and wisdom of your trip, carrying it with you as you go forward. Make note of any lessons you've learned. Know that you can return to your healing place at any time . . . and so you will.

We've come to the end of Step 7, and you've learned a lot about the mind-body connection. You've begun to identify the way your body talks to you and figure out how to implement its lessons. You've created some affirmations and guidelines to help you work this step, considered whether a psychotherapy consultation could benefit you, and learned how to use a guided-imagery tool to facilitate your Step 7 Take-Charge efforts.

This work is ongoing, because your body will be talking to you forever. As you continue to use the techniques of this step, you'll become increasingly fluent in the language of your body and adept at using its voice in your healing. Like Sandra, Frank, John, and Lisa, you can master this process, and I know you will!

STEP 8

Share Stories and Build Connections

We need one another. Even the Bible, an ancient record of human history, tells us that when God created Adam, he determined that it wasn't good for man to be alone. So he created a life partner for Adam, and woman was "born." As in the biblical tale, we need one another to face and solve life's problems, care for each other, and ensure the survival of our species.

Whether you believe that the Bible is divinely inspired or not, this lesson is enduring. Connection fosters health, fulfillment, and well-being; while loneliness, isolation, and lack of social support lead to illness and suffering. I often say, "Isolation fuels depression. Disconnection promotes anxiety. Despair destroys lives. Love heals."

We humans are profoundly relational. Our brains, bodies, and spirits are wired to put ourselves in each other's shoes and feel for one another; we want to reach out and help those less fortunate. We also ache to be seen, heard, touched, and understood. We want our stories to be known, to have someone care about what happens in our day, and to matter to our friends and neighbors. We're happiest when we're in fulfilling relationships. We thrive when we know that others are there for us—that someone will drive us to the doctor when we're too ill to take ourselves, lend us money if we come upon tough times, and remember our birthdays.

We've evolved in communities for a good reason. Many studies have shown the importance of love and connection to wellness and longevity. When you feel cared for, nurtured, and supported, you're more likely to be happy and healthy than when you feel lonely and isolated. Furthermore, when you get sick, you have a much greater chance of getting better if you aren't on your own. Dr. Dean Ornish has compiled a lot of studies that show the relationship between connection and well-being in his book *Love & Survival* (which I mentioned earlier). He demonstrates that loneliness and isolation increase the likelihood of disease and premature death from all causes by 200 to 500 percent or more! We really do need one another.

Unfortunately, when it comes to respect for this enduring wisdom, we're living in particularly scary and challenging times. Recent advances in technology, globalization, and economic forces that keep us at work for most of our waking hours have conspired to destroy much of what has kept us connected and healthy for countless generations. Too many of us are living on the edge of despair, disconnection, and burnout. As a result of our isolation and time-challenged lives, we're experiencing more depression, anxiety, distress, disease, and addiction. More and more college students have serious mental-health issues each year, and baby boomers face a growing incidence of clinical depression. We're in a lot of trouble as a society, and it isn't getting better.

Think about it: How many people really know your story? How many of those are paid by you in some way (such as your masseuse, housekeeper, hairdresser, or therapist)? How much time do you spend hanging out—without every minute scheduled—with people you care about? Do you routinely drop in to see your neighbors? Do friends often call you to talk? If so, do you have time to visit with them when they do? How often do you do two things at once, such as drive and talk on the phone, or check your messages while you're in line at the supermarket?

How many nights a week do you eat a family (or household) meal at home? Do you take the time to cook or prepare your food? When is the last time you borrowed an egg or a cup of sugar from a neighbor? How much television do you watch? What games do you play on the computer, when you could be visiting with another person instead? How often do you e-mail someone because it's easier than finding the time to talk? And how many times do you leave voice-mail messages or play "phone tag" without actually connecting with the other party?

How much of your life do you actually share with your best friend or life partner (if you have one)? If you're a parent, how often do you visit with your child or children without distractions—just sharing stories, ideas, concerns, and observations? What would you rather do: read a book or see a movie? How much of a real "neighborhood" do you live in—in other words, are there kids on the street playing ball or riding bikes in good weather? Do you take walks around the block and know most of the people you pass along the way? Where do you feel a sense of belonging in your life?

How long have you lived in the same town, county, state, or even country? How many long-term relationships do you have? How often do you choose FedEx over "snail mail," e-mail over a phone call, or fast food over a home-cooked meal?

How many people are "there" for you? Who would you call to take you to the emergency room, lend you money, or sit with you if a loved one were in surgery? How many folks would step in to support you if your home burned down or you got sick? How many would help you out in times of need? How much do you give back, sharing of your time, energy, and gifts? Would others notice if you went away for some weeks without telling them that you'd be gone? Who would call to check in on you? How many people know your routines? Do you know anyone else's habits? More than one person? How many?

If you're like most people, you're working more hours than your parents had to for a comparable lifestyle. You have less leisure time, are more stressed, feel routinely anxious and behind on your responsibilities, and see no end to the challenge. You go on vacation to relax but get overwhelmed with what you need to do in order to get away. You then come home to more pressure than you left originally. Upon returning, you may even question the value of leaving in the first place!

Like many others, you probably grew up in a more connected world than you now inhabit. You spent more time playing with friends without needing the structure and entertainment that characterizes kids' playdates today. You often made last-minute plans to eat dinner with a friend, comparing menus and deciding which one was more appealing. You could do that because everyone ate at home at about the same time. Very few families do that anymore; and most kids have too much homework, participate in a bunch of extracurricular activities, and are running just as hard as their folks.

If you're like many, you have very few real intimate and enduring relationships and can count on one hand the number of people that you rely on to be there in a crisis. You may feel lonely, isolated, and disconnected more often than you'd like to admit.

You see, I know what goes on in the intimacy of people's lives, because I hear about it all the time. Almost everyone is feeling this pain of disconnection. And I know from my own personal life as a wife, mom, doctor, and teacher how lonely it can be to live in our "advanced" society. We're too busy to be there for ourselves and for one another.

To be connected to others, we must first be in touch with ourselves, and as you know from Step 7, our inner connection can only come if we make space for solitude. But we don't seem to be good at doing that. We're bombarded with stimulation, and we're always running because we can't seem to get caught up. But this frenetic life we lead is a real crisis, a disaster, and even a potential death sentence. We crave connection; we need one another.

I've learned, both from my own life experiences and from having the opportunity to hear about the lives of many brave souls, that no matter how hard it is, we need to stop running. We've got to take time to be with ourselves and listen to our thoughts, bodies, and inner wisdom. We've got to shut out the distractions, silence the background noise, and force ourselves to create and protect be-with-myself time. We must recharge.

And then, from our place of greater wholeness, we've got to *work* at building connections into our lives. We have to swim against the current, making sure that what has healed us as a people from one generation to the next doesn't get lost in the race to advance. This isn't easy to do. The concept is simple, but it takes a big effort to implement . . . and doing so is crucial to our survival.

See, we all know deep down that we'll never get everything done and that there's always more to do. We know that we can fill every moment of our lives trying to succeed and wind up on our death beds wondering what we did with our precious time here on Earth. When most people are asked what they want to be remembered for, what matters most to them in life, or how they'd spend their remaining days if they only had a few left, the majority focus on relationship issues. They want to matter to someone, to love and be loved, and to contribute to making someone's life better.

We most value oneness, love, and connection, yet we don't make these things enough of a priority in our lives. As a result, we're unhappy and unwell. We're making ourselves sick, and we've got to stop it. We have to change our focus and build connections. We can take charge of our love lives, and we can heal.

In this step, you'll consider the degree of connection and isolation you experience in your life. How often do you share your story or really listen to others? You'll learn communication skills to foster intimacy. And after studying a list of ten tools that you can use to build your Step 8 Take-Charge strategy, you'll choose to implement the ones best suited to your needs.

In answering the questions I posed earlier in this chapter, you've already begun examining your life for connections and disconnects. As you move into deeper self-reflection, I'd like to talk to you about the healing power of sharing our stories. What happens when we do that? Why is it so beneficial?

WHY SHARE STORIES?

We need to talk to others so that when we lose touch with ourselves, they can remind us of who we are and what we've lived. In sharing our tales, we can gain perspective; balance out our negativity; be accepted when we have trouble approving of ourselves; and clarify our own thoughts, feelings, and ideas. We each exist in relationship to others. As we listen and respond to one another, we come to know and understand ourselves a little better. Let's look at some examples of these benefits of sharing our stories. (Although there's overlap among all these concepts and examples, we're examining each of them individually so that you get a good sense of why you need to share your story in order to take charge of your emotional life.)

OTHERS REMIND US OF WHO WE ARE AND WHAT WE'VE LIVED

I see this first benefit active in my work all the time. Often, patients will come in overwhelmed, down on themselves; or hopeless about their ability to change, grow, or make progress. But having worked with them for some time and seen dramatic change take place already, I can say something such as: "Remember when you first came to see me—depressed, unemployed, and on the verge of divorce? You've climbed out of that hole, found a new job, and turned your life around. Your marriage is on the mend, and you often see light at the end of the tunnel. Perhaps you're having a bad week, but you're nowhere near the dark place you started from."

Here's another example of how sharing our stories enables others to remind us of our own tales. This one is about my son Gabriel (again!). He recently came home from basketball practice upset and said, "I played great. I've been doing really well all week, and I'm not getting recognition!"

"Gabe," I said with a smile, "you're doing *great?* And you're upset *not to be recognized?* I thought you were going to tell me that you played badly. It wasn't that long ago that you considered dropping the sport because you weren't good enough. What's this about?"

In a split second, Gabe's mood and facial expression changed. With a big smile on his face, he said, "You're right, Mom! What's important is my improvement. It's about the sport." And off he went to get a snack from the kitchen—full of joy in his progress.

Here's a third example. To be fair, I'll share an anecdote about my older son, Benjamin—a high school senior who's applying to colleges right now. A lot of the essay questions he must complete require him to describe his goals, passions, career plans, and accomplishments. But, like most 17-year-olds, Ben hasn't thought about his story in that way.

He's known for a long time that he wants to be a pediatrician and that he's great with kids and adults of all ages. But before our family caucuses about filling out college applications, he didn't even remember all the places where he'd worked that involved teaching and caring for kids. Once we reviewed his work history with him, he recognized how his passion had been manifesting for years. In coming to know himself better through our feedback, he figured out what to write on his applications.

Think about the power of having others know you well enough to be able to remind you of your own story when you most need to hear it. When have you had experiences like that in your life? Could you benefit from more? Record your thoughts here or on a separate piece of paper:

_____

_____

_____

Sharing Our Stories to Gain Perspective

The first illustration of this powerful benefit is from my own life. I'll never forget one especially painful time when I was feeling a lot of financial pressure to provide for my family and my marriage was in its rocky phase. I planned to do a day-long seminar on whole-person heal-ing—out of my own desperation, I think. The program was to include a large workbook and many other materials. Brochures went out, and people began to register.

But I was in no place to create all the needed materials by the seminar date. Since I'd said I would do so, I began to feel like a failure. This was one of the only times in my life when I'd committed to something and then felt unable to follow through. I did realize my error several months in advance, in plenty of time to refund registration fees and cut my losses, but I'd let myself down and couldn't stop beating myself up.

Finally, I shared my self-critical perspective with my husband, who was loving and humorous. "You never do things like this," he said. "You always do whatever you say you're going to—you're amazing that way. But you're only human. This mistake you made, I make regularly. I often have trouble meeting deadlines and balancing my time. Give yourself a break. It's no big deal."

Upon hearing Rick's words, I was able to regain perspective. What he said was completely correct and totally true. I needed to learn my lesson and let go of my self-flagellation. It *was* "no big deal."

In my clinical practice, I often help my patients by offering perspective. We all need this when we're anxious, overwhelmed, or depressed. When overwrought, we see things in ways that are out of whack and need reality checks to get back on track. Remember Sam's story in Step 6? He was convinced that his job was in jeopardy when his boss hadn't responded to his messages, but he later learned that his boss had the flu. His therapy session involved helping him regain perspective.

How often do you get a more realistic view of the situation from sharing your story with others? What comes to mind? Could you benefit from more input?

Balancing Our Negativity by Sharing Ourselves with Others

Perhaps you've read my first book, *There's Always Help; There's Always Hope.* If so, you know the story of Gillie, a woman in her 40s who came to me with dissociative identity disorder, and who's now well. In my many years of work with this patient, I'd routinely hear her say, "I'm bad. I'm ugly. I'm stupid," and many other self-critical things.

Invariably, I responded, "I don't see you that way." I'd go on to tell her how I *did* view her. I believe that hearing my consistent, supportive remarks—my antidotes for her negative judgments—played a big role in enabling Gillie to transform her self-concept and heal.

In my work, I often hear people say, "I can't do that," when they don't really know for sure, or "No one values my opinion," when they haven't even tried to share it. I'm regularly struck by how self-critical we all seem to be—how much we focus on the ways we're fat, unattractive, poor, stupid, friendless, loveless, or just not enough. By sharing our stories, our inner dialogue, with those who care about us, we open ourselves up and come to realize that we're not alone. Many of our friends—the ones we see as "more than" us—feel about themselves the way we do about ourselves. This learning is healing: We're not alone in our pain, and we're not as bad off as we often believe.

Think about the ways in which sharing your stories with others (or hearing theirs) have helped or would help challenge your negativity. Write your thoughts below or on a separate piece of paper.

_____

_____

_____

OTHERS ACCEPT US WHEN WE HAVE TROUBLE APPROVING OF OURSELVES

Perhaps the *greatest benefit* you'll gain from sharing of yourself in this way is the acceptance you'll feel from others—even when you're unable to accept yourself. I think that this is why all the 12-step recovery-program meetings are set up to encourage personal sharing. And no matter what people say after being called on to speak, they're always thanked for their participation.

In AA it's said, "You're only as sick as your secrets." When you give honest voice to whatever you carry, you'll be received, and you'll heal. They also say, "Just keep coming back." Whoever you are, whatever your journey, just show up and let others in. In doing so, you will recover.

Another example of the deep healing power that comes from acceptance is to be found in the statement "I love you." What a heartwarming, validating, change-the-world experience we have in hearing those words! When we let others in enough to know and love us through thick and thin, we open ourselves to great joy, fulfillment, peace, and self-acceptance. Remember, love heals, and without it, we die.

Think about times you've been accepted and/or loved by others, whether or not you felt worthy. What comes to mind? Who, when, where, and how? Do you make yourself (safely) vulnerable enough to others in order to experience the depth of love and commitment you want to have in your life? If not, what gets in the way? Record your thoughts on the next page or on a separate piece of paper.

_____

_____

_____

Talking about Ourselves Clarifies Our Thoughts, Feelings, and Ideas

My patients frequently apologize to me as they begin telling me about something—for not having thought it through enough, for not really knowing exactly what's bothering them or what they need. But I reassure them: "That's exactly why you're talking about this. You know that something is bugging you—something needs to be figured out—but you're not sure what yet. As you talk and I ask you questions, we'll figure it out together." Often, they'll even realize what they're thinking or feeling *as they hear themselves* speaking!

At other times, patients will describe inner dialogues or share scenarios because they need help in making sense of them. For example, a woman named Karen told me: "I'm feeling restless, and I've been feeling that way for a while. It's coming to me that I want to change almost everything about my routine, my life, where I live, how I go through my day, and who I talk to. But I know that's just a restlessness—it's not edited or clear at all, this desire to start over somewhere else."

I listened to her describe her dream and devalue her inner voice. Knowing her well enough to realize that her "restlessness" made a lot of sense as she pursued her healing journey, I said, "Karen, what you said was beautiful. It was very clear, and it makes a lot of sense to me. You live where you've lived your whole life, yet you have negative associations with many of the people and places around you. Much of your history here has been traumatic. And you're at a point in your healing journey where you can begin to choose where you want to live and what you want to do from a healthy place. Honor the restlessness. It's healthy to do so, because it's there for a reason."

Karen listened carefully to my words and thanked me once I'd finished. Through her tone of voice, she conveyed her sense of relief and powerful validation. I'd helped her realize the meaning of her musings.

On another occasion, my patient Patricia said, "Can I just talk about what happened between me and my mother-in-law? I'm not exactly sure what to say, but we had a big fight. I know I need to learn something about my issues and about how to deal with her differently, but I have no idea how to understand the problem or what I'm doing wrong."

As we visited the history of the relationship and the specifics of the recent fight, it became clear that Patricia was looking to her mother-in-law for love and validation that she wasn't going to get there. Having been abused by her own mother for many years, she was looking for someone to fill this maternal role in the wrong place. Oftentimes, when her husband's mom would behave as in-laws often do and treat her as just a relative by marriage, Pat would feel wounded. She'd get angry and demand things that the woman wasn't prepared to give. Fights would invariably ensue.

As soon as Pat saw this dynamic clearly, she knew what to do to better care for herself and to repair the relationship. The insight that came from sharing her dilemma was powerfully healing.

Think about the ways and times that you've clarified your own thoughts, feelings, and ideas by opening yourself to others. What have you learned? Who has helped you, and in what ways? Do you talk about yourself enough or too much? Do you ask for input and listen to what others have to say? Write your reflections below or on a separate piece of paper.

_____

_____

_____

CULTIVATING INTIMACY: ISSUES IN COMMUNICATION

By now you've devoted a lot of thought to how much connection you experience in your life. You've also explored the ways you share and withhold your story. You understand the importance of cultivating intimacy as you take charge of your emotional life. You probably recognize that you need to push yourself to be more open and trusting with others.

But you may be fearful of making yourself more vulnerable. Or you may be trying to connect but keep finding that you have trouble getting close to others in spite of your attempts to do so. So let's look at fear and communication issues a bit.

It's always scary to share ourselves. In doing so, we make ourselves vulnerable to criticism, rejection, or abandonment. As I discussed in Step 5, we're powerfully driven by the need for approval. As kids, we all need this from our parents in order to survive. The teaching to be what others want or need you to be is deeply ingrained. We can carry the dread of disapproval forward in profound ways. In some deep and primitive fashion, we may fear for our survival when we aren't accepted for who we are.

Additionally, the more we open ourselves to others—the more we share our weak, sensitive, and vulnerable spots—the more likely we are to be hurt. Those who know us best can support us most, but they can also injure us very deeply. They can attack us in ways that wound, and they can abandon us both emotionally and physically. Whenever we step into intimacy, we invariably accept great joy and deep pain. They come together; we can't have one without the other.

But we're not in danger the way we were as kids. As adults, we can weather, survive, and grow stronger each time we're hurt. In fact, from our pain we learn about joy. In losing someone, we learn what we have; when in the valley, we often develop a greater love for the mountain. We need the downs of life to recognize and appreciate the ups. And most people who love or have loved deeply say that the heartache is a small price to pay for the magic, wonder, and deep joy found in the bond with another.

So I urge you to push yourself to be open. Use affirmations, visualizations, psychotherapy, prayer, and whatever else you need to empower yourself to take risks. Open your heart, mind, and soul to other human beings. Don't allow fear to limit, govern, or control you. Step into your life fully, wholly, and optimistically. The universe will support you in your efforts. You need not fear.

But how are you supposed to talk to other people? And what does it really mean to listen? What is healthy, effective communication? These are crucial questions for us to explore. We often think that we're communicating, when we're actually building walls and setting up barriers. We routinely judge, devalue, and criticize one another without even realizing what we're doing. We focus on the other people instead of ourselves, and we usually tell them what they should do or what they're doing wrong. But the kind of sharing that fosters intimacy is accepting, supportive, respectful, humble, and most important, nonjudgmental.

In order to help you communicate more effectively, I want to give you a template to use when talking about yourself and working to connect with others:

Say the following, inserting a statement of fact and a feeling word:

When you _____**[a]**_____ *, I feel* _____**[b]**_____ .

[a] = a nonjudgmental statement of fact, such as "walk out of the room while I'm speaking"

[b] = a feeling word or a description of an emotional state, such as "hurt" or "devalued"

Be sure not to add the words *like, that,* or *as if* after the word *feel* in the above template. As soon as you do so, you shift the focus away from you and your feelings, onto the other person. You're then likely to say something critical about him or her.

You probably realize that judgments create distance between people. In contrast, when we share our pain, struggles, joys, and challenges with one another, we foster empathy and connection. This honest kind of sharing in which you make yourself vulnerable is healing.

Use the template from this section to increase the degree of connection you experience as you work Step 8 of your Take-Charge program.

TOOLS TO BUILD A CONNECTION

In the final portion of this chapter, you'll consider a series of connection-building tools or strategies. As you read through each of the ten suggestions, think about which ones you'd like to incorporate in your Take-Charge process. At the end of this section, you'll find a place to record your thoughts and commit to your plan on paper. The suggestions you'll explore are:

1. Be present.
2. Listen to learn.
3. Share feelings.
4. Commit to being there.
5. Open yourself to the experiences of others.
6. Reach out and touch someone.
7. Join a group.
8. Plant a garden.
9. Care for a pet.
10. Create partnerships.

1. Be present. So much of the time when we're in the company of others—even when we're talking to them—we aren't really present. We answer our cell phones in the middle of discussions, work on our computers while listening to our spouses, and pay bills while on the phone with our dear friends and relatives. Think about this phenomenon for a moment. Do you feel heard and received by others when they're multitasking as you're trying to share an experience with them? How often are you the one who's not *really* there for someone else?

So often when we could be present for the person next to us in line at the supermarket or the beauty of the sunrise just in front of us, we're really elsewhere. We're on the phone, checking our Blackberries for e-mail, or tuned in to our iPods. We're busy planning or worrying about tomorrow and losing all connection to today. We're strung out, unsettled, and out of touch with whoever and whatever might heal us.

Suggestion: Choose to do one thing at a time for an hour each day, week, or even month. Decide to keep your cell phone off whenever you're visiting with a friend. Or, out of the myriad of internal and external distractions you bring into your own life, pick one to cut down or eliminate all together.

2. Listen to learn. How often do you listen to others just so that you know when it's time for you to talk and share back? And how many times have you spoken of your needs, hurts, or challenges only to feel misunderstood or dismissed by the other person?

Although few of us do this, we need to step into the other person's experience as we visit with one another. Many faith traditions teach the ideas *Treat your neighbor as yourself* or *Do unto others as you would have them do unto you.* We must learn what it's like to be the other. An ancient Native American proverb says: "Do not criticize your neighbor until you have walked a mile in his moccasins." Cultivating empathy should be the goal of communicating. And empathy—love of the other—is what heals.

Suggestion: Look at how often you engage in conversation to learn about the experience of another. Think about someone in your life whose story you barely know, or reflect on a time when you gave advice before fully understanding the challenge that someone was trying to describe. Consider your prejudices, your unchallenged beliefs about those less fortunate or privileged than you.

Decide to get to know someone better, to listen longer in conversation before giving advice, or to expand your mind and consider new ideas about what might lead a group of people to be as they are. Figure out some way to cultivate more empathy for others in your life.

3. Share feelings. Remember the lesson you learned in the "Cultivating Intimacy" section of this chapter? You make the greatest connection to others when you use "I feel . . ." statements in conversation. Becoming proficient in this way of communicating takes practice, and you might even want to pick up a copy of my first book, *There's Always Help; There's Always Hope,* to work on this skill. It contains a Feelings Vocabulary, an extensive list of words that you can use to become adept at naming your emotional state. It's really important to your growth to let others know how you're feeling. Strange as it may seem, the more ashamed, scared, isolated, less than, or alone you feel, the more benefit you'll gain from letting others in. You're never as bad off as you think or feel you are.

Suggestion: Look at how often you let others know what you're feeling. Is this an area of strength for you? How can you improve? Pick one person in your life with whom you'll try to be more open. It could be a friend, relative, or therapist. What do you need to share? Commit to telling them.

4. Commit to being there. One of the most important things you can do to build connection is to resolve to be there for others. This may mean getting married; choosing to become a parent; being someone's best friend or exercise buddy; or joining a committee at your local church, school, or town hall. It might involve signing up to deliver meals to the homeless every Tuesday, walking your friend's dog twice a week, or even participating in the Big Brothers Big Sisters program and helping a needy child.

The most crucial element of this suggestion and what makes it healing is its consistency in your life. You do it on a regular basis. You know you'll be there, and others can count on your presence.

Suggestion: Examine your commitments. Are there enough of them in your life? What do you reliably do? What can people count on you for?

Plan to add an additional responsibility to your life, or adjust your involvement in one of your ongoing roles or activities to reflect your desire for greater connection. Or stop doing something you're already committed to in order to take on something that you can do more regularly or wholeheartedly.

5. Open yourself to the experiences of others. We can build connections by learning about others through magazines, newspapers, lectures, classes, films, and excursions. This is a way to immerse ourselves in another's way of life, day-to-day challenges, and individual triumphs without even knowing that person. We tap into our own potential for pain, pleasure, hope, despair, triumph, and inspiration by visiting the journeys of our fellow travelers. In doing so, we're often moved to make a difference.

Suggestion: Think about how often you step into someone else's experience through mediums other than conversation. Would you benefit from doing more? Consider taking a class, reading a memoir or social commentary, joining a book group, or watching a documentary. Choose one way to increase your knowledge of another person's world.

6. Reach out and touch someone. There are so many ways to connect with one another. We can, of course, do so physically with a handshake, hug, kiss, or even massage. But we can also do it with a smile, a compliment, a willingness to let someone pull in front of us in traffic, a thank-you, a "thinking-of-you" note, a piece of candy, a charitable donation, an invitation, a volunteer job, or a home-cooked meal.

We touch one another when we offer or receive help, support, concern, or acknowledgment. And it takes so little from us to say, "Have a blessed day," "Thank you for thinking of me," or "I'm so glad you're in my life." We don't do this enough. Instead, we often ignore, criticize, and attack one another way more than we reach out and give back. But remember, love is what heals.

Suggestion: Think about how much you do to reach out and touch others. How often do you offer little niceties to those you care about? How about to strangers? How much do you share of what you have?

Choose someone to connect with, and list three things that you'll do to make their week just a little more pleasant. Decide to say "Thank you" whenever someone extends themselves to you, or to engage in a few random acts of kindness every Sunday. Pick anything else you want to do to reach out and touch someone, and then make sure you do it!

7. Join a group. Whenever people come together around shared interests, values, or needs, miracles happen. The immediate connection that results from sharing a challenge or purpose is deeply healing. I've seen wonderful things occur when people join regular yoga or exercise classes, meditation groups, churches, synagogues, ashrams, book clubs, or supportive gatherings (such as AA, OA, Weight Watchers, and bereavement groups). In fact, I could make a list of possible organizations for you to join that would fill an entire book! The number of psychotherapy and support groups alone is huge.

Suggestion: Think about the groups you belong to. How many are there? What's the purpose of each one? Do they fit your values and needs? Are you a regular participant? Would you do well to join an additional community or to increase your level of involvement in one you belong to already? Make a list of those that appeal to you, and compare it with a rundown of your current activities. Then bring the two lists into alignment. Commit to increasing your involvement in things that matter to you, because you'll build connections this way.

8. Plant a garden. Life is about planting seeds. Much of what we do is like planting a garden—digging holes; putting possibilities into the ground; nurturing what might grow with sun, water, fertilizer, and love; and waiting to see what emerges from our efforts. The bulk of what happens is unseen and silent, under the ground. But then, wonder of wonders, a tender shoot pokes through the earth, and before we know it, we're looking at a marigold, a daisy, or a morning glory.

Taking charge of your emotional life is like planting a garden. You're doing things moment by moment that have no obvious impact at the time; sometimes they may even seem useless or crazy. But then, like the shoot that pokes up through the earth, they begin to pay off. You start to see dramatic change, transformation, and real healing in yourself.

Given these similarities, it probably won't surprise you to learn that caring for plants is deeply healing. Having and maintaining a relationship with the wonder of trees and flowers—living things that depend on you and enrich your life in return—fosters a sense of meaning, peace, and deep connection to the mystery of existence. Many spiritual journeys inward occur in nature, whether beneath a tree, beside a river, or on a mountaintop. Connection to the natural world is deeply beneficial for personal growth . . . and it might just start with pulling weeds.

Suggestion: Think about your connection to plants, trees, flowers, and nature in general. Do you spend enough time outdoors, tending to plants, or arranging flowers? Do you even take the time to smell a rose or walk barefoot upon freshly cut grass? When is the last time you collected beautiful fall leaves or visited an arboretum?

Plan to spend some time in nature each week. Decide if this means tending to a houseplant, weeding a garden, or taking a walk beneath the tall oak trees in your neighborhood. Figure out what it means to you to plant a garden, and start doing so.

9. Care for a pet. How many times have you smiled upon seeing a cute puppy, a tiny kitten, or a foal struggling to stand for the first time? Do you feel better after petting a bunny or cuddling an affectionate dog? Would you rather buy a calendar with scenes of baby animals or still-life paintings on each page? What feelings come up when you remember a beloved animal from your childhood?

Pets heal. Our ongoing relationships with these creatures augment our immune function, increase our experiences of meaningfulness, and lengthen our days. We live longer if we have these companions in our lives.

Suggestion: Think about your involvement with animals. Do you have pets? Have you had them in the past? Do you volunteer at a local animal shelter or feed the ducks at your local pond? In what ways does being with these creatures heal you? Is it through viewing pictures, petting them, observing them, joining the Sierra Club, or caring for them yourself? How might you bring a relationship with animals into your life? Pick some action that makes sense to you and begin doing it. You'll probably be surprised to discover how healing this activity can be.

10. Create partnerships. You've probably heard these expressions:

- The whole is greater than the sum of its parts.

- One plus one equals more than two.

- What we create together is more wonderful than what either one of us could come up with alone.

These statements all speak to the notion that there's greater potential between "us" than there is within each person alone. Remember what you read at the beginning of this chapter, that ancient biblical message: *It is not good for man to be alone. We need one another.*

How many people do you partner with in life? Consider your spouse, lovers, aunts, uncles, cousins, siblings, children, friends, colleagues, therapists, personal trainers, mind-body healers, doctors, lawyers, coaches, accountants, committee members, fellow church members, and whoever else comes to mind. Think about the nature and quality of each relationship. Which ones enhance your life? Are there enough of them?

Suggestion: After taking a careful inventory of the number and quality of your partnering relationships, reflect on how well you build connections that change an "I-you" dynamic into a "we." With whom on your list can you reasonably say one plus one is greater than two? Can you say that often enough?

Decide to increase the number or quality of your partnerships. Do so by hiring a coach, revisiting the rules of engagement with a friend, or cultivating relationships with co-workers who are like-minded. Do whatever works for you to build productive connections in your life. You need to partner, and you can do so to great personal advantage.

You've come to the end of Step 8, so take some time to reflect on what you've learned. How have you benefited from sharing your story with others? Where do you get hung up? What are you planning to change? Which connection-building strategies do you intend to implement as part of your Take-Charge program? Record your insights and plan below, or on a separate piece of paper.

_____

_____

_____

I want to congratulate you on how far you've come. You've now visited and worked eight steps and have acquired many more tools! You deserve hearty acknowledgment: Bravo to you! I encourage you to say these words to yourself: *Bravo to me!*

Celebrate your successes to date, and allow the pleasure you generate by doing so to spur you on in your healing journey. You *can* take charge of your emotional life, and you are *well* on your way to doing so!

STEP 9

Live in the Power of the Possible

Welcome to Step 9: Live in the Power of the Possible. We live in seemingly impossible and challenging times. We're bombarded with negativity and a focus on what doesn't work, on all that's wrong. Most of our "breaking news" is about death, danger, disease, violence, and corruption. As we watch TV, listen to radio news broadcasts, read the headlines on our computer screens, and peruse our local newspapers, we're absorbing a lot of negative energy. We're struck by what a miserable world we inhabit, and we may even find ourselves feeling depressed, anxious, overwhelmed, or numb. We can only take so much of this, but it may seem as if we're surrounded by blackness. We hear so few stories about the power of human potential, the ability of humankind to triumph over adversity, or the benefits that come from doing good deeds.

Whether we recognize it or not, messages such as "The world is dangerous," "Bad things constantly happen to good people," and "You never know who you can trust" begin to seep in. Our anxiety, self-doubt, and potential for despair are activated by the media. Beyond that, marketing messages that encourage us to focus on our faults, problems, and limitations (in order to sell us the solutions) further feed our experiences of personal failure, impossibility, and hopelessness. We may think, *I'm not enough, and I never will be. Why bother?*

I'm deeply troubled by how often we're told to "be realistic," that achieving our hopes and dreams is impossible, and that we need to accept our lot in life and defer to those who "know better." I worry about how little we're encouraged to trust our guts; to believe in the power of what's possible; and to search for guides, mentors, doctors, and supporters who can help us actualize our gifts. I wish that I'd been given a flowering plant each time a person told me that my first book wouldn't sell or that I'd never find a "partner" in a publishing house. I'd have a beautiful garden by now!

So much of the anxiety, distress, and depression that we all experience is a result of how much we live in the power of *impossibility*. We've learned to tell ourselves: *I'm not good enough, I can't do that, There's no use in trying, They're out to get me,* and *The little guy can't succeed against the behemoth corporation.* We've learned to feel helpless. Progressively more victimized by the messages that surround us, we're prone to despair, checking out, and giving up.

But we *can* overcome! I have unflagging faith in the power of the human spirit to triumph over adversity. I believe in you and your capacity to create miracles. I know that by learning to live in the Power of the Possible, you can transform your life. You can find options where there were none, joy where there was only pain, and fulfillment where there was just despair. In Step 9, I intend to teach you how to do that.

But what does it mean to live in the Power of the Possible? What must you tell yourself day in, day out? How can you neutralize and transform the forces of negativity within your mind and in the world around you?

Do you remember *The Little Engine That Could?* If not, go out and get yourself a copy of this wonderful children's book, and read it over and over. It's the story of how a poor, tired little blue engine who'd never made it over the big hill before was willing to take a chance and try to help out another train whose engine had broken down. The broken train was carrying toys for all the children on the other side of the mountain. Many more powerful engines had already come by and refused to help; they were full of excuses.

But the little blue engine was willing to step into the power of possibility. Wanting to help, she was committed to trying to accomplish what would be a huge feat for her. She chose to attempt what many would say was impossible, and she was successful!

So how did she do it? First, she was willing to say yes. And then, mustering every single bit of energy she had, she began pushing herself and pulling all of the cars full of toys behind her. As she slowly but surely began to climb the hill, she kept affirming herself, *I think I can— I think I can—I think I can.* And believing in the possibility that she could triumph, she did.

You see, she didn't know for sure. So she didn't say, "I will succeed," but she surely didn't know that she couldn't either. Unlike many of the more able and powerful engines who said, "I can't," she chose to open herself to the possibility that she could. She was willing to believe in what might be, to act in accordance with it, and thus bring it about. This is what it means to live in the Power of the Possible. You must be willing to believe in the energy of what *might be* and then choose to step fully into doing what must be done to enable that possibility to be actualized.

Living this way means challenging your negativity, false assumptions, and laziness. It involves committing to affirm yourself, push yourself, and surround yourself with those who believe in you. It requires you to monitor yourself for those "impossible" messages, to challenge them whenever they arise, and to remind yourself of what just might be.

Think about it. How often do you say: "I can't," "They won't," "It's hopeless," or "It will never work," when you don't know for sure you're right? And how frequently do you tell yourself (or others): *It's too much effort, It's not worth it,* or *Why bother?* when doing whatever "it" is could yield awesome results? Have you ever been heard to say "That's impossible" when the reality is that it's not, or "It's crazy to think I could do that" when you're just too scared to try? Have you said "I give up" before you put forth your very best effort? Have you ever refused to get help when you were struggling with something because you thought, *If I can't do it myself, it can't be done?* How many times have you given up on a relationship that mattered to you—be it with a friend, co-worker, or relative—without even talking about the problem because it was "too difficult" or "it just couldn't be worked out"?

Record your thoughts below or on a separate piece of paper.

If you're like most of us, you've done all of the above many times. We all get stuck in "impossible" thinking some times, and we're never well served when we do.

I'd like to tell you a story about the power of possibility that relates to how I "ended up" in Tucson, where I've been for about two and a half years. I'd lived in the northeastern part of the United States almost my whole life, and until about 14 years ago, I hadn't even known that a place like Tucson really existed. I came here on a brief vacation when my two now-teenage sons were still in preschool, and something magical happened: A seed got planted. It was the seed of possibility, a wondrous little spark of what might someday be.

I fell in love with Tucson, this jewel of a city in the blooming Sonoran desert, surrounded on all sides by mountains that are visible from almost anywhere. That December, as my husband and I hiked in the easily accessible peaks, it was 60 degrees and sunny. The birds were chirping up a storm, and I was shedding layers of clothing. The saguaro cacti towered all around me, and I felt the presence of the spirits of the ancestors that Native Americans believe reside in the plants.

Tucson is the only city in Arizona that has a medical school, and no matter where people live in the community, they can easily get to the school and its hospital complex. There's a Jewish community here, which matters to me, and an openness to holistic thinking about life and human well-being that isn't nearly as prevalent as it ought to be in our world. Tucson reaches out and grabs you if you're meant to be here. And that December, lo those many years ago, it grabbed *me.*

But I had a full outpatient psychiatric practice in Philadelphia. I was involved with a lot of folks, committed to seeing them through the long healing journey to wellness. And my husband had a busy urogynecology practice of his own. He couldn't readily leave it, and he had no interest in doing so anyway. "Tucson is way too hot in the summer," he told me. My folks were in the Northeast and were unable or unwilling to move. I was their main support at the time.

But the power of possibility spoke to me on that visit, and it wouldn't quit. So when I got back to Philadelphia, I contacted the Arizona medical-licensing board. Believing that I was someday meant to move to Tucson, I became licensed to practice here. And without knowing for sure if I'd ever come, I regularly renewed my license. There was something about paying my 400-plus dollars each time the bill arrived that was about living in possibility. I never questioned my need or desire to keep doing it; I just wrote my check and sent it off.

Meanwhile, I maintained a busy psychiatric practice in Philadelphia, where I saw patients for 45 hours a week, year after year. But as time went by, I became increasingly distressed about how broken our models of care and intervention are. I kept helping people recover and graduate from treatment who, before meeting me, had been stuck in a never-ending cycle, searching for solutions and getting nowhere. I felt the need to share what I was learning about the power and ways of whole-person healing. I wanted to assist the myriad individuals like you, whom I might never have the opportunity to meet as a solo practitioner.

I realized that I needed to start writing, teaching, and speaking publicly to do this. But I couldn't pursue that and maintain a full-time clinical practice. So as each one of my patients graduated, I kept the slot that had been theirs open in my schedule. I didn't take on new patients. Eventually, I had enough time available to write *There's Always Help; There's Always Hope,* in which I recorded some of my patients' stories.

There was an amazing side benefit to making that dramatic and conscious change in my clinical practice: My work no longer tied me to Philadelphia! During that time, my mother died, and my father would have gone anywhere with me. And it just so happened that my husband had given up clinical work some years before—a casualty of the rising cost of medical-malpractice insurance, coupled with the decline in reimbursement for patient care. Unable to make a living in medicine, he'd taken a job in industry. While committed to his work, he was no longer tethered to Philadelphia either.

One day when Rick came home from work, we sat together in our living room to talk. It was a cold, gray winter day. Ice had covered the ground for weeks, and I'd been unable to take my daily walk outside for at least a month. "I really hate it here," I told him. "And I don't want to live in this area for the rest of my life. The kids [we now had four] are all at a reasonable enough point in their education to change schools without too much disruption. I'd like to go to Tucson over their spring break to research what it might be like to live there. The kids can visit the schools they would go to; and we can explore the Jewish community, look at job options, houses, whatever. Let's see if it's possible for us to move there—if we're willing and ready to leap into something new. We'll have to do it this summer or wait until the boys both finish high school."

The passage of time brings about wondrous things. My husband sat in rapt attention and listened to me, as tears poured down my cheeks. "I'm ready to do that now, too," he said. "Let's go and see how we feel. I can imagine making a life there. I surely haven't been able to experience the life I thought I'd be having here, so I'm willing to check it out."

You, dear reader, know the end of this story, because I've told you that I live in Tucson now. But I want to share how clear it became that following my hunch, trusting my gut sense, and choosing to believe in the power of possibility enabled me to actualize what *was meant to be.*

We came to Tucson over spring break, and the kids immediately fell in love with this place. As soon as our plane landed and we began walking through the airport, the magic took hold. The sun was setting, and as we looked out the windows while walking toward baggage claim, we saw mountains everywhere. The sky glowed a gorgeous red, yellow, and orange.

The children gasped and—each seemingly more moved than the others—said, "It's awesome, Mom! Let's move here." Within the next few days, they visited the schools they might attend, and they each had a positive experience. All four were willing to make the change. My husband and I found a house to buy within two days, sold our Pennsylvania home for more than the asking price in just 24 hours on the market, and made the contact that ultimately led to my husband's current job. Rick and I returned to Philadelphia with a very deep sense that this was *meant to be.*

Today is January 16th. At sunrise I started my day off walking a path that I often follow. As I hiked up the steep hill around the corner from my home, I watched the sun rise over the mountains and listened to the birds sing as they darted from the saguaros to the mesquite trees to the palo verdes all around me. The air was crisp and cool for Tucson—winter mornings in the desert are awesome. The temperature was probably about 55 degrees when I started out, but as the sun rose, the air warmed quickly. You can't help but feel it. Living here means you're immersed in nature—it's part of the magic of this place.

This morning as I crested the hill, I found myself thinking, *I love Tucson.* I thought back to that time in my life many years before when the city reached up and grabbed me in its loving arms. Had I not listened to the call, trusted in the power of possibility, and been willing to be patient and brave, I'd still be living in Pennsylvania, and I wasn't happy there. So here I am, living my dream, all because I was willing to trust in the Power of the Possible. If I can do it, so can you!

I'd like you to begin thinking about your hopes, prayers, and wishes for yourself. What do you want to see happen? What would you like to imagine could come to pass? I urge you to suspend your disbelief. Almost anything is possible; almost nothing is *im*possible. Let everything that comes into your mind, body, and spirit matter. Each message is there for a reason. Make notes of what you wish for here or on another sheet of paper.

_____

_____

_____

Perhaps you hope for inner peace, more free time, a life partner, children, career success, self-acceptance, self-love, good health, financial security, joy, a pet, a garden, or a dwelling that really feels like home. Whatever it is, it's possible . . . but you may not believe that. You most likely tell yourself "impossible" things such as: *Get real, Who are you kidding,* and *That will never happen.* You probably cut yourself off from realizing your dreams before you even get started naming them. We all do that sometimes.

Devote some thought to how you shut down your wishes for your life. How do you extinguish hope? What do you say?

_____

_____

_____

When you live the Power of the Possible, you banish your naysayers, your inner critics, and your doom-and-gloom voices. You work to identify them and then stop them in their tracks by using tools such as the thought-stopping technique and affirmations described in previous chapters. If, for example, you don't know with absolute certainty that you can't find a life partner, then you must *stop it* whenever you hear yourself say, "I can't." Instead, you must say, "It's possible that I will," and step fully into doing whatever must be done to actualize that possibility. It might involve online dating, letting your friends know that you're looking, or participating in social activities with other like-minded individuals. It could mean giving the people you meet more of a chance than you do now, adjusting your expectations of others, or challenging your notions of romantic love. You *must trust that it is possible* for you to find a life partner if you really want one, and then do whatever you can to make it happen.

Living in the Power of the Possible means many things. While the concept stays the same, it may take time to recognize how to apply it to a series of different situations. Since you probably need to practice bringing this idea into your life, I'd like to walk you through a group of ten possibility questions, with anecdotes that demonstrate the lessons of the first five. As you read and consider the possibilities presented, ask *yourself* the questions, too. Think about how you can apply the teachings in each section to your own story.

Consider-the-Possibilities Exercise

1. Is it possible that you're wonderful just the way you are, and that your *self-doubt* or *anxiety* is the problem? I was seeing Fred in my office for a consultation. He'd just finished his first semester of college and was home on winter break. His dad, a colleague of mine, had asked me to see the young man because he'd had a tough term. A straight-A and honor student in high school, he'd found the rigor of college courses and the lack of structure quite challenging. He'd done fine (his grades were mostly B's), but he was convinced that he wasn't smart enough to make it in college. He didn't even know if he wanted to go back.

As Fred talked about his experiences at school, I began to see a pattern. He'd started each course with optimism and openness, but he'd gotten a B on the first test or paper in each class. Although he hadn't yet learned how to succeed in college at the level he was accustomed to in high school, he was immediately devastated. He started telling himself, *I'm not smart enough to excel,* and convinced himself that he was right. He chose not to go for the extra help that all the freshmen were encouraged to make use of because he was sure it wouldn't make a difference. Although he made it through the rest of the semester without his performance suffering even more, he found the whole experience so overwhelming and demoralizing that he didn't want to return.

Fred struck me as a very bright young man. When he described the courses he'd taken during his senior year of high school—in which he'd excelled—I could tell that he was a brilliant kid. But he'd never before had to work at his studies to do well, and he clearly didn't know how to do so.

"Fred," I said, "you're a gifted student who can do phenomenally well in college, but you have to learn how to study. You've never had so much work to do on your own time, so few hours in the classroom, and such a need to be focused in your study hours. I really believe that your self-doubt, and consequent unwillingness to go for coaching help, is the problem.

"Would you be willing to start the next semester believing that *it is possible for you to excel?* Will you sign up for study-skills coaching right away and give yourself every opportunity to succeed? I'd be glad to see you again if you have trouble improving your performance, but I doubt that will happen. What do you think?"

Fred decided to trust my assessment of the situation enough to do what I recommended. We shook hands, and I wished him well.

Some months passed and I hadn't heard from Fred. Then one spring morning I ran into his dad in the hospital where we both worked. "I can't thank you enough," he said. "Fred did exactly what you suggested. He's getting straight A's again, but more important, he's excited about being in school. And he was so moved by the power of your lesson that he decided to teach study skills to incoming freshmen. He goes around the dorms sharing his story to get his fellow students to sign up for help."

Grateful to hear of these developments, I told Fred's dad, "I only suggested that your son banish his self-doubt and consider the possibility that he could excel. I'm so glad he chose to do that."

Consider whether your self doubt or anxiety is the problem. Is it possible that you're wonderful just the way you are?

2. Is it possible that the little things you worry about all the time aren't nearly as important as you think they are? You probably have an immediate "yes" response to this question, as almost all of us relate to this dynamic. I believe that the universality of this problem is the main reason that the book *Don't Sweat the Small Stuff . . . and It's All Small Stuff* is such a success. We all "sweat stuff" a lot and think our worries matter. But we also know deep down inside that we're often spinning our wheels, wasting energy, and focusing on insignificant issues.

When I was about 18 years old, I escorted groups of adults two, three, and four times my age to Eastern Europe and what was then the Soviet Union. I worked for a U.S.-based tour-packaging company, and my job was to travel with the groups and make sure that everything ran smoothly. I worked with the local city guides, hotels, airlines, and so on. For some reason, I found very little of it overwhelming, but I did always worry, *What if we get to Moscow or Leningrad and the local guide with the bus doesn't meet me at the airport? This could be a big problem.*

You see, in the USSR at that time, the government owned and ran all tourist operations—including the hotels and local tour-guide agencies. For reasons of "security," tour groups weren't told where they'd be staying in advance. The Intourist guide who met us at the airport would tell us what hotel we'd be going to and have a bus ready to take us there. *How will I possibly know where to go and what to do with my group of 30 to 40 tourists if no local help appears?* I would worry . . . a lot!

And then, guess what? It happened! I got to Moscow with 35 travelers, and no guide appeared. It turned out that I had no time to worry. I designated one group member as the leader, parked all my tourists around him, and told him to keep everyone together until I returned. I'd find out what to do.

And off I went. I quickly found an Intourist representative in the airport who got on the phone immediately. In rapid-fire Russian, he sorted out what had happened, secured a bus for us, ascertained where we were meant to stay, and told me that our guide would be at the hotel by the time we got there.

In no time flat, my group was en route to our accommodations—and no one besides me and the driver had any idea that there'd even been the slightest glitch in the plans. As I sat at the front of the bus, microphone in hand, pointing out and describing the sights along the way, I realized that my long-standing worry had been much ado about nothing.

Today, whenever I hear myself or any of my patients say, "What will I do if . . . ?" and then go on to describe some worry about *what might be,* I reply, "We'll deal with it when we get there." Reminding myself and those I serve that there will be a solution when the time comes is deeply comforting. It allows the worrier to relax and let go.

Consider whether the small things that you worry about all the time are as important or worrisome as you make them out to be. Is it possible that you're more capable than you give yourself credit for?

3. Is it possible that your assumption about what will happen is wrong? We so often play the role of prophet, convinced that we know what will happen when we actually have no reason to believe that our predictions are correct. "I can't do that because . . ." we say. The latter part of our sentence is, of course, some statement about what will absolutely happen if we do whatever it is.

My patient Denise had finally agreed to meet with a sales rep, Jack, who kept hounding her. She couldn't keep saying no, but she had no intention of buying anything from him. Beyond that, she was very busy and didn't want to spend an hour over coffee with him. "Well, just tell him the truth," I told her. "You're not in a position to place an order with him at this point, and you can't spare the time."

"I can't do that," Denise said. "I'll hurt his feelings. And I see him in social situations."

The two of us began to explore her response. "Is it possible you're wrong?" I asked. "Jack is a salesman, so he's used to being turned down like this. Pushing to get together is what he does to make and close deals. But he, like everyone in his profession, knows that 'No, thank you' comes with the territory. What makes you think he's so fragile?"

As Denise sat with the question, she realized that she could, of course, be wrong. Empowered to set the boundaries she needed in order to take care of herself, she called Jack to cancel the meeting.

"No problem," he replied. "I'm sure we'll have other opportunities to get together in the future."

Denise was impressed with his resiliency. "I learned a big lesson," she said.

Consider whether your assumptions about what will happen are wrong. How often do you play prophet? Is it possible that you hold yourself back by assuming you know things that you really don't?

4. Is it possible that you're attributing an incorrect motivation to someone else's behavior and suffering as a result? One day when Georgette came for her regular psychotherapy session, she said, "I need to talk to you about what happened last night." As she tried to complete her next sentence, she began to cry.

"It's okay, Georgette," I said. "You're clearly upset, but that's why you need to talk. When you're ready, just start telling me what happened."

Within a minute, she calmed down enough to share her deep pain of rejection. An old friend named Violet had been withdrawing more and more, and the previous night's events had been the culmination of Georgette's growing distress. Violet was at home but wouldn't come to the phone when my client called and reached Violet's husband. He said that she "didn't want to talk."

I asked Georgette to describe the history of the friendship. Before her move away two years earlier, she and Violet had lived in the same city for many years. They spent most mornings working out at the same gym, eating breakfast together, talking on the phone, and taking trips. They were close buddies who shared the details of their lives on a regular basis.

But in the last several years, they'd grown more and more apart. Georgette would reach out and call Violet, get together with her when she returned to her old town, and invite her to come visit her in her new home. But Violet initiated few contacts and never paid Georgette a visit.

My client began to feel hurt. She said to herself, *Maybe she doesn't really care about me the way I thought she did. I don't know what I'm doing wrong.* She carried this pain forward. Then, when Violet was too wiped out to come to the phone that night, she cracked, and all the pain burst forth.

But as we began to examine the relationship history, a lightbulb went off for Georgette. When I asked her to tell me how Violet was at maintaining long-distance relationships, Georgette realized that her friend didn't do that at all! When people left, they were no longer part of her life. She was great at maintaining intimacy with those she saw on a regular basis, but she was awful at extending herself and maintaining connections across time and space.

Her withdrawal wasn't personal; she was just being how she always was. Georgette's move had destabilized the relationship. It probably couldn't continue as it had been, but it had nothing to do with issues of caring or my client doing something wrong.

"I feel better already," Georgette said upon realizing that she'd attributed incorrect meaning to inevitable developments in the relationship. She left feeling more prepared to deal with Violet, and was more assured of her own value to her many other friends.

Consider how often you attribute incorrect motivation to the behavior of others and suffer as a result. Is it possible that your assumptions about why people behave as they do are incorrect? Might you feel better off if you stopped doing that?

5. Is it possible that your "failure," setback, or loss is really an opportunity in disguise? How many people do you know who had to lose their jobs in order to find their passion? What about those who had to fail in their own businesses in order to discover that they work best when someone else establishes and maintains the corporate structure? Are you close to anyone whose addictive illnesses had to escalate to the point that they hit rock bottom and lose everything in order to find and reclaim their lives? How many folks do you know who needed to get divorced in order to find true love or experience a home robbery in order to become grateful for the gift of continued life? Think about the individuals who have found profound meaning in life only because they're helping others cope with the traumas that they've endured themselves.

Have you ever experienced a business loss that you thought would do you in, only to emerge better off financially? Perhaps you've lost a friendship, only to discover how damaging it had been to you; or become clinically depressed, unduly anxious, or physically ill because you were pushing yourself beyond your limit and needed to learn how to take better care of yourself.

Have you ever gotten to the point where you felt that you couldn't handle one more loss or setback, only to discover a strength within yourself or your relationships that you never knew existed? Have your relationships with others grown deeper because you were touched by a serious illness or the death of a loved one? Have you ever been hurt so badly by someone that you never wanted to deal with that person again, but found that the two of you grew closer once you worked together to repair the wound?

Have you ever found healing in *the way* that a parent, sibling, or friend died? Have you grown closer to your children as a result of being there through their countless temper tantrums, or learned how to live your dreams by studying the parts of your life that have been such a nightmare?

I'm sure you said yes to some of the questions you just read. I hope that you relate to the expression "Whenever a door closes, a window opens." Our lives are constant manifestations of this fact: We're denied admission to our first-choice college and meet our soul mate at our second-choice school. We're devastated by infertility and adopt a child who becomes the light of our life. We can't afford to live in the community we most desire but make lifelong friends with the neighbors we do have. Perhaps our car breaks down and a stranger helps us out.

Whenever a door closes, a window opens. If you really believe in this, you'll be awestruck by how frequently you see it manifest. But you do really have to look for it.

Make a list of at least three times in your life when you've seen a door shut and a window open—a loss led to a gain, a hurt called forth a joy. Then *consider* how often you focus on your failures, setbacks, and losses and feel overwhelmed by them. Is it possible that you're looking at your painful experiences in the wrong way? Might they actually be opportunities in disguise? How would it change your life if you started searching for the window each time a door closed in your face?

I think you're getting the hang of the "Consider-the-Possibilities" exercise. As you read each of the following questions, start creating your own examples to illustrate each concept. You now know, of course, that for each "Is it possible?" question, the answer is yes. It *is* possible, so prove it!

6. Is it possible for you to outlive the odds? Could you have a spontaneous remission if you develop a supposedly fatal illness? Might you prove the experts wrong?

7. Is it possible that being forced to confront your own mortality—whether through cancer, diabetes, addiction, depression, heart disease, or the like—can teach you how to live?

8. Is it possible that you deserve to heal? Are you meant to experience fulfillment? Do you have gifts the world needs you to share?

9. Is it possible that your enemies can become your friends? Do more people care about you than you realize? Are you loving and lovable?

10. Is it possible for you to take charge of your emotional life? Can you master a ten-step program designed to do so and thus live your dreams?

ADDITIONAL STRATEGIES

You *can* take charge of your emotional life, and you've come a long way in doing so. You're deep into the ninth step already! In working this chapter's concept—live in the Power of the Possible—you've come to understand the importance of believing in your dreams, quieting and challenging your inner critics and naysayers, affirming yourself, continuing to ask if it's possible to look at a situation differently, and making sure that you search for the windows that will appear whenever doors close in your life. I'd like to offer you five additional guidelines to follow as you propel yourself into the wonderful world of possibility:

1. Monitor the company you keep.
2. Share your dreams.
3. Cultivate patience.
4. Visualize yourself already there.
5. Use varied-volume affirmations.

As you read the description of each idea, imagine yourself using the tool. All of these techniques are readily available to you for your immediate use!

1. Monitor the company you keep. Some folks heal us, while others unsettle us. People who are loving, accepting, encouraging, upbeat, and optimistic are most apt to inspire us and nurture our spirits. Those who are critical, negative, and pessimistic are most likely to destabilize us.

To stay in touch with the power of possibility, surround yourself with individuals who nurture, calm, inspire, and encourage you. Keep far away from those who tell you, "You can't succeed," "You're not good enough," or "Bad things are bound to happen."

Pay attention to how you feel in the company of different folks. Notice when your energy picks up—when you feel excited, at peace, at home, and at ease. Also, register when you become anxious, have a less-than feeling, or are overcome by hopelessness. Observe your body language when it somehow tells you *I like that person,* and when it says *Beware* or *I need space.* Your inner wisdom is brilliant, and your body is always talking to you. It knows where you can thrive and where you'll be held back. Listen to it, and honor its messages.

For example, I'm immediately unsettled by those who are critical, pessimistic, preoccupied with themselves, or who always seem to think that they know what's best for me better than I do. As soon as I begin to feel anxious around someone, I look long and hard at what's going on. I ask myself, *Is there something about associating with this individual that's destructive for me?* If the answer comes up yes, I set a boundary as soon as possible. I cut my losses (no matter how great) and find a way to walk away.

By contrast, if I'm drawn to someone—that is, excited, energized, or joyful in their company—I consider the healing power of associating with them. If it becomes clear that they nurture me somehow, and the opportunity allows, I try to build more of a relationship with them.

I honor my body messages at work and in play. I hire and partner with those who support my efforts to make a difference in the world, and run for the hills from those I believe interfere with my mission. I surround myself with friends who want to know what I'm doing, believe in me, and want to see me succeed. I don't allow folks that doubt me to become or remain my friends.

Tip: Pay attention to what your body's telling you. Surround yourself with those who believe in you. Avoid spending time in the company of anyone who makes you feel anxious, self-critical, negative, or hopeless. Ask yourself: *Does this person help me live in possibility, or push me into impossible thinking?* Monitor the company you keep, and make sure that your relationships support your Step 9 work.

2. Share your dreams. You may carry a silent dream for a long time, but until you give voice to your hope, it doesn't fully exist. And in that state, it can't be actualized. So you must share your hopes, wishes, dreams, and prayers. Living in possibility requires you to do that.

But whom should you tell? Who is safe? You sure don't want to hear that you're foolish, grandiose, or unrealistic, and lots of stuck-in-the-muck folks tell dreamers those things. So who's your ally? Look for someone who heals you and whose company you're drawn to, a person who has encouraged or supported you in the past. Perhaps it's a friend, relative, therapist, coach, or pastoral counselor.

Remember my story about how I "ended up" in Tucson? I would never have gotten here if I hadn't shared my dream with my husband and, in another way, with the Arizona medical-licensing board! The telling made the dream real. Once it existed with a life of its own, it could manifest.

Tip: Find someone who believes in you. If that means hiring a therapist or coach, do so. Share your hopes, dreams, prayers, and fears with that person. Let him or her help you banish all doubts. You can realize your dreams. This is positively possible!

3. Cultivate patience. This is a biggie. After all, there's a reason we all know the expression "Rome wasn't built in a day." We need to be reminded of the pace at which real change happens. When we're bothered by something or wish things were different, we want the situation to change overnight. *I want what I want, and I want it now!* we seem to be screaming inside. We're unrealistic and impatient. Although we may know that true growth, substantial change, or actual transformation takes a long time, we don't really get that. We expect miracles and often get down on ourselves when we fall short of our crazy ideas.

When this happens, we feel like failures, become hopeless, and quickly give up on our attempts to effect change. Think about it: How long do most people stick to their New Year's resolutions, diets, and debt-busting plans? How many describe their brief efforts by saying, "I tried that, but it didn't work"?

We lose perspective quickly and need to be reminded to hang in there. It *is* possible to effect change, but it takes time.

Tip: When you notice self-doubt, hopelessness, or despair creeping in, cultivate patience in yourself by challenging your negativity with the questions: *Is it possible that I'm making more progress than I can see? Might I be asking too much of myself?*

Remind yourself that Rome *wasn't* built in a day. It took you a long time to get where you are now. You've carried certain ideas with you and enacted your particular behavior patterns for quite a while. It may be some time before you see a substantial alteration in yourself, but change is possible, and if you hang in there long enough, it *will* come.

4. Visualize yourself already there. The more we see ourselves where we want to end up, the more likely we are to believe in our potential to get there. Think back to the story of Carol, the runner who was able to qualify for the Olympic team after injuring her leg because she trained her mind—and thus her body—to be there.

So often we cut off the possibility of achieving what matters to us by refusing to consider that it could happen. But what if each time you thought, *I'd like to get to know Jim better* or *I'd love to own my own flower store,* you chose not to silence the desire with a *No way* response. What if you just started imagining yourself socializing with Jim or arranging flowers in your new shop? How might you feel if you daydreamed yourself into being where you wanted to go? Do you think this exercise would make your goals easier to achieve?

Most people who achieve great feats use this strategy, whether they're athletes, entrepreneurs, performers, or sales reps. Time and time again, they'll tell you that the secret to their success was the decision to see themselves, in their mind's eye, succeeding. It makes sense, doesn't it? If we can envision something, we're more apt to try to realize it. And if we work toward it, we're more likely to make it real. It seems pretty basic when you get down to it.

Tip: Visualize yourself where you want to be, whether or not you trust in your ability to get there. This exercise will nurture your belief in the possibility of realizing your dreams. And that, of course, is the first step to actualizing them.

5. Use varied-volume affirmations. Here's the affirmation you're going to use to practice this technique: *I can take charge.* To begin, stand up and say the affirmation out loud five times. The first time, you'll use a loud voice and a lot of emphasis only when you say the first word, *I.* So you'll say: *I can take charge*—where the underlined word is loud. The second time you say the affirmation, you make the second word loud, and so on. Your first four affirmations will be like this:

1st time: *I can take charge!*
2nd time: *I CAN take charge!*
3rd time: *I can TAKE charge!*
4th time: *I can take CHARGE!*

Then you will say *all four* words in a loud voice and with a lot of emphasis: *I CAN TAKE CHARGE!*

Stand up now (unless you're in the car, a public library, or some such place) and do this exercise. You'll feel an amazing surge of energy and sense of hope when you're through. It's awesome! I often use this tool when working with large audiences to quickly demonstrate the Power of Possibility. When hundreds of people do this together, the energy is unbelievable. Everyone feels empowered by it!

You can use any affirmation you want for this exercise, but it works best with short sentences (three or four words is best) and single-syllable words. Also, it falls flat with an ending word such as *it* or *so.* Try to finish with an action word, such as *heal: I can heal!*

Tip: Pick a varied-volume affirmation statement that speaks to you; use one of the examples I've provided or create your own. Try using this technique every day for a few weeks. You'll be amazed by the power it has to keep you living in possibility.

You've come to the end of Step 9. You're amazing! You've learned so much and grown so beautifully thus far. I'm really proud of you. I'm impressed with your willingness to learn, your persistence in staying with the process, and your commitment to keep on going. I hope you feel as good as I do about what you've accomplished.

In your last and final step, you'll learn how to nurture your spirit. I'm sure you'll enjoy the stories and exercises in Step 10.

STEP 10

Nurture Your Spirit

Welcome to Step 10! In this chapter, you'll focus on bringing spiritual practices—whether faith-based or not—into your Take-Charge program. The relationship between spirituality, health, and emotional well-being has been understood for countless generations. In many ancient cultures, healers were the spiritual leaders of their communities. Only recently (as you learned in Step 4) has our biomedical model of healing and treatment gotten so disconnected from crucial teachings and enduring wisdom.

Step 10 is a particularly powerful part of your Take-Charge program because it's all-encompassing. You see, the biological interventions—such as the medications and herbal remedies that you worked on in Steps 1 through 4—operate predominantly on the inner-limbic emotional areas of your brain in order to effect change. By contrast, the cognitive interventions—such as thought stopping and reprogramming brain circuits covered in Step 6—work on the outer cortical areas of your brain to bring about transformation. But with spiritual pursuits, you get a double benefit.

These systems and practices work on the deep emotional brain and its outer cortical structures. All spiritual traditions include ideas, beliefs, values, and philosophies about life. When you immerse yourself in those teachings, you process and live them through your *thinking, cortical* brain. But these faith systems also include actions, such as meditation, song, prayer, yogic breathing, and postures. When you engage in those activities, you involve your *deep emotional* brain to bring about a response. Involving yourself in spiritual pursuits on a consistent basis is therefore a particularly powerful way to take charge of your emotional life.

I believe that spirituality is fundamental to your mental and physical health, but I want you to understand what I mean when I say *spirituality.* I believe that spirituality involves the meaning and purpose of existence. It includes notions of a higher calling, your sense of connection to something bigger and grander than yourself, and the belief that we're meant to share our gifts to help enrich one another. It answers the question "Why am I here?" and includes the realms of religion, mysticism, meditation, and the sacred. It's the root of life and the source of the infinite within each one of us.

Spirituality encompasses the experience of connection and oneness that unites all creatures—that *healing force* that reverberates between two or more people, or between a single soul and the universe. This energy is also sometimes apparent in an astonishing moment when we feel that the wisdom of the world has been revealed to us. Spirituality is the whole, which is infinitely greater than the sum of its parts. It's the holy or the miraculous in the mundane.

This doesn't necessarily have to involve organized religion. Many people are extremely religious, but they may not be spiritual; others are extraordinarily spiritual, but have no affiliation with a church, temple, or other congregation.

Whether you're a devout religious follower or not, your search for meaning can offer you a sense of hope and self-worth. If nothing else, your connection to the world can lift you out of yourself, shed new light upon the struggles you face, and offer you a momentary reprieve from those challenges. In a world as chaotic and complex as ours, it's certainly easy to lose your way; a sense of faith and purpose can be your guiding thread through this labyrinth.

You mustn't underestimate the power of spirituality when it comes to your physical, mental, and emotional well-being. I've personally seen the miraculous emerge from a tiny sliver of faith, and devastation take over when all hope was snuffed out. I've watched the power of love transform lives, and isolation and alienation destroy them. I've seen children excel when told that they're smart, and fail when told that they aren't. I've observed patients with hope survive illnesses that were thought to be fatal, and others in despair die of curable diseases.

And finally, I've experienced the healing power of love, hope, and acceptance in my own life. I've been lucky enough to learn how to offer these gifts to others. My faith in the value, purpose, and potential of each of my patients helps them heal; and by teaching them to see themselves in kind, they blossom.

In *Essential Spirituality,* Roger Walsh, M.D., Ph.D., demonstrates that each of the great spiritual traditions shares a common belief: The sacred and divine exists both within and around us. In his book, he does a wonderful job of showing the universality of that teaching. He put together the following statements—central messages that are clearly consistent over time and space:

- "The kingdom of heaven is within you. (Jesus, Christianity)"

- "Those who know themselves know their Lord. (Mohammad, Islam)"

- "He is in all, and all is in Him. (Judaism)"

- "Those who know completely their own nature, know heaven. (Mencius, Confucianism)"

- "In the depths of the soul, one sees the Divine, the One. (The Chinese *Book of Changes*)"

- "Atman [individual consciousness] and Brahman [universal consciousness] are one. (Hinduism)"

- "Look within, you are the Buddha. (Buddhism)"

His book is filled with practices you can use to awaken your heart and mind to this truth. I highly recommend his work as a way to cultivate healing through kindness, love, joy, peace, vision, wisdom, and generosity.

THE BENEFITS OF SPIRITUAL PRACTICES

Lots of studies have demonstrated the power of spiritual practices—such as yoga, prayer, meditation, and tai chi—to augment the healing response. People who engage in these activities regularly often live longer and healthier lives. You know from Step 4 that most Americans believe in God or some universal spirit. Gallup polls have shown this to be true of about 95 percent of us! Nearly 60 percent of respondents say religion is "very important" to them, and at least 54 percent believe in spiritual healing. Many pray for their own health or for the recovery of loved ones who are ill. Overwhelmingly, people believe that their prayers are answered.

All spiritual practices connect individuals to something larger than themselves. They also promote a positive worldview in which every person matters. They encourage self-love and caring for others, and prescribe the performance of acts of kindness: "Love your neighbor as yourself" or "Do unto others as you would have others do unto you." They validate the experience of suffering and offer perspective, hope, guidance, and support in negotiating life's challenges. Engaging in spiritual practices decreases the stress response—the fight-or-flight reaction—that releases cortisol and depresses the immune system. They allow our bodies to return to their innate self-healing states.

SPIRITUAL PRINCIPLES

The wisdom of spiritual teachings is enduring; its practices are clearly life affirming and enhancing. I personally believe that hope heals, prayer and other spiritual pursuits transform lives, and that anyone can find a spiritual home. In Step 10, you'll examine your spiritual history and work at creating your own spirit-care plan. You'll explore such topics as your beliefs about God and religion, what gives your life meaning, and where you can find support for what matters to you.

You'll examine your involvement in spiritual pursuits and consider what you might want to add or alter. This part of your Take-Charge program is crucial because spirituality is fundamental to physical and emotional health.

Before beginning your own exploratory work, please review the following list of spiritual principles. All of these beliefs are embodied in the Take-Charge program, and some of them will be familiar to you already. My comments on these concepts are italicized and in parentheses. As you read through these statements, think about which ones you already believe and live, which ones make sense to you but aren't active in your mind or behavior, and which ones you have trouble accepting could be true.

1. You're amazing, wondrous, and a piece of the divine—that is, you're enough, and you deserve to be free and well. *(Because I see you this way, I'm committed to helping you heal.)*

2. Your inner wisdom is brilliant; if something doesn't *feel* right, it isn't. *(My job is to help you find your personal right answers.)*

3. Your inner healer is looking for partners. *(That's why you're reading this book and working this program.)*

4. There's a reason for your symptoms, distress, or difficulty, and you can discover it. *(You've already identified much of what you need to know.)*

5. You're here for a reason and needed in the world. *(I need you as much as you need me.)*

6. What matters to you is of the utmost importance. *(What matters to you is what you're meant to express.)*

7. You can live the life you want and are meant to lead. *(Rumi, one of Islam's great mystics, taught: "Everyone has been made for some particular work, and the desire for that work has been put in our heart." Through the Take-Charge program, you'll find your place in the world.)*

8. Where there's a will, there's a way. *(I've found this to be true with every patient I've ever known. You're no different.)*

9. Although you may not understand "why" tragedy strikes, you can always learn from it and be transformed for good. *(I've never found the "Why me?" question to be helpful in trying to explain tragedy. But I've seen many people transcend devastation by trying to learn from it.)*

10. There's a right answer to every question, but it's always a *personal* right answer. *(My clinical work has taught me this.)*

11. There's a spiritual path that you're meant to travel—a spiritual home that's right for you—and you can find it. *(There's a place for you. You must look deep within yourself as you search the world around you to find your spot.)*

12. You're a blessed child of the universe. *(Whether you recognize it or not, you're blessed. We all are.)*

13. In giving, you receive. *(We're transformed, healed, and uplifted when we share.)*

14. There are no small acts of kindness. *(Think about how many times your day has been transformed by a simple compliment, a smile, or some other little nicety.)*

15. An attitude of gratitude transforms lives. *(Both feeling grateful and offering thanks heal us. The former affects the feeler, while the latter alters both parties!)*

16. You can take charge of your emotional life. *(I'm sure you're seeing this reality play out already.)*

17. Love is *almost* all you need! *(While love is crucial, it can't substitute for guidance and direction. You need all three!)*

18.   You're never alone. *(Reach out for help, and you'll be answered.)*

What came into your mind as you read the 18 spiritual principles and my comments? Did you identify with any, some, or many of them? Were my comments helpful? Record your thoughts below or on a separate piece of paper.

_____

_____

_____

Because my life and work have shown me how fundamental faith is to the recovery process, I'm committed to helping you bring the spiritual dimension into your Take-Charge plan. You may already have a deep sense of faith, trust, or spirituality but have no idea how to use it to support yourself in your journey to heal. By contrast, you may be skeptical of religion and spirituality and feel challenged by the mere notion that faith heals or that belief matters when it comes to your mental well-being. I've worked with individuals from both ends of the spectrum, and I can help you no matter where you are.

Interestingly, it's been my experience that many sufferers who believe in God or have a profound sense of spirituality don't know how to apply the teachings and practices of their faith in their own healing. For example, many folks believe that a piece of the divine resides in every human being but still see themselves as worthless. Do you relate to this conflict?

These two beliefs do not fit together; they can't logically coexist. So if you have a sense of faith, your Step 10 work may focus on challenging your self-concept with what you know to be spiritually true about humankind, or it might involve learning how to use your traditions more directly to enhance your healing. Later in this chapter, you'll read Miguel's story. This deeply religious man learned how to use prayer phrases to take charge of his emotional life and heal his trauma. You can learn a lot from studying his journey.

If you question the meaning of existence, doubt that a higher power exists, or feel deeply disconnected from spiritual principles and concepts in your life, your Step 10 work will be different. You'll need to nurture a sense of hope in what's possible, increase your involvement in activities that offer the opportunity for human connection and sharing, and begin to explore ways to find meaning in your life. Later in this chapter, you'll also read Juliette's story. When she came to me, she doubted God's existence and saw no role for spiritual pursuits in healing. But she ultimately found her anxiety disorder transformed when she added activities to her Take-Charge program that fostered connection, service, inner peace, and meaning. You'll learn a lot from her tale, too!

In order to help you figure out where you are on your spiritual path and what you might need to do to nurture it, I've included some questions for reflection. As you go through the "Spiritual-Assessment" exercise, reflect on the meaning and purpose of existence. What's your notion of a higher power or God? What gifts do you have that you're meant to share? What matters to you? Why do you think you're here? If you happen to have had a devout upbringing, what did you learn from it? What was constructive and what wasn't? For example, did you learn about a loving, compassionate God or a punishing one Who's out to get you for your sins? Are you able to use helpful religious teachings in your life? Can you let go of difficult or harmful messages? What do you do with what you've learned?

As you go through the additional questions on the next page, document whatever comes to mind. This will help you figure out where you need to start your Step 10 work. I want you to know that there are no objective right or wrong answers here, only those that are *personally* correct. You can feel moved and uplifted when you're singing in a choir, climbing a mountain, donating your time to a charitable organization, or sitting in a quiet chapel. Your spiritual connection can take many wonderful forms.

Spiritual-Assessment Exercise

- What do I value most in life?

- What are my most precious memories? What are my dearest belongings?

- Whom do I respect the most? Why?

- Where, when, and with whom do I feel the most calm or at peace?

- What words heal me?

- What words harm me?

- Do I have a spiritual home? If so, where? If not, why not?

- Do I see myself as a child of the universe? If so, do I treat myself like one? If not, why not?

- Do I show myself as much love as I show my children, pets, partners, friends, relatives, and neighbors? If not, why not?

- Do I offer to help others?

- Do I allow myself to ask for assistance when I need it?

- Do I treat my body like the physical temple that houses my soul? If not, why not?

- Do I give and receive love with a full heart?

- Do I act from a place of self-love and affection for others?

- Do I allow judgment and criticism to rule my life?

- Do I approach pain with humility and a desire to learn from it?

- Do I give thanks for the many blessings in my life? Do I even know what they are?

- Do I take the time to watch the sunrise or sunset, to smell a flower, or to say a prayer?

- Do I strive for peace and harmony, or would I rather be right?

- Do I say "I'm sorry" often enough? Too much?

- Do I believe in magic, miracles, and wonder?

- Do I allow myself to experience pure joy?

- Do I give myself permission to be silly, playful, and creative?

- Do I allow myself to laugh and cry enough?

- Do I hear my spirit when it sings? Do I allow myself to dance to its music?

- At the end of my days, what do I hope to be remembered for? Am I living a life that supports that vision? If not, why is that?

- Do I surround myself with people who nurture my spirit? If not, why don't I?

- Do I spend the bulk of my time pursuing what matters most to me? If not, what gets in the way?

- Am I generous with my time, money, self, and gifts? If not, why not? Am I afraid that they'll get used up?

Each time I read through the questions in this exercise, I feel moved. In fact, when I do healing workshops, I often have an attendee read the list aloud to the group before we journal or share with one another. By the time the last question is read, most people feel deeply touched. There's something very powerful—almost meditative or prayerlike—that happens when we step into contemplation of meaning, beauty, self-love, love of others, and the sacred. We're transformed as we explore questions of purpose, wisdom, humility, and gratitude; we're reminded of what truly matters.

Please take some time to reflect on your reactions to the "Spiritual-Assessment" exercise. What did you learn from it? What might you want to explore or change?

I suggest that you take time to write more extensively than you may have in earlier parts of the book, perhaps in a journal or on your computer. Why? Because figuring out where you are on your spiritual path and what makes sense for you to do for personal growth is an exercise in deep self-exploration and reflection. While I can give you some suggestions about what to consider and teach you how to approach particular types of challenges, you'll need to find your unique spiritual path "home."

To emphasize this point, I'd like to paraphrase the wise words of one of my favorite authors, Kahlil Gibran in *The Prophet: No one can teach you anything but what is already asleep in the dawning of your own knowledge. . . . Each one of us must be alone in our knowledge of God and in our understanding of the earth.* Meaningfulness is deeply personal. I can lead you to the doorway of your journey, and I can even give you some directions to follow along your way. But ultimately, you'll need to wrestle with your own demons and find your own personal path to purpose, wholeness, and maybe even God.

I'd like to share a few stories with you to illustrate how you can use spiritual beliefs and practices to transform challenge. In the first tale, you'll see how I helped a religious man use his faith to overcome a sleep/trauma problem. Then you'll learn how a woman who lacked faith in God learned to use spiritual questions (about meaningfulness and purpose) and pursuits (acts of charity) to transform her anxiety disorder. As you read these stories, think about how they relate to you and your Take-Charge needs. Are you religious? Do you believe in God? Do you know how to use your faith to support your own healing? Or do you lack faith in God? Do you have a sense that some spiritual values, ideas, approaches, or practices could help you? Do you know how to use them for wellness? Let yourself learn from the experiences of others.

Faith Heals: Miguel's Story

Miguel, a deeply religious man of 68, asked me to help him overcome a sleep problem. He'd immigrated to the United States as a young man to escape persecution in his birth country. He'd made a good life here and was grateful to God for his salvation. He attended church regularly and prayed several times each day.

But several years before meeting me, Miguel had begun having terrible dreams every single night that would awaken him—usually screaming—and scare him so much that he was often unable to fall back to sleep. He'd been to many doctors and therapists, but nothing had helped. He'd tried some sleep medicines, but they made him groggy and confused. He was at his wit's end, and wondered if there was something I could do.

As you know by now, I needed to hear Miguel's story to figure out how to understand his problem and determine the route to his recovery. So, I asked him to tell me his tale. We began to explore questions such as: What was the content of his dreams? Had he ever had similar problems? Did he suffer from any psychiatric condition? What was happening in his life when the sleep problem began? And so on.

I learned that as a child, Miguel had witnessed and suffered great trauma. His life had often been in danger. He saw many he knew and loved die. After coming to the U.S., it had taken him some time to stop reliving the horror of his childhood, but he had been well for many, many years.

Although he hadn't realized that there could be a connection, he'd written a memoir several years before I met him. It won't surprise you to learn that writing the book required him to revisit the trauma of his past, and in doing so, it came alive again. His body memories became activated, and he began to have nightmares of being in danger, unable to escape.

So, first of all, I helped Miguel understand why he was having a reemergence of his symptoms—that is, his body was back in the past. Then I taught him what to do to heal. When he awoke in fear, I told him to remind himself that he was now safe. The dream was history coming alive—but the trauma was over. He was at no current risk.

As I explained all this, something told me that Miguel needed more than the explanation and affirmation to combat the reappearance of his severe-trauma experience. So I asked him if there were any prayers or teachings from his religion that he might utter when he awoke in fear—phrases that could soothe him.

Miguel had never thought of using his faith in such a specific, self-healing way, but he immediately remembered a prayer phrase that he could use. It spoke of the role of God as the healer—something along the lines of "My Lord heals me," as I recall. I suggested that he say those words over and over when he awoke. I believed that because they had such meaning and power for him, they'd settle his nervous system and allow him to drop off again.

By the time I saw Miguel the next week, he was sleeping through the night. He'd begun using the affirmation and prayer phrase immediately. The first night he'd awoken several times but was able to fall back to sleep each time. As the week went on, he awoke fewer and fewer times, and he was able to drift off again quicker and quicker. After eight nights, he was no longer waking up at all. His faith, in a sense, had healed him.

Yes, he did need to understand the reason for his troubles and begin an affirmation practice to combat old fears. We can't minimize the role of these other steps in his recovery. But the bulk of his cure involved a very specific use of his prayer practice. Once he learned how to apply the teachings and words of his faith to his particular challenge—in just the right way and at just the right time—he quickly transformed a problem that he'd been dealing with for years. This story is a great example of the idea that faith heals, don't you think?

Do you relate to Miguel's story? How might you benefit from applying the teachings of your belief system to your difficulties or self-concept?

_____

_____

_____

Before I move on to tell you the second story, I want to share "Footprints" with you. This is an amazing little story that I first heard from a recovering addict whom I used to work with. You may know this tale, because it's on cards and bookmarks in many stores. But I'm including a short summary of it here because if you *aren't* aware of it and have some faith in God, you might find it helpful whenever you're feeling particularly overwhelmed or challenged—I know that I do.

> A man dreamed that he was walking along the beach with the Lord as he saw moments from his past. There were often two sets of footprints in the sand: his and the Lord's. But sometimes there was only one set of marks, often during the most trying experiences.
>
> He asked about this, since the Lord had promised to be with him always. He didn't understand why he'd been left alone during his worst trials.
>
> The Lord told him that when there was only one set of footprints, it was because He was carrying the man in his arms and bringing him to safety.

I love the image of being carried in times of great need. In fact, before I'd ever even heard of "Footprints," I used to envision and feel myself resting in the hands of God whenever I was overwhelmed. I think the image came to me from hearing the song "He's Got the Whole World in His Hands," where, you may remember, there's also a line about the "tiny little baby in His hands." I see and feel these huge hands, cupped lovingly together, as I—tiny in comparison—sit or lie within them. Does an image like that comfort you? Think about it. If so, use it to soothe, heal, grow, and empower you as you work to take charge of your emotional life.

Bringing Meaning to Life: Juliette's Story

Juliette was 58 years old and married, without children, when she was referred to me by her gynecologist. She had severe pelvic pain but no identifiable problem; all her examinations and medical tests were normal, so her doctor wasn't sure what to do. He'd given her medication for her pain, but nothing seemed to help.

When Juliette came to see me, I saw a beautiful, fit, and friendly woman who was quite anxious and prone to tears. "I'm not sure what to do," she told me. "I'm in constant pain, and nothing seems to help much. When I take enough medicine to control it, I can't stay awake. This is just awful."

Juliette began to tell me her story. She'd been raised with minimal exposure to her religion and didn't believe in God. She liked the holidays but didn't know much about their origins or purpose. She'd retired from a satisfying and successful career in the financial industry when the bank she worked for had been acquired two years before. She took an early retirement plan that was too good to pass up, but she was now feeling sort of lost.

She was also disturbed about her path and legacy. "I'm not sure what I'm meant to be doing with my life," she said. "I don't feel that I've made—or will make—much difference in the world. I never had kids because my husband didn't want them, so there's nothing there either. And I'm anxious all the time."

I began to wonder if Juliette's pain and excessive worry were due to a lack of meaning in her life. She met diagnostic criteria for panic disorder, but the anxiety attacks had begun around the time of her retirement. She'd never had such symptoms before. And interestingly enough, her pelvic pain had appeared soon thereafter.

I began to explore this idea with her. At first, she doubted the possibility, but as time went on, it began to make sense to her. I gave her anti-anxiety medication to use as needed and taught her how to employ thought stopping and affirmations to decrease her worry. With these tools, she improved a great deal, but her problems didn't resolve completely until she began bringing meaning and spirit-nurturing activities into her life.

So what did she do? She explored a lot of things, adding one pursuit after another, staying with those that felt satisfying or nurturing and abandoning the ones that didn't. Ultimately, Juliette chose to sponsor a child in need in another country, volunteer regularly at a local soup kitchen, plant a garden, and practice tai chi. After doing those four things for about six months, her anxiety and pelvic pain disappeared. She still participates in these activities, and to this day—several years since her graduation from my care—she's pain and panic free.

Do you relate to Juliette's story? Might you do well to bring more meaningful pursuits and spiritual practices into your Take-Charge plan? Write your reflections below or on a separate piece of paper.

_____

_____

_____

Before we go on, I need to say something to those of you who've had negative experiences with religion. If there's something particularly traumatic or tough to get past in your history, don't despair. Start with what's comfortable for you now. Do nothing that feels wrong, and be open to seeking counseling if you get to a point where that calls to you. You can use a therapist, counselor, or spiritual director—whatever feels right. It's also possible to work this step without a God-focus at all. Just look at the list in the next section, and you'll find that very few of the suggestions are religion or God oriented. You can find your way!

SUGGESTION LIST: WAYS TO CULTIVATE A SPIRITUAL CONNECTION

While I can't tell you exactly what to do to bring meaning, hope, and purpose into your Take-Charge program, I can offer you the following list of 24 things you can do to enhance your spiritual life. These are all simply suggestions, so pick out the ones that speak to you and try using them. See what works for you in building your Step 10 plan. Be open and notice what happens.

1. Give thanks. Take time to notice what works in your life. What do you appreciate? Commit to saying "Thank you" to someone every day, or send a message saying "Thank you for being in my life" to a friend, relative, or co-worker. Start a gratitude list and write down three things you're thankful for each day.

2. Help others. Decide to practice small acts of kindness, such as opening the door for someone pushing a stroller or carrying a bag of groceries. Cook dinner for a friend who's ill, volunteer your time at Habitat for Humanity, or donate money to a worthy cause. Make giving a daily practice.

3. Forgive yourself/others. Ironically, in forgiving others, we receive the benefits of health and inner peace. Sometimes we can't bless those who have hurt us until we've honored our hurt, pain, and anger and found appropriate ways to work through it. But we *can* shift our focus to compassion and forgiveness. Ask yourself, *Do I have room in my heart to forgive?* Strive to make that space. As you do, avoid fanning the flames of hurt and anger. Be gentle with yourself and others; cultivate compassion.

4. Love. You've already devoted a full step to building connection, but you may not have recognized the spiritual nature of loving and being cared for in return. All spiritual traditions revolve around the power of this emotion. Tell someone dear to you "I love you," or reach out and show how you feel.

5. Nurture acceptance. So often we strive to control or change what isn't in our power to effect. Remind yourself that you are *as you're meant to be.* Let those parts of yourself that you don't like—but can't alter—be okay. See if you can begin to tolerate them, then accept them, and ultimately, grow to love them (and yourself) fully. Let others and the universe around you just be. Stop trying to change those who hurt you. Care for yourself by altering what you have the power to effect, and simply make some space between yourself and those who unsettle you. Accept what is without judgment.

6. Study, learn, and expand your awareness. Study the Bible, spiritual or religious books, philosophy, or theology. Open yourself to the wisdom of ancient texts, traditions, practices, and laws of life. Challenge yourself to apply some of their enduring lessons to your current experiences.

7. Cultivate humility and banish judgment. You're both a wondrous being and a tiny piece of the infinite, so don't allow yourself to become too self-important. We're all of equal value. Catch yourself when you start thinking that you know better or *are* better than someone else. Ask yourself on a regular basis *Am I humble enough? Do I sound critical or judgmental?* Monitor yourself daily for arrogant thinking and behavior.

8. Don't criticize. I love the lesson that Thumper's mother teaches him in the film *Bambi*, which I remember as "If you don't have anything nice to say, don't say anything at all." We're so quick to criticize, attack, and find fault with others. Practice raising your concerns with those who hurt or anger you in a respectful way. Use this template: "When you_____, I feel _____," to confront them. Always ask yourself, *Am I being respectful in my communication?* If the answer is no, apologize and try again!

9. Look for the blessing in challenging, painful, or difficult situations. As my dad lay dying of cancer recently, my heart was breaking. He was "my person," my champion, support, and soul mate in a very profound way. He and I were the only two in my immediate family of origin who believed in God, felt comfort in our faith tradition, and shared a commitment to helping those less fortunate.

In one way, living through my father's decline was one of the most challenging and deeply painful experiences I've ever endured, but it was probably one of the most healing as well. During that time, we had so many conversations about our history, relationship, mistakes, regrets, and love. Everything that had ever hurt me in my 47-year history with him was healed in those final months. And as we sat together, my dad often said, "I so enjoy these conversations we're having," and so did I.

The fact that my father was meant to leave this earthly life because of what felt to me like an early call "Home" was deeply challenging for me. But I searched for, and found, amazing blessings in my loss. And as you know from this book's dedication, my dad did, too.

He died "ecstatic" that I was helping so many people, feeling deeply loved, and without fear. *"Adonai li v'lo y'rah,"* he would say. "My Lord is with me; I will not be afraid."

You can find blessings in the smallest of life's challenges and in the greatest experiences of pain. Look for the silver lining of every cloud, the rainbow after each storm, and the present in every loss. There's always a blessing there.

10. Search for the divine and the wonder in others. There's an ancient Jewish parable about a community where no one was getting along; there was abuse, violence, and stealing. The inhabitants began to call out, crying to God for the Messiah to come—to transform the community and bring peace. A message came back: *The Messiah is among you.*

Not knowing who it was, each villager began to treat all the others with the love and respect due to a messenger of God. Very soon, the community was transformed. Joy, respect, and compassion reigned once more, and there was no longer a need to be rescued. This change in perspective and behavior had healed the whole town.

This parable is no different in its message from what we learn in studies showing that teachers who think their students are smart wind up with gifted scholars, while those who think their classes are quite limited find their students failing simple exams.

We each have unique gifts. We're uplifted and transformed when we look at ourselves and others that way. Search for the wonder in yourself and in those you meet, reminding yourself to do this on a regular basis. You'll be amazed at what comes back if you do.

11. Always give the benefit of the doubt. Assume the best of others until proven otherwise. We're so quick to assume the worst of others. We can't find a ring, and before searching our drawers, we assume that our housekeeper took it. We don't receive an invitation to a close friend's party, and without checking out what happened, we decide that she's trying to get back at us for something. We're passed over for a promotion—for a job we're actually ill suited to perform—but decide that our boss is trying to get us to quit. . . . I could go on and on, but you get the idea.

Start to notice how often you assume the worst, and commit to challenging yourself whenever you see it happening. Ask yourself, *Do I know that for sure? What if I were to give the benefit of the doubt?* Change your behavior and change your life.

12. Pray: Offer thanks and ask for strength, wisdom, acceptance, and healing of self/others. Prayer changes lives. You may know that already, and perhaps you even pray sometimes. I suggest that if this resonates for you, plan to pray daily. Take a moment or two each morning or evening to offer thanks or ask for strength. Talk to God or your personal Higher Power. This communion with something larger than yourself will heal you.

13. Exercise, dance, meditate, or do yoga or tai chi. Many people find that settling into their bodies in these ways connects them with what's healing in the universe. Find an activity that does that for you and use it regularly. Make it part of your plan, routine, and schedule, growing into it and through it. You'll love the results!

14. Spend time being present in nature. Sometimes when I feel down or distressed, I push myself to get out. Even if I spend just a few minutes walking among the birds and cacti around my home, I feel renewed. There's something about Mother Nature's work that calms and heals us. Gazing up at the tiny arc of the moon in the night sky, walking through a carpet of wildflowers at dusk, or sitting on a mountaintop at sunrise and feeling the breeze can be awe inspiring and deeply grounding at the same time.

Commit to spending some time in the natural playground each week, and pay attention to the wonder of the scene and space. Notice the scent of a flower, the shape of a cloud, the pattern of leaves on a tree, or the sound of water rushing over smooth rocks in a stream. Be in nature—really *be* there, and be uplifted!

15. Be generous with your time, resources, and spirit. We're so quick to focus on why we can't share and spend almost no energy trying to figure out how we can do more. But our strategy is a recipe for disaster. The tighter we hold on to what we have—the more we close our hands into fists—the less we ultimately end up with. We destroy what *is* there. Yet the more we open ourselves to those around us, the more we get back. We increase our material and spiritual resources by sharing them.

You probably know the expression "If you need something done, ask a busy person." That seems counterintuitive. Shouldn't these folks have less time? Not according to the spiritual laws of the universe. You see, the more we do, the more we're able to do; the more we give, the more we get.

Devote some thought to how often you say "I can't" when asked to share your time, resources, or spirit. Figure out how you can say yes more often, and then open your hands and heart more regularly.

16. Visualize yourself in the palm of God's hand. This is the lesson of "Footprints," the story you read a summary of earlier in this chapter. If being carried, buoyed, or supported physically by God or some other loving being comforts you, then visualize yourself there. Allow yourself to see and feel the experience. Call it up whenever you feel the need for protection, love, or support; it's always available to you.

17. Paint, draw, sing, sculpt, garden, or write. These are, of course, all art forms. And for many people, something deeply spiritual happens when they enter the creative process. A bigger force takes over and expresses itself as the separation between artist and art disappears. The creator is elevated by this experience. If any form of art appeals to you, start puttering around with it. Perhaps you'll find something to do on a regular basis that heals, uplifts, and empowers you. If you do, use it!

18. Listen and receive another in pain. Really hear the story. You already know from your Step 8 work how important it is to share stories and build connections, but there's something particularly healing in receiving someone else in pain. We're touched at a deep, heart-healing level when we're really there for another in that way.

We often withdraw from people when we believe they're in pain. We tell ourselves, *I don't want to make them feel worse by coming around or asking them how they're doing.* But when we run for cover at these times, we're copping out and abandoning those who need us. Challenge yourself to call or stop by when you hear of a friend's loss or other challenge. Don't assume that someone's cancer diagnosis, death in the family, or loss of a job means that she needs space. Call her and make room for sharing. Let her tell you what she needs to say. You'll be healed for being there.

19. Explore spiritual homes, religious institutions, or Quaker meetings. Begin a regular ritual practice. You can't find your spiritual home if you don't go searching for it, and you won't feel connected to that community if you don't regularly engage in any of its ritual practices. So start visiting different churches, synagogues, ashrams, prayer groups, bible-study classes, Quaker meetings, or any other institutions that could be options for you. Talk to congregants, other participants, leaders, and clergy to find a good fit. Then begin a regular practice.

20. Feed yourself well—treat your body with the respect of good nutrition. Your physical self is the temple that houses your soul or spirit, and nurturing yourself spiritually means treating your body with respect and care.

Do you eat healthfully, getting enough fruits, vegetables, good protein sources, fats, and carbohydrates? Do you eat a lot of junk food? Take a careful inventory of your diet, and resolve to improve your nutrition a little bit at a time.

21. Surround yourself with people who believe in you. You can't cultivate faith if you're immersed in criticism, doubt, and negativity, so examine the company you keep. Work actively and aggressively to cultivate nurturing relationships, and avoid those that hold you back.

22. Nurture hope. This is one of the most crucial suggestions I have to offer you. As you know, belief in what could be heals people, and a lack of it kills them. Do everything you can to be hopeful. Read inspirational literature, listen to speakers who encourage you to trust in possibility and potential, surround yourself with optimistic friends, and only go to doctors who believe in your healing powers.

Avoid doom-and-gloom news, people, movies and Websites. Stick your head in the sand if you have to at times! Negativity is rampant in our culture, and sometimes we have to play ostrich to get away from it all.

Remember, you're wonderful. You *can* take charge of your emotional life and be well. Where there's a will, there's a way. Don't allow yourself to believe those folks who tell you otherwise.

23. Ask for help. You'll be answered. The universe wants you to be well. Don't let yourself get stuck in thinking: *No one cares, I deserve to suffer,* or *I ought to be past this need by now.* Push yourself to find the support that's waiting for you. Reach out; try, try, and try again. With persistence, you *will* be answered.

24. Never give up. I believe in you and know that you can heal. You can take charge of your emotional life. You have the ability to overcome your anxiety, distress, and depression through whole-person healing. There's always help, and there's always hope for you. If you don't believe me, read my first book; immerse yourself in its powerful tales of transformation. If those folks can do it, so can you! Have no doubt: *You can transform your life.*

I've given you 24 suggestions for ways to cultivate your spiritual connection. I could go on, but it's time for me to stop. Your inner wisdom is aching to point you in the right direction. Now you can begin to create your own spirit-care plan. Think about what you've learned in this chapter. What do you need to do to nurture your spirit? What are you ready and willing to take on? What might you choose to do in the future? Record your thoughts below or on a separate piece of paper.

_____

_____

_____

Congratulations! You've just finished a comprehensive ten-step plan to take charge of your emotional life. You'll need to revisit and work with these steps forever, but you've come a long way in healing yourself already. I'm proud of your accomplishments.

In the Afterword that follows this chapter, you'll have a chance to review what you've learned in the Take-Charge program. After revisiting each step, you'll create your own Take-Charge mission statement—your personal summary and action plan. But, before we move on, I'd like to close this step with my blessing to you.

My Prayer for You

May you live to see your dreams fulfilled.
May you appreciate your wonder, your bountiful gifts.
May you recognize your divinity reflected back at you.
And may love, hope, and purpose suffuse your being.
Amen.

AFTERWORD

It's time for you to review each of the ten steps of your Take-Charge program. Read through each one as listed below and think about what you want to do in order to work that step. You might find it helpful to revisit the appropriate chapters to refresh your memory. Record your observations and plans for each step in the space provided or on a separate piece of paper.

Step 1: Consider your story and its lessons: Do you have a medical condition or chemical imbalance?

_____

_____

_____

Step 2: Explore your need for medication.

_____

_____

_____

Step 3: Follow treatment guidelines when medication is necessary.

_____

_____

_____

Step 4: Include complementary and alternative interventions.

_____

_____

_____

Step 5: Make life choices that fit your nature.

_____

_____

_____

Step 6: Identify the beliefs that imprison you and reprogram the brain circuits involved.

_____

_____

_____

Step 7: Learn the language of your body and make friends with your inner healer.

_____

_____

_____

Step 8: Share stories and build connection.

_____

_____

_____

Step 9: Live in the power of the possible.

_____

_____

_____

Step 10: Nurture your spirit.

_____

_____

_____

Now review your reflections and write your personal Take-Charge mission statement below or on a separate piece of paper.

My Take-Charge Plan

In reviewing my history, I realize that I need and want to do the following:

_____

_____

_____

_____

_____

_____

_____

_____

I understand that my needs and my plan will change over time. I commit to working on what I've written now, and to altering my plan as it makes sense to do so in the future.

I can take charge of my emotional life. I can overcome anxiety, distress, and depression. I will heal.

Now, make some copies of your Take-Charge plan. Post a few in prominent places, and carry one with you wherever you go. Read and work your plan daily, updating and changing it as you grow. In this way, you'll take charge. You'll overcome your challenges, find fulfillment, and heal! You're amazing and deserve to be well. My hopes and prayers are with you.

— **Eve A. Wood, M.D.**

GLOSSARY

Acupuncture ("AK-yoo-pungk-cher") is a method of healing developed in China at least 2,000 years ago. Today, this word describes a family of procedures involving stimulation of anatomical points on the body using a variety of techniques. American practices incorporate medical traditions from China, Japan, Korea, and other countries. The technique that has been most studied scientifically involves penetrating the skin with thin, solid, metallic needles that are manipulated by the hands or electrical stimulation.

Aromatherapy ("ah-roam-uh-THER-ah-py") involves the use of essential oils (extracts or essences) from flowers, herbs, and trees to promote health and well-being.

Ayurveda ("ah-yur-VAY-dah") is an alternative medical system that has been practiced primarily on the Indian subcontinent for 5,000 years. It includes diet and herbal remedies and emphasizes the use of body, mind, and spirit in disease prevention and treatment.

Chiropractic ("kie-roh-PRAC-tic") is an alternative medical system. It focuses on the relationship between bodily structure (primarily that of the spine) and function and how that relationship affects the preservation and restoration of health. Chiropractors use manipulative therapy as an integral treatment tool.

Dietary supplements were defined by congress in the Dietary Supplement Health and Education Act (DSHEA) of 1994. A dietary supplement is a product (other than tobacco) taken by mouth that contains a "dietary ingredient" intended to supplement what you eat. Ingredients may include vitamins; minerals; herbs or other botanicals; amino acids; and substances such as enzymes, organ tissues, and metabolites. These supplements come in many forms, including extracts, concentrates, tablets, capsules, gelcaps, liquids, and powders; they have special requirements for labeling. Under DSHEA, dietary supplements are considered foods, not drugs.

Electromagnetic fields (EMFs, also called "electric and magnetic fields") are invisible lines of force that surround all electrical devices; the Earth also produces them. Electric fields are created when there's thunderstorm activity, and magnetic fields are believed to be produced by electric currents flowing at the Earth's core.

Homeopathic ("home-ee-oh-PATH-ic") **medicine** is an alternative medical system. In this discipline, there's a belief that "like cures like," meaning that small, highly diluted quantities of medicinal substances are given to cure symptoms, when the same substances given at higher or more-concentrated doses would actually cause those same symptoms.

Massage ("muh-SAHJ") therapists manipulate muscle and connective tissue to enhance function of those tissues and promote relaxation and well-being.

Naturopathic ("nay-chur-o-PATH-ic") **medicine,** or naturopathy, is an alternative medical system proposing that there's a healing power in the body that establishes, maintains, and restores health. Practitioners work with the patient with a goal of supporting this energy through treatments such as nutrition-and-lifestyle counseling, dietary supplements, medicinal plants, exercise, homeopathy, and traditional Chinese medicine.

Osteopathic ("ahs-tee-oh-PATH-ic") **medicine** is a form of conventional medicine that, in part, emphasizes diseases arising in the musculoskeletal system. There's an underlying belief that all of the body's systems work together, and disturbances in one system may affect function elsewhere. Some practitioners use osteopathic manipulation, a full-body system of hands-on techniques to alleviate pain, restore function, and promote health and well-being.

Qi gong ("chee-GUNG") is a component of traditional Chinese medicine that combines movement, meditation, and regulation of breathing to enhance the flow of *qi* (an ancient term given to what's believed to be vital energy) in the body, improve blood circulation, and enhance immune function.

Reiki ("RAY-kee") is a Japanese word representing Universal Life Energy. The practice is based on the belief that when spiritual energy is channeled through a practitioner, the patient's spirit is healed, which in turn heals the physical body.

Therapeutic touch is derived from an ancient technique called "laying-on of hands." It's based on the premise that it's the healing force of the therapist that affects the patient's recovery. Healing is promoted when the body's energies are in balance, and by passing their hands over the patient, practitioners can identify energy imbalances.

Traditional Chinese medicine (TCM) is the current name for an ancient system of health care from China. TCM is based on a concept of balanced qi (pronounced "chee"), or vital energy, that's believed to flow throughout the body. This is thought to regulate a person's spiritual, emotional, mental, and physical balance and to be influenced by the opposing forces of yin (negative energy) and yang (positive energy). Disease is thought to result from the flow of qi being disrupted and yin and yang becoming imbalanced. Among the components of TCM are herbal and nutritional therapy, restorative physical exercises, meditation, acupuncture, and remedial massage.

INDEX

ACKNOWLEDGMENTS

Whenever I write, teach, or parent, I put my whole self in. I don't know how to do it any other way. I share my perspective, but I also go out on a limb and reveal my own pain, joy, secrets, and ongoing challenges. In doing so, I make myself vulnerable to the world.

There's a part of this that's scary. As a result, I'm eternally grateful to those who support and encourage me in my work. I need every one of you to enable me to pursue my mission, which is to help as many people as possible heal or become whole in a broken world.

I must start by thanking Reid Tracy, the president of Hay House and a wonderful human being. Reid saw the power and potential of my work and welcomed me into my new home. He has been a champion and a great support. I adore him.

Hay House is an author's dream. Every single person I've had the pleasure of working with since June 2005 has enriched my life and work. You are Jacqui Clark, Georgene Cevasco, Rocky George, Amy Gingery, Roberta Grace, Louise Hay, Jill Kramer, Nancy Levin, Jeannie Liberati, Shannon Littrell, Summer McStravick, Diane Ray, Kyle Rector, Christy Salinas, Sonny Salinas, Stacey Smith, John Thompson, Angela Torrez, and Jessica Vermooten. It's not often that an author has the pleasure of developing true friendships with those behind the scenes of her work. But I feel so blessed to have my editor Jill, publicist Angela, producer Diane, and event coordinator Nancy in my life. Thank you all for your wisdom, support, and love.

I am also awed and grateful for the caring and encouragement of my colleague friends Victoria Maizes, Tieraona Low Dog, Ann Marie Chiasson, and Joan Borysenko. It's such a delight to find like-minded spirits who want you to succeed. You four are true blessings in my life.

This is the second time I've sent a brainchild out into the world for endorsements and had a series of angels step in to encourage and acknowledge my manuscript. You dear folks are Daniel Benor, Joan Borysenko, Susan Cooper, Frederic Craigie, James Lake, Tieraona Low Dog, Victoria Maizes, Michelle May, Belleruth Naparstek, Christiane Northrup, Candace Pert, and Andrew Weil. I'm grateful to every one of you for taking the time to read what I had to say and offering me such validating feedback.

While many other people support me in my efforts, there are a number of additional individuals who deserve special mention. My mother-in-law, Helene Isenberg, has been so loving and proud of me that it warms my heart. My Aunt Marcine and Uncle Arty Weiner are like second parents to me. My dear friend and publicist Cate Cummings continues to enrich my life and work. My children, Benjamin, Gabriel, Shira, and Glory, light up my life and willingly allow me to share their stories in my books. And my biggest behind-the-scenes supporter is my husband, Rick Isenberg, who keyboards every word I write and encourages me to keep going, no matter what sacrifices are involved.

I can't close the acknowledgment section of any book without thanking all of my patients. You're my greatest teachers. I offer a special thanks to those of you who have allowed me to share your stories in this book.

I must also thank my father, Leonard Wood, of blessed memory, for his past and continuing love and support; and my mother, Glory Ann Wood, God rest her soul, who believed in me from day one. I thank God for all the gifts I've been given, and thank you, my dear readers, for welcoming me into your lives.

ABOUT THE AUTHOR

Eve A. Wood, M.D., the award-winning author of *There's Always Help; There's Always Hope,* has devoted nearly two decades to the care of troubled individuals from all walks of life. Her therapeutic approach has attracted attention and acclaim from the nation's leading authorities in the fields of medicine, health, and spiritual well-being. She's the author of numerous articles for medical and professional publications, is a feature columnist for *Massage Therapy Journal,* and is a frequent speaker at national workshops and conferences.

She has served on the faculty of the University of Pennsylvania School of Medicine, the executive committee of The Institute of Pennsylvania Hospital, and is Clinical Associate Professor of Medicine at the University of Arizona Program in Integrative Medicine. Uniting body, mind, and spirit In One™ in an empowering treatment model, she helps people take charge of their emotional lives. Dr. Wood lives in Tucson with her husband and four children.

For more information, please visit: **www.DrEveWood .com.**

NOTES

We hope you enjoyed this Hay House book. If you'd like to receive our online catalog featuring additional information on Hay House books and products, or if you'd like to find out more about the Hay Foundation, please contact:

Hay House, Inc., P.O. Box 5100, Carlsbad, CA 92018-5100
(760) 431-7695 or (800) 654-5126
(760) 431-6948 (fax) or (800) 650-5115 (fax)
www.hayhouse.com® • www.hayfoundation.org

Published in Australia by: Hay House Australia Pty. Ltd.,
18/36 Ralph St., Alexandria NSW 2015
Phone: 612-9669-4299 • *Fax:* 612-9669-4144
www.hayhouse.com.au

Published in the United Kingdom by: Hay House UK, Ltd.,
The Sixth Floor, Watson House, 54 Baker Street, London W1U 7BU
Phone: +44 (0)20 3927 7290 • *Fax:* +44 (0)20 3927 7291
www.hayhouse.co.uk

Published in India by: Hay House Publishers India,
Muskaan Complex, Plot No. 3, B-2, Vasant Kunj, New Delhi 110 070
Phone: 91-11-4176-1620 • *Fax:* 91-11-4176-1630
www.hayhouse.co.in

Access New Knowledge.
Anytime. Anywhere.

Learn and evolve at your own pace
with the world's leading experts.

www.hayhouseU.com